History of the Underground Railroad in Chester and the Neighboring Counties of Pennsylvania

DR. R. C. SMEDLEY.

HISTORY

OF THE

Underground Railroad

IN

CHESTER AND THE NEIGHBORING COUNTIES OF PENNSYLVANIA.

BY

R. C. SMEDLEY, M. D.

ILLUSTRATED.

"Verily I say unto you, inasmuch as ye have done it unto one of the least of these, my brethren, ye have done it unto me."

MATTHEW xxv : 40.

"If there is one attribute of our nature for which I thank God more, than for any other, it is that of sympathy."

PRINTED BY JOHN A. HIESTAND,
LANCASTER, PA.

TO THE

SURVIVING MEMBERS OF THOSE HOUSEHOLDS IN WHICH

THE FUGITIVE SLAVE WAS FED,

CLOTHED, AND ASSISTED TO A LIFE OF FREEDOM,

THIS VOLUME

IS AFFECTIONATELY INSCRIBED BY

THE AUTHOR.

would be none left but their descendants to tell of the perils and privations they endured to relieve and set free a "brother in chains," while they were confronted by a Government, and surrounded by a people adverse to negro liberty.

To visit the aged throughout the country who could relate their experiences better than write them, to correspond with others who were connected with the work, and thus to glean reminiscences of facts and record them in an interesting manner, worthy of preservation, was a task the writer felt himself unable to perform as fully as the intrinsic merits of the cause called for. But, admiring the unselfishness and sympathizing spirit of those noble-hearted men and women who sacrificed comfort and imperiled property to aid the fugitive to freedom, endured obloquy and maintained their independence and firmness in the face of all opposition in pleading for the rights of an oppressed and down-trodden race, he commenced the work, humbly trusting that his labors in collecting and writing this traditional history might prove interesting to the reader, and rescue from oblivion the works of a quiet, unpretending, liberty-loving and Christian people.

Heroes have had their deeds of bravery upon battlefields emblazoned in history, and their countrymen have delighted to do them honor; statesmen have been renowned; and their names have been engraved upon the enduring tablets of fame; philanthropists have had their acts of benevolence and charity proclaimed to an appreciating world; ministers, pure and sincere in their gospel labors, have had their teachings collected in religious books that generations might profit by the reading; but these moral heroes, out of the fullness of their hearts, with neither expectation of reward nor hope of remembrance, have, within the privacy of their own homes, at an hour when the outside world was locked in slumber, clothed, fed, and in the darkness of night, whether in calm or in storms, assisted poor, degraded, hunted human beings on their way to liberty, despite the heavy penalties fixed by law for so doing. If the Government was wrong, as they claimed, in holding one race in bondage for the emolument and aggrandizement of a few—and that upon no other grounds than the color of their skin—they could not tacitly acquiesce in that injustice, but prompted by their conscientious convictions of duty, raised their voices against it, and advocated universal freedom and equality before the law.

It is not the object of the writer in this work to treat

of the anti-slavery principles and movement in general, nor of the pro-slavery principle combatted, except so far as these relate to, or have a direct bearing upon the management of this secret passage of the slave to freedom. Nor was it the intention at first to enter into a description of this route of the assistance given fugitives, except incidentally, beyond the limits of Chester county. But the sections of the line in contiguous counties being such important parts could not be omitted. Hence the labors of the author in collecting reminiscences, and the size of the volume, have been proportionately increased.

He has endeavored to glean only well-authenticated facts, unadorned by the glowing colors of fancy, which lend such a charm and fascination to many descriptions of adventures.

As the narration of incidents, amusing and .pathetic, of well-devised plans, promptness of action, and hair-breadth escapes, are as necessary to a history of this kind as the description of battles is to the history of a war, the author has endeavored to be punctiliously exact and truthful in relating those events as described to him by the families having immediate knowledge of the transactions, or who were themselves participators in them.

It is with feelings of much gratification that he is able to present to the readers the portraits of many of the leading men and women who were actively engaged in the "Underground Railroad," who dared to open their houses to the fugitive slave, and to do unto him as they would be done by. With the exception of a few cuts, furnished through the kindness of William Still, all have been engraved expressly for this work from the best likenesses in the possession of the families.

When we consider that from the beginning of the anti-slavery conflict until after the breaking out of the Rebellion, the whole North was, by a vast majority, pro-slavery; when abolitionists were individually reviled and persecuted, even by churches of all denominations; when their country meetings were frequently broken up by ruffians, and their city conventions dispersed by mobs; when Faneuil Hall, the "Cradle of American Liberty," was refused by the Board of Aldermen to abolitionists for holding a convention, and afterwards used for pro-slavery purposes; when but three ministers in all Boston could be found who would read to their congregations a notice of an anti-slavery meeting; when Miss Prudence Crandall, of Canterbury, Conn., who opened a school for colored persons, was refused all supplies and accom-

modations in the town, was arrested and imprisoned
according to a law passed by the Legislature of that
State, *after* the commencement of her school, *expressly
for the purpose of suppressing the education of the colored
people*, and that, too, in intelligent New England, where
a system of public school education received its earliest
support; when a convention for the purpose of forming
a State Anti-slavery Society in Utica, N. Y., was broken
up and dispersed by a mob, headed by a former Judge
of the county; when newspapers refused to publish anti-
slavery speeches, but poured forth such denunciations
as: " The people will hereafter consider abolitionists as
out of the pale of legal and conventional protection
which society affords to its honest and well-meaning
members," that " they will be treated as robbers and
pirates, and as the enemies of the human kind;" when
the offices of anti-slavery papers were broken into and
the presses and the type destroyed; when William Lloyd
Garrison, then editor of *The Liberator*, was seized and
dragged bareheaded through the streets of Boston by a
mob, many of whom sought to kill him; when Elijah P.
Lovejoy, for the same offence of editing an anti-slavery
paper, was mobbed and shot to death in his office in
Alton, Ill.; when Northern merchants extensively en-

gaged in Southern trade, told abolitionists that as their pecuniary interests were largely connected with those of the South, they could not afford to allow them to succeed in their efforts to overthrow slavery, that millions upon millions of dollars were due them from Southern merchants, the payment of which would be jeopardized by any rupture between the North and South, and that they would put them down by fair means if they could, but by foul means if they must; with all this violent pro-slavery spirit existing throughout the North, and the Fugitive Slave Law, like a sword of power in the hands of slave-holders, ready to be wielded by them against any one assisting a slave to freedom, we must concede that it required the manhood of a man, and the unflinching fortitude of a woman, upheld by a full and firm Christian faith, to be an abolitionist in those days, and especially an Underground Railroad agent.

It need scarcely be reiterated that this malevolent spirit was wrought up to white heat in the South. An abolitionist could not travel there without persecution and threats of death; from five to twenty thousand dollars reward was offered at different times by Southern *gentlemen* for the arrest and delivery into their hands of William Lloyd Garrison, Arthur Tappan and others.

Yet slave-holders could travel through the North without any fear of personal or physical violence from abolitionists. Their principles and their teachings were against using brute force or encouraging a feeling of hatred for their adversaries.

Aside from the direct antagonists to anti-slavery, there were apathetic people who heard recitals of tales of torture inflicted upon slaves, of the labors of abolitionists to educate people against the tyranny of the system, and the persecutions inflicted upon them for so doing, without giving a thought or manifesting a feeling upon either side. William Lloyd Garrison became quite warm in conversation one time when alluding to these two classes and the sin of slavery. His friend, Samuel J. May, said to him: "Do try to keep cool, my friend; why, you are all on fire." Laying his hand upon May's shoulder with a kind and sympathetic pressure, he said slowly, and with a deep emotion: "Brother May, I have need to be *all on fire*, for I have mountains of ice about me to melt."

Thanks to an over-ruling Providence, those mountains have melted, and their clear waters have descended to Southern fields of recent carnage, and washed away the crimson stains of a fratricidal war growing out of the institution of slavery—a rebellion against the Government which had recognized and protected the system, and still offered protection to it that the Union might be preserved. By the Proclamation of Lincoln, as a means to acquire victory, to hasten the termination of war and to establish a peace, the fetters of four millions of human beings were struck off and they were declared henceforth and forever free.

The stars and stripes of American liberty are now no longer fanned by the mingled breath of master and slave, and the American eagle looks down exultantly from his majestic soarings upon a broad, free country, of which he is the proud and honored National emblem.

The one great cause of sectional animosity being now removed, let us devoutly hope that all will be united in one common brotherhood, actuated by one common purpose—the prosperity, welfare and happiness of the whole people living under the protection and regulation of a wise, well-administered, general Government.

Trusting that this volume may fulfill the limited mission for which it is designed, it is humbly submitted to the public as a brief record of a few incidents in the lives of those who, although environed by constant danger in the days of slavery, successfully managed the

Underground Railroad in Chester and adjoining counties, until universal freedom made it no longer a necessary pathway of the slave to liberty.

ROBERT C. SMEDLEY.

West Chester, Pa., 10th Mo. 9th, 1882.

ILLUSTRATIONS.

THE AUTHOR,----------------------FRONTISPIECE.

PAGE.

WILLIAM WRIGHT,----------------------------- 37

DANIEL GIBBONS,----------------------------- 53

RESIDENCE OF DANIEL GIBBONS,--------------- 54

HANNAH W. GIBBONS,------------------------- 56

DR. JOSEPH GIBBONS,----------------------- 59

THOMAS WHITSON,---------------------------- 67

CALEB C. HOOD,----------------------------- 80

LINDLEY COATES,---------------------------- 84

SARAH MARSH BARNARD,----------------------137

JOHN VICKERS,-----------------------------143

RESIDENCE OF JOHN VICKERS,----------------144

GRACEANNA LEWIS,--------------------------170

NORRIS MARIS,-----------------------------191

ELIJAH F. PENNYPACKER,--------------------206

DR. JACOB L. PAXSON,----------------------222

THOMAS GARRETT,---------------------------237

ISAAC MENDENHALL,-------------------------249

DINAH MENDENHALL,-------------------------250

DR. BARTHOLOMEW FUSSELL,------------------260

JOHN COX,---------------------------------273

HANNAH COX,-------------------------------274

EUSEBIUS BARNARD,-------------------------288

	PAGE.
SARAH P. BARNARD,	290
NATHAN EVANS,	338
JAMES LEWIS,	344
JAMES T. DANNAKER,	347
ROBERT PURVIS,	353

CONTENTS.

CHAPTER I.

Opposition to Clause in Constitution Sanctioning Slavery.—Origin of Organized System of Underground Railroad work in Columbia.—Early Settlement of Friends There.—First Attempt at Kidnapping. —WILLIAM WRIGHT.—Increasing Number of Fugitives.—Routes and Agents Established.—Origin of the Term, Underground Railroad. PAGE 25

CHAPTER II.

Slaves Escape in Large Numbers from Harford and Baltimore Counties, Md.—Agents at Gettysburg.—At York Springs.—William Wright.—Twenty-Six Fugitives.—Another Party of Sixteen.—Another of Four.—Death of WM. WRIGHT, York Springs.—Agents in York.—Attempts to Intercept Fugitives at Columbia.—SAMUEL W. MIFFLIN.—Incidents. 36

CHAPTER III.

DANIEL AND HANNAH GIBBONS.—JAMES GIBBONS.—Incidents.—Daniel Gibbon's Method of Questioning Fugitives.—Other Incidents. 53

CHAPTER IV.

DR. JOSEPH GIBBONS.—Early Education.—Studies Medicine.—His Wife PHEBE EARLE GIBBONS, a Contributor to Literature.—Dr. Gibbons Establishes The Journal.—DR. J. K. ESHLEMAN.—Incidents. 59

CHAPTER V.

THOMAS WHITSON.—Member of First National Anti-Slavery Convention.—Incidents.—JACOB BUSHONG.—Incidents.—JEREMIAH MOORE. —Incidents. 67

CHAPTER VI.

JOSEPH AND CALEB C. HOOD.—Women Aided by Rev. Charles T. Torrey on His Last Trip to Maryland.—Sketch of the Life of TORREY.—Three Men Who Had Been Engaged in the Christiana Riot.—Other Incidents.—LINDLEY COATES.—Incidents.—JOSHUA BRINTON.—Incidents.   80

CHAPTER VII.

JOSEPH FULTON.—Incidents.—Assists Wives of Parker and Pinkney.— MOSES WHITSON.—Colored Man Betrayed by Fortune-Teller.—Incidents.—William Baer Assists in Capturing a Slave at Marsh Chamberlain's.—ABRAHAM BONSALL.—Elisha Tyson.—THOMAS BONSALL. Meeting of Abolitionists.—Clarkson Anti-Slavery Society Formed. —Incidents.—Marriage to Susan P. Johnson.   90

CHAPTER VIII.

THE CHRISTIANA TRAGEDY.—Sketch of Life of William Parker.—Dickerson Gorsuch Lay Wounded, and was Cared for at the House of Levi Pownall.—Castner Hanway Tried for Treason.—Other Cases Removed to Lancaster.—Acquittal.   107

CHAPTER IX.

J. WILLIAMS THORNE.—Incidents.—Kidnapping at Michael Myers.— SEYMOUR C. WILLIAMSON.—JAMES FULTON, JR., AND GIDEON PIERCE.—Incidents.—GRAVNER AND HANNAH MARSH.—Incidents.— Sarah Marsh marries Eusebius Barnard.—Work of Station Closes.
                                                            131

CHAPTER X.

John Vickers, Early Education and Domestic Life.—Incidents.—Abner Landrum.—Other Incidents.—Paxson Vickers.—Charles Moore. Micajah and William A. Speakman.—Sarah A., daughter of Micajah, marries J. Miller McKim.   143

CHAPTER XI.

THE LEWIS FAMILY.—Descent.—Labors for the Slave.—Clothing Furnished Fugitives by Friends.—Incidents.—DR. EDWIN FUSSELL.— Experience and Incidents.   168

CHAPTER XII.

NORRIS MARIS.—LEWIS PEART.—A Dream.—EMMON KIMBER.—Sketch
of Experiences of RACHEL HARRIS.—"Cunningham's Rache."—
Abbie Kimber.—Gertrude Kimber Burleigh.   191

CHAPTER XIII.

ELIJAH F. PENNYPACKER.—Incidents.—Parentage.—Member of Legislature.—Marriage.—Enters Ministry.—JOSEPH P. SCARLETT.—
Saved Life of Dickerson Gorsuch at Christiana.—Arrested.—Acquitted.—THOMAS LEWIS.—THOMAS READ.—Incidents.—Daniel
Ross.—Amusing Incident at Company.—Public Opinion.—DR.
JACOB L. PAXSON.—Assists Parker, Pinkney and Johnson.—Interesting Colored Family.   206

CHAPTER XIV.

JOSEPH SMITH.—Incident in Canada.—Marriage and Death.—OLIVER
FURNIS.—JOHN N. RUSSELL.—THOMAS GARRETT.—Inspiration.—
Marriage.—Arrested and Fined.—Prospered Afterward.—Reward
Offered.—Plan of Management.—Woman Escaped in Wife's Cloth-
ing.—Death.—JACOB LINDLEY.—Earliest Worker.—Death.—LEVI
B. WARD.—Kidnapping.—JAMES N. TAYLOR.—Assisted Parker,
Pinkney and Johnson.   227

CHAPTER XV.

ISAAC AND DINAH MENDENHALL.—Interesting Incidents.—HARRIET
TUBMAN.—Assists Parker, Pinkney and Johnson.—'Squire Jacob
Lamborn.—Sarah Pearson Opens Free Produce Store in Hamor-
ton.—Isaac Mendenhall Disowned.—Assist in Organizing Society
of Progressive Friends.—Reunited to Original Society.—Golden
Anniversary of Wedding.—Original Estate.   249

CHAPTER XVI.

DR. BARTHOLOMEW FUSSELL.—Parentage.—Teaches Colored School
in Maryland.—Studies Medicine.—Lydia Morris Fussell.—Influence
of Charles C. Burleigh.—Incidents.—About Two Thousand Fugitives Passed.—Women's Medical College.—Death and Burial.—
Incidents Related by His Son.—JOHN AND HANNAH COX.—Incidents.—Take Active Part in Anti-slavery Societies.—Golden Wedding Anniversary.—Greeting.—Death.   260

CHAPTER XVII.

SIMON BARNARD.—Differences at Kennett Square.—Incidents.—Arrest of Charles C. Burleigh.—EUSEBIUS BARNARD.—Incidents.—Eusebius R. Barnard's tedious journey.—Eusebius Barnard's Ministry. —William Barnard with Eusebius and Others Assists in Founding Society of Progressive Friends.—Kidnapping at house of Zebulon Thomas.   282

CHAPTER XVIII.

ISAAC AND THAMAZINE P. MEREDITH.—MORDECAI AND ESTHER HAYES. —MAHLON AND AMOS PRESTON.—CHANDLER AND HANNAH M. DARLINGTON.—BENJAMIN AND HANNAH S. KENT.—A Large Party of Fugitives.—ENOCH LEWIS.—Conscientious Labors.—Redeems a Negro at Great Risk.   301

CHAPTER XIX.

BENJAMIN PRICE.—His Father, Philip Price, Assists Runaways.—Incidents.—Golden Weddings.—SAMUEL M. PAINTER.—Abraham D. Shadd, John Brown and Benjamin Freemen.—NATHAN EVANS. 323

CHAPTER XX.

JAMES LEWIS and JAMES T. DANNAKER.—Many Fugitives Taken to the Anti-slavery Office, Philadelphia.—ROBERT PURVIS.—The Dorsey Brothers.   344

APPENDIX.

Letters Received by William Still, 363.—American Anti-Slavery Society, 368.—The Fugitive Slave Law, 381.—Lincoln's Caution and Conscientiousness, 387.—Letter to Horace Greely, 388.—Visit From Delegation of Ministers, 390.—Proclamation of Emancipation, 391.— Extracts From Messages, &c., 393.—Amendments to Constitution, 394.

HISTORY

OF THE

UNDERGROUND RAILROAD.

CHAPTER I.

Opposition to Clause in Constitution Sanctioning Slavery.—Origin of
Organized System of Underground Railroad work in Columbia.—
Early Settlement of Friends There.—First Attempt at Kidnapping.
—WILLIAM WRIGHT.—Increasing Number of Fugitives.—Routes
and Agents Established.—Origin of the Term, Underground
Railroad.

When the convention to frame the Constitution of
the United States met in Philadelphia in May, 1787,
many were opposed to the clause sanctioning negro
slavery. They felt it to be incompatible with the principles of the Declaration of Independence which had
inspired, encouraged and supported them during their
long and arduous struggle for liberty,—"that all men
were created equal; that they were endowed by their
Creator with certain inalienable rights; that among
these are life, liberty and the pursuit of happiness."
And they felt it to be an abjuration of the solemn promise made at the close of that Declaration, that "for
the support of which, with a firm reliance on the protection of *Divine Providence*, they mutually pledge to
each other their lives, their fortunes, and their sacred
honor." And they further held it to be inconsistent
with the principles of the free government they were

. B

about to establish, to hold any class of people in a
bondage more oppressive, more degrading, and more
tyrannical than that from which they had just emancipated · themselves through the trials, vicissitudes and
privations of a seven years' war.   After much discussion
and dissension, they yielded to the adoption of this
clause, with the hope that ere long the wisdom, humanity
and justice of the people would annihilate forever the
obnoxious system of human slavery from a soil they had
nobly fought to make free.

This relic of ancient despotism, making chattel property of man, having now been incorporated as a part
of the Constitution, the friends of universal liberty assumed very little direct antagonism toward it until some
cases of kidnapping and shooting of fugitives who attempted to escape, occurred in Columbia, Pa., in 1804.
This incited the people of that town, who were chiefly
Friends or their descendants, to throw around the colored people the arm of protection, and even to assist
those who were endeavoring to escape from slavery to a
section of country where they might be free.   This gave
origin to that organized system of rendering aid to fugitives which was afterward known as the " Underground
Railroad."

The active and determined position to which the opponents of slavery were now aroused, and the large
number of colored people who had settled in Columbia,
made that place the goal of the fugitive to which he
directed his anxious footsteps with the reasonable hope
that when arriving there he would receive aid and directions on his way to freedom.   His expectations were
not disappointed.

More than a passing allusion is due to Columbia, as
it was there those sentiments were fostered and feelings
aroused which developed into a secret and successful
plan of transporting the slave through friendly hands
from bondage to freedom.   In 1726 John Wright and
Robert Barber removed from Chester, Pa., and settled
there.   In the following year Samuel Blunson also
removed there from the same place.   These persons
were Friends, or Quakers.   Barber and Blunson owned
a number of slaves, mostly domestics in their families.
When Samuel Blunson died, in September, 1746, he
manumitted his slaves and provided for them.   The
descendants of Barber gradually quit owning slaves
and came to hate slavery.   Their influence and example
made an impression upon the small community which
lived upon their lands at and around Wright's Ferry.

In 1787 Samuel Wright, grandson of John Wright,
Esq., laid out the town of Columbia.   The lots were
disposed of by lottery and all sold, and many substantial persons from Bucks, Montgomery and Chester
counties, and Philadelphia settled there.   A majority
of them were Quakers, who bore a decided testimony
against the holding of human beings in slavery.

Gradually all the colored people in the vicinity collected in the northeastern part of the borough upon
lots given them by the Wrights.   Being thus brought
into one community it was quite natural that any
strange colored persons going that way would seek shelter
among them.   •

In 1804 General Thomas Boude, of Columbia, a revolutionary officer of distinction, who had been a member
of the State Legislature, and who had represented Lan-

caster and Chester counties in Congress two terms,
purchased a young slave, named Stephen Smith, of a Mr.
Cochrane, living a few miles south of Harrisburg.
Smith would have been free at 28, but was given his
liberty before that time. In the same year Smith's
mother ran away from Cochrane and went to General
Boude's. In a few weeks a spinster rode up to the
house, dismounted, and walked into the kitchen without
any ceremony. Meeting Mrs. Smith she ordered her
to " pack up her duds and come with her." Mrs. Smith
refused, whereupon she seized her and endeavored to
carry her to the horse and bear her off. Young Stephen
ran out and told the General, who came to the house
and ordered the woman away. This was the first case
of attempted kidnapping that occurred in Columbia so
far as is known. The General afterwards purchased
Mrs. Smith.

About this time a wealthy planter of Virginia manumitted his slaves, fifty-six in number. The heirs endeavored to retain them as their property, but after two
years of litigation the Legislature of Virginia and the
courts decreed their freedom. They were brought to
Columbia in wagons.

A year later Sally Bell, a Friend, of Virginia, emancipated about 75 or 100 slaves, who also settled in
Columbia. Quite a number of slaves fled from their
masters and went there. Frequent attempts were made
by pursuers to capture and return them to slavery,
some of which were successful.

WILLIAM WRIGHT.

William Wright, of Columbia, who had become an
uncompromising hater of slavery, was an active man of

strong nerve power, possessing a thorough knowledge of
the law pertaining to the institution, and a presence of
mind equal to any occasion.   He assisted all fugitives
who applied to him, and when he heard of any being
captured, he lost no opportunity by his broad deep
strategy, in court or out of it, to secure the captive's
escape.

On several occasions when fugitives came to his place
closely pursued by their hunters, he hastily dressed
them in women's clothes and sent them to Daniel
Gibbons, about six miles east of Lancaster.

The slaves were now escaping in such large numbers,
and passing through Columbia, that the slaveholders determined to intercept them by employing men to watch
the place and arrest every fugitive.   They paid a man
named Eaton several hundred dollars a year to remain
there and give information; and also stipulated with
Charles Taylor, who drove stage between Columbia,
York and Baltimore, for the same purpose.   Notwithstanding this, few arrests were made, and of those apprehended some were rescued by the active abolitionists
before they could be returned to bondage.   The colored
people of the town manifested no particularly tender
feelings toward any one that came there for the purpose
of carrying them back into slavery.   They made a
swoop one day upon a slave catcher, named Isaac
Brooks, bore him through a deep snow to the back part
of town, stripped him of his clothing and whipped him
soundly with hickory-withes.   He was never seen in
Columbia afterwards.

The increased numbers now arriving made it necessary to establish other and reliable agencies along some

direct line to the Eastern States and Canada, whither most of the fugitives desired to go, although many preferred remaining with friendly farmers along the road and taking their chances for safety. This line very naturally shaped itself by way of some of the noblest hearted, earnest, sympathizing Abolitionists in Adams, York, Lancaster, Chester, Montgomery, Berks and Bucks counties to Phœnixville, Norristown, Quakertown, Reading, Philadelphia and other places. The two first stations nearest the Maryland line were Gettysburg and York. When ten or twenty fugitives arrived in a gang at Gettysburg, half were sent to Harrisburg and half to Columbia. The Columbia branch was chiefly used as it had better facilities for escape. Stations were established southward from Columbia toward the Maryland line, and northward or eastward at distances about 10 miles apart.

The principal agents on the line running northward and eastward were Daniel Gibbons, Thomas Peart, Thomas Whitson, Lindley Coates, Dr. Eshleman, James Moore, Caleb C. Hood, of Lancaster county; James Fulton, Gideon Pierce, Joseph Haines, Thomas Bonsall, Gravner Marsh, Zebulon Thomas, Thomas Vickers, John Vickers, Micajah and William A. Speakman, Esther Lewis and daughters, Dr. Edwin Fussell, William Fussell, Norris Maris, Emmor Kimber, and Elijah F. Pennypacker, of Chester county; Rev. Samuel Aaron, Isaac Roberts, John Roberts, Dr. Wm. Corson, Dr. Jacob L. Paxson, Daniel Ross, colored, and others of Norristown. This was subsequently called the northern route through Chester county.

Thus was the Underground Railroad established and

put into successful operation until, as Thomas Garrett
said, "the government went into the business, and made
a wholesale emancipation." And to William Wright,
of Columbia, grandson of John Wright, is due the
credit of being one of the first anti-slavery advocates
who arranged and put into practice, at the risk of his
life, this well-known but secretly conducted transit of
the slave from bondage to freedom.

The inherent spirit of liberty now impelled still
greater numbers along the border counties, and further
south, to leave their masters, and in pursuing a northern
course the majority of them came through the southern
part of Lancaster and Chester counties. The ever
benevolent abolitionists assisted them from friend to
friend, until another route, more travelled than the first,
was, almost as if by spontaneity, established among
them. This, with its branches, was called the southern
and middle route. Being contiguous to the border
slave States, a rapid transit of passengers had to be
made, which was not unfrequently attended with exciting incidents of close pursuit and of narrow escapes.

Many who came on this route crossed the Susquehanna at points in the vicinity of Havre-de-Grace, and
were forwarded by Joseph Smith, Oliver Furniss, and
others in Lancaster county. A still greater number
came from Wilmington through the hands of Thomas
Garrett, Benjamin, William and Thomas Webb, and
Isaac S. Flint. Many others came direct from the more
Southern Slave States, travelling by night only, and
guided solely by the North star—their universal guide—
until they reached some abolition friends along the line,
who fed them, secreted them by day, and either took

them to the next station at night, or gave them notes
with the names of agents, and directions how to find
them.

` Every slave that came from the South knew the
North Star, and that by following it he would reach a
land of freedom. Trusting to this beacon light before
them as a celestial pilot, thousands successfully made
their escape. The slaveholders knowing this, freely expressed their hatred for that star, and declared, if they
could, they would tear it from its place in the heavens.
But Josiah Henson, who was the character selected by
Harriet Beecher Stowe as "Uncle Tom" in her "Uncle
Tom's Cabin," said, "Blessed be God for setting it
there."

Some of the branches of this line interlaced with the
northern route, particularly at the Pierces and the
Fultons in Ercildoun; Levi Coates, near Cochran-
ville; Gravner Marsh, Caln; Esther Lewis and daughters, Vincent; John Vickers, near Lionville, and Elijah
F. Pennypacker's, near Phœnixville. At this place
quite a number crossed the river into Montgomery
county, and were sent in different directions, many of
them to Norristown.

One route from Havre-de-Grace was by way of
Thomas, Eli and Charles Hambleton's in Penn township to Ercildoun, thence to Gravner Marsh's, John
Vickers', and so on. Those who were sick or worn out
were taken to Esther Lewis's and carefully nursed until
able to proceed further.

After leaving Wilmington, the main route came by
way of Allen and Maria Agnew, Isaac and Dinah
Mendenhall, Dr. Bartholomew Fussell, and John and

Hannah Cox, near Kennet; Simon and Sarah D. Barnard, East Marlborough; Eusebius and Sarah Marsh Barnard and Wm. Barnard, Pocopsin; Isaac and Thamazine P. Meredith, Mordecai and Esther Hayes, Newlin; James Fulton, Jr., and Gideon Pierce, Ercildoun; Dr. Eshelman, Zebulon Thomas and daughters, Downingtown; Micajah and William Speakman, Uwchlan; John Vickers and Charles Moore, Lionville; Esther Lewis and daughters, Mary, Elizabeth and Graceanna, William Fussell, Dr. Edwin Fussell and Norris Maris, West Vincent; Emmor Kimber, Kimberton, and Elijah F. Pennypacker, near Phœnixville.

Another branch passed by way of Chandler Darlington, Kennet; Benjamin Price, East Bradford; the Darlington sisters and Abraham D. Shadd, West Chester. Dividing here, one portion united with the northern and middle routes at John Vickers', and the other went to Nathan Evans, Willistown. Again dividing, one branch went to Philadelphia, the other to Elijah F. Pennypacker's, near Phœnixville.

When fugitives arrived at any of the stations in large numbers, and close together, many were frequently sent off the direct route to well known abolitionists in order to elude pursuit should slave-hunters be on their track. Among these, on the northern route, were Jeremiah Moore, Christiana; Dr. Augustus W. Cain, West Sadsbury; Joseph Brinton, Salisbury, Lancaster county; Joseph Moore, Sadsbury, Lancaster county; Joseph Fulton, West Sadsbury; J. Williams Thome and James Williams, Sadsbury—the latter known as "Abolition Jim," in contradistinction to one of same name near by, but of opposite principles—Seymour C. Williamson,

B*

Caln; William Trimble, West Whiteland, and Charles
Moore, Lionville.

Along the lower route were Mahlon and Amos Preston, and Wm. Jackson, near West Grove; Benjamin
and Hannah Kent, Penn township, and others who occasionally gave willing aid when required, but whose
residences were not so located as to give them advantages
whereby they could expedite travel to the safety of the
fugitive.

To convey passengers successfully over the great
trunk lines and branches of this road from its beginning
to its terminus, to prevent captures, and to escape arrests and the mulcting punishments attached to slave-
holding laws, required men of firmness, courage, sagacity, coolness and intrepidity in time of danger, pre-
dominant philantrophy impelling them to do unto the
liberty-seeking slave as they would be done by under
similar circumstances, and having firm reliance on Him
who commanded to "undo the heavy burdens, and to let
the oppressed go free." And it is a notable fact that
nearly all who thus assisted the fugitive to freedom were
members of the Society of Friends; although the majority of that society, while averse to slavery, took no
part in the labors, and, with few exceptions, refused the
use of their meeting-houses for anti-slavery lectures.

In the early part of this concerted management
slaves were hunted and tracked as far as Columbia.
There the pursuers lost all trace of them. The most
scrutinizing inquiries, the most vigorous search, failed
to educe any knowledge of them. Their pursuers seemed
to have reached an abyss, beyond which they could not
see, the depths of which they could not fathom, and in

their bewilderment and discomfiture they declared *there must be an underground railroad somewhere.* This gave origin to the term by which this secret passage from bondage to freedom was designated ever after.

CHAPTER II.

Slaves Escape in Large Numbers from Harford and Baltimore Counties, Md.—Agents at Gettysburg.—At York Springs.—William Wright.—Twenty-Six Fugitives.—Another Party of Sixteen.—Another of Four.—Death of WM. WRIGHT, York Springs.—Agents in York.—Attempts to Intercept Fugitives at Columbia.—SAMUEL W. MIFFLIN.—Incidents.

The counties of Frederick, Carroll, Washington, Harford and Baltimore, Md., emptied their fugitives into York and Adams counties across the line in Pennsylvania. The latter two counties had settlements of Friends and abolitionists. The slaves learned who their friends were in that part of the Free State; and it was as natural for those aspiring to liberty to move in that direction, as for the waters of brooks to move toward larger streams.

Among the most active agents at Gettysburg, the station nearest the Maryland line, was a colored man whose residence was at the southern boundary of the the town, and Hamilton Everett, who lived a short distance north of the suburbs. Thaddeus Stevens, as a young lawyer, first practising his profession, rendered valuable assistance.

There was a very friendly feeling in Gettysburg towards the abolitionists. The professors at the College and at the Theological Seminary were anti-slavery in sentiment and contributed to the cause; but they had to do it cautiously, as many of their students were from the Southern States.

At the next important station, York Springs, Adams

WILLIAM WRIGHT.

county, one of the most noted and successful managers was WILLIAM WRIGHT, a Friend. While possessing wisdom, sagacity and firmness to an eminent degree, he was as unassuming in manner as he was earnest and efficient in action.

He was born 12th mo. (December) 21st, 1788. In 11th mo. (November), 1817, he married Phebe Wierman, sister of Hannah W. Gibbons, the wife of that sage and sympathizing friend of the slave, Daniel Gibbons. William and Phebe Wright resided during their entire lives in a very old settlement of Friends, near the southern slope of South Mountain, a spur of the Alleghanies, which extends into Tennessee. This location placed them directly in the way to render great and valuable aid to fugitives, as hundreds guided by that mountain range northward, came into Pennsylvania, and were directed to their home.

A party of twenty-six came to York about 1842, from Anne Arundel county, Md. It was one night's walk from there to Wrightsville, the next important station. The night being cloudy they became bewildered on their way, and concluded they could travel in day time. They turned around and were coming back, when they met a colored man near York who knew they were slaves, and told them they were going toward Maryland. He put them on the right road, with directions northward. Early next morning, when near Wrightsville, they followed some wagons which they knew were going there. After crossing the bridge into Columbia they were happy, and lay around on the ground, thinking they were safe in Canada. They were spoken to by a person who knew they were fugitives, and told of their danger.

They looked astonished, and asked if they were not in
Canada. When told not, they were frightened, and
some started off in the midst of his talking, and could
scarcely be persuaded to wait for directions. They were
armed with clubs, pistols and guns. He finally induced
them to listen to him long enough to give them directions how they should pass through Columbia. But
they started off in one gang through the streets, defying
any authority that might attempt to apprehend them.

When nearing Lancaster they met a man who knew
from their appearance that they were slaves. He
stopped and tried to converse with them; but they
seemed to distrust his purpose, and appeared determined
to proceed headlong despite all counsel. But finally he
convinced them that he was their friend, and that there
was a large town a short distance ahead where they
would be in danger unless they listened to and obeyed
his directions. He then told them how to enter the
town, to pass the Court-house, and to go on until they
came opposite an office—describing it so they would
know it. They were then to enter and walk up to a
man, who was Thaddeus Stevens, and give him a paper
upon which had been written an account of the men.
They did so. He told them to sit down and he would
get them something to eat. After refreshing themselves
he gave them directions to Daniel Gibbons.

Daniel was sitting on his piazza when they came up.
He accosted them with, "come in boys; I know who
you are; I have been looking for you." After giving
them food he separated the party, and sent them in different directions.

A party of sixteen came to York about 1843, and were

consigned to Joel Fisher of that place, who was in constant correspondence with William Wright and Dr. Lewis, of Lewisburg. When they arrived, William Wright and Dr. Lewis happened to be at Joel Fisher's house. The fugitives were taken into a neighboring cornfield and hidden under the shocks. The following night Dr. Lewis piloted them to hear his house at Lewisburg on the Conewago, where they were concealed several days, the doctor carrying them provisions in his saddle-bags. When their pursuers had ceased hunting for them in William Wright's neighborhood, he went down to Lewisburg, and in company with Dr. Lewis took the sixteen across the river, fording it on horseback, taking the men and women behind them, and carrying the children in their arms. It was a gloomy night in November. Dark heavy clouds swept across the sky, obscuring at intervals the light of the moon, and casting their sombre shadows upon the waters which, swollen by recent rains, were rolling in a dangerous torrent. When the last one had got safely over, the doctor, who professed to be an atheist, looked upon the party and their midnight surroundings, and upon the efforts being made in behalf of these poor creatures, and from the depth of a heart filled with sympathy he exclaimed: "Great God! is this a Christian land; and are Christians thus forced to flee for their liberty?" William Wright took the party to his house that night, and concealed them in a forest near by until it was safe to start them on their way to Canada.

In the early part of harvest, 1851, four slaves came to William Wright's house from Maryland. They were in a state of semi-nudity, their clothing being nearly all

torn off and hanging in tatters.   At this hospitable
home they were furnished with clothing and shoes.
Learning that the slaveholders had gone to Harrisburg
in search of them, two were concealed at William
Wright's place, and the other two sent for concealment
to Joel Wierman, his brother-in-law, two miles distant.
In a day or two while William Wright with the colored
men and some workmen was at the barn, a party of
hunters came up and recognized the two slaves as belonging to one of their numbers. The negroes, apparently giving themselves up, said they had left their coats
at the house.   William Wright told them to go and get
them.   One was seen by the family to take his coat
hastily from one of the out-buildings.   Giving them
time to get their coats, William Wright and the slaveholders walked leisurely to the house.

Stepping upon the piazza where his wife was seated,
he said, giving her a significant and piercing glance,
"Phebe, these are Mr. —— and Mr. —— and Mr. ——
from Maryland, and Mr. —— from Pennsylvania.
Gentlemen, this is my wife.   These gentlemen claim to
be the owners of Tom, Fenton, Sam and George.   Gentlemen, be seated."   Taking from her husband's look
that they were to be entertained and thus delayed for a
purpose, Phebe Wright arose in her dignified manner
and seconded her husband in his invitation.   Her eldest
daughter coming to the door she cast at her a glance
that told the story.   William Wright sent for some
fresh water and some cherries that were near by in the
dining room.   After these elaborate preliminaries, which
took some time, had been gone through with, Phebe
Wright said, in rather a surprised tone: " Do I under-

stand you to say that you claim to be the owners of these
colored men?" On their replying in the affirmative,
she said: "Do you recognize the Scripture as the guide
of your lives?" "Certainly, madame," said one, assuming a a very sanctimonious air, "I am an elder in the
Baptist church." He proved, although, as subsequent
events showed, a very bad man, to be not without fear
of the higher law, for, when Phebe Wright, sending for
the Bible, proved to him from its pages the sin that he
was committing in holding slaves, his teeth chattered
with terror. After three-quarters of an hour thus spent,
they arose saying that it was time to proceed to business,
and asked William Wright to produce the men. He
replied: "Oh! that is not my business at all; if they
are you slaves, as you assert, you saw them, it was your
business to take them." In answer to their assertion that
he was hiding their slaves, he said: "Haven't I been
here all the time? How can I have concealed your
slaves? If you have your lawful authority here is the
house; search it. I shall not help you, but I can't prevent you." With this they showed their warrants and
proceeded to search the house. After this they went
through the out-buildings, William Wright saying: "I
will go with you. You charge me with being responsi-
ble for your slaves; this I deny, as they were within
your grasp half an hour ago." Continuing, he said:
"Gentlemen, I protest against this whole proceeding
and consider the Fugitive Slave Law no law in that it
contravenes the law of God. But, you have the wicked
law of the land on your side. I can't prevent you."
Of course all this was done to detain the slaveholders
and to give the slaves a chance to escape. In the search

they passed the carriage-house, which stood a little to
one side of the path between the house and the barn.
They never seemed to think of entering this building.
After the search was over, they having been induced to
enter every nook and corner and to look into the most
out-of-the-way and absurd places William Wright stood
in the path a little beyond the carriage-house and indi-
cating it, his out-buildings and house with a sweeping
gesture of the hand, said : " Now, gentlemen, you will
acknowledge that you have searched my house and out-
buildings to your hearts' content. If you are still un-
satisfied, we'll search the barn." So they searched the
barn and then departed, expressing, with muttered
oaths, much discontent at being, as they said, "hood-
winked."

After their departure, the old slave Tom was found in
the carriage-house, between the seats of the carriage, on
his knees. He said that all the time the search was
going on he was praying that the Lord would blind the
searchers' eyes and confuse their understandings. To
Phebe Wright's question, whether he was afraid, he replied, "No, madame, no. I felt dat de Lawd was
about dah." It then appeared that William Wright, as
he was escorting the slaveholders from the barn to the
house, had seen this man's heels disappearing within the
carriage-house door.

Fenton, who, by the way, was the son of the Baptist
deacon, had taken refuge in a rye field. Beyond the
house was a ditch which, at this time, was overgrown
with reeds and tall grass. Into this he jumped and
crawling, on his hands and knees, the distance of one
field, entered the second which was the rye field afore-

said. Here he remained till eleven o'clock at night when he came to the house, indicated his presence by whistling and rejoined Tom. They were fed and sent back to the rye field where they remained for several days, being fed at night.

The other two were taken to the farm of Joel Wierman, where they remained concealed for several days in the barn. One of them, tiring of the monotony, begged to be allowed to go into the corn field where there were some men at work. Joel Wierman did not wish him to do this, but he persisted. ·To this field came the masters, fresh from their search at William Wright's. As soon as he saw them he ran across two fields, they following at full speed, and Joel Wierman bringing up the rear. Coming to a large stream, he plunged in and reached the opposite bank, which was very steep. As he began to climb it, they shouted to him that if he persisted, they would shoot him, they having fair aim. In dread of sudden death, he hesitated and they caught up with and captured him. His hands were tied behind him, the master holding the rope. Thus he was brought to . William Wright's house. Phebe Wright quoted Scripture to the master, and used every argument she was mistress of, to induce him to promise not to sell Sam to the far South. "I assure you, madame," was his reply, "I am a paternal master. I don't desire the money this man would bring or even his services, but only to make him comfortable. Just look at the rags he is in. He would make you believe that he is kept in this way. I assure you he is not. He has run away and hidden in the mountains till he is in this condition. I shall take him home and clothe and shoe him." While this was going on at the house, one of the daughters went down to where the poor negro was tied, and said, "Sam, is your pistol with Fenton's things in the house?" "No, Miss, I left my pistol in the barn at Mr. Wierman's." Then she filled his pockets with cherries—all she could do, alas! and advised him to run away again the first chance that he had. This he promised to do. The "paternal" master was seen dragging him through Gettysburg tied as has been described. Instead of taking him to his home in Washington county, Md., he took him to Frederick City and sold him to a slave dealer who, at that time was getting up a drove for the far South! He was never heard of again. The other three men, with the help of the managers of the Underground Railroad, reached Canada in safety.

One amusing incident occurred at this house. A large number of fugitives came at one time, among whom was a mother with a young child. Their masters following them quickly, all were disposed of except the infant, whose cries, it was feared, would lead to detection. A stratagem was resorted to that showed these anti-slavery people were quick-witted as well as philanthropic. A young woman staying at the house went to bed, taking the baby with her. When the slaveholders came they were requested to be very careful in searching as there was a lady with a young infant in the house. When they came to the room in which this supposititious recent arrival was, they opened the door a little, the action being accompanied with a "Sh!" and a finger uplifted in warning by their guide, while the "mother" pinched the baby and made it cry in order to convince the unwelcome visitors that they were not being deceived. These are a few among the scores of incidents that occurred in this family and among those that helped them in their work.

William Wright believed in political action against slavery and took considerable part therein. He was one of the founders of the Free-Soil or Liberty Party in Pennsylvania. For many years his name, with that of Samuel W. Mifflin, stood at the head of the Liberty Party electoral ticket. He attended Anti-Slavery and Liberty Party Meetings and Conventions whenever his business would permit, and was a delegate to many of these, notably to the convention that met in Pittsburg in 1844, and nominated Dr. F. J. Lemoyne for Governor of Pennsylvania, and to that which met in Philadelphia in June of 1856, and nominated John C. Fremont and William L. Dayton, for President and Vice President of the United States.

The long, well-spent life of William Wright closed on the 25th of Tenth month (October), 1865. He had the satisfaction of seeing the principles of liberty and justice for which he had labored triumph over Slavery and oppression. In his death he calmly resigned his spirit to the Maker whom he had so earnestly and meekly served.

"Mark the perfect man, and behold the upright; for the end of that man is peace."

Joel Fisher, a Friend, living in York, was also active and prominent in the cause.

William C. Goodrich, a wealthy and very intelligent light mulatto was an active and valuable agent at that place. Whenever he received information that "baggage" was on the road which it was necessary to hurry through, he sent word to Columbia the day before it was expected to arrive. Cato Jourdon, colored, who drove a team which hauled cars over the bridge, brought all "baggage" safely across, where the agents had another trusty colored man to receive it. The fugitives were then taken through Black's hotel yard to another portion of the town, and concealed over night; when Wm. Wright, of that place, generally took them in charge and sent some to Daniel Gibbons, and some direct to Philadelphia, in the false end of a box car, owned by Stephen Smith and William Whipper, colored men and lumber merchants of Columbia. They got off at the head of the "plane," near Philadelphia, where an agent was in waiting to receive them.

After his removal to Lancaster Thaddeus Stevens gave money, and also assisted those who came to Columbia. Mrs. Smith, who kept house for him for more than twenty years, and nursed him at the close of his life, was one of the slaves he helped to freedom.

An old man named Wallace, living at York, was an ardent abolitionist and rendered efficient aid. Many threats were made to kill him, and his life was often in danger.

The agents at York had pass-words, which they used on occasions when required for the purpose for which they were intended. One was "William Penn." This name they frequently signed when addressing notes to each other.

William Yokum, constable at York, was favorable to fugitives, and instrumental on various occasions in securing their protection. He had the "pass-words," and made good use of them. When called upon by slave-catchers to hunt or arrest fugitives, and he could ascertain through the agents where they were, he led the hunters in a different direction, or managed to have the slaves removed before he reached the place.

Many and curious devices were resorted to by the active abolitionists to conceal fugitives, or to rescue them from the hands of their captors. When the slave catchers were taking John Jones, a "runaway slave," by the residence of Robert Barber, some one tripped the officer, and Jones darted into an open cellar-way under Barber's house, and out the back door and escaped.

Thomas Bessick, a colored man, who ran cars in Columbia, was one of the boldest and most useful agents there. On one occasion when the slave-hunters were in town, he took two fugitives they were in search of boldly to the station, purchased tickets, and put them in a passenger car while their pursuers were in a hotel close by.

When slave-hunters heard of slaves being on the York route they hastened to Columbia to intercept them. A party of seven were on the way from York station when their masters hearing of it, rode with all possible speed, arrived in Columbia in advance of them. Not expecting their chattels for a few hours they stepped into a hotel to "take a drink." The agents there heard of this and went to the Wrightsville end of the bridge just in time to meet the slaves as they were approaching it. They were quite happy and jocund, singing songs, and exultant in the thought that as soon as they crossed that bridge they would be free.

"Their footsteps moved to joyous measure;
Their hearts were tuned to notes of pleasure."

The idea prevailed to a considerable extent among the slaves that when they crossed the Susquehanna they were on free ground, and were safe. But when told how near they were to where their masters were lying in wait for them they were struck with amazement and fear.

They soon, however, became wild with consternation, and began running like frightened sheep in every direction. By skillful effort and the assurance of protection, the agents succeeded in gathering them together again, and they were conducted to a place of safety.

A base practice connected with the slave-hunting business was that of unprincipled men sending South the description of free colored persons, and having these descriptions printed in hand-bills, then capturing and carrying into slavery such as were thus described. This aroused the sympathies and fired the hearts of abolitionists to more determined efforts to protect the rights and liberties of the colored people.

Samuel Willis, of York, was also one of the active agents at that place.

SAMUEL W. MIFFLIN.

Samuel W. Mifflin, son of Jonathan and Susan Mifflin, of Columbia, Pa., was an abolitionist by birth and education. His mother's family never owned a slave, and his grandfather, John Mifflin, of Philadelphia, was the first to respond to the demand of the Yearly Meeting that Friends should liberate their slaves. His mother was the sister of that early and earnest abolitionist, William Wright, of Columbia, an agent on the Underground Railroad from the days of its earliest travel. As far back in his boyhood as he can remember Samuel was accustomed to seeing fugitives passed along by different members of their family. When he saw the tall fugitive stride across the yard in women's habiliments that reached but to his knees he wondered that any one could think him disguised in such short garments. But when he saw him seated by the side of his aunt on the back seat of a dearborn, with all the appearance of a woman, it excited no suspicion or remark other than that "Mrs. Wright was too much of a Quaker to mind riding alongside of a nigger."

On another occasion, when a boy, a fugitive was hid in a corn-field and fed day after day by a cousin who went out with his gun, and his game bag filled with provisions. The spot where he lay is now occupied by Supplee's machine shops on Fourth and Manor streets, Columbia.

In early life Samuel engaged in civil engineering, which required him to be from home the greater part of the time until after his father's death which occurred in 1840.

On one of his visits home, just before his father's last illness, he found the parlor occupied by thirteen fugitives. They comprised two families of men, women and children whom his elder brother found wandering in the neighborhood. The windows were closed to prevent discovery, and a lamp kept burning all day. They were thus guarded during two days and nights of stormy weather and high water in the Susquehanna which prevented their crossing the river. On the third night they were transferred to the care of Robert Loney who ferried them over to the Columbia shore.

C

A woman with her daughter and grandson were sent there one time from York, and remained a night and a day until means were found to forward them to Philadelphia. The claimant of this family was a woman from Baltimore who was then on a visit to Philadelphia, and while there boasted that her slaves would never run away from home. At that same moment this family of her slaves was safe in the Mifflins' house. They were sent over to Columbia, thence forwarded to Philadelphia where members of the Vigilance Committee met them outside the city.

A party of five came one summer night, who, instead of stopping at Mifflin's, went directly to the bridge. Four of these were slaves until they should arrive at the age of 28. The other was a slave for life. He stood back while the others knocked at the toll-gate. Immediately the kidnappers rushed out and seized the four, but the fifth man jumped over the parapet and disappeared. The place from which he leaped was thirty feet high, but a lot of coal had been piled up there to within ten feet of the top, down which he rolled uninjured. Then climbing up at another point he reached the towing path of the canal bridge, and on that made his way to Columbia, where Stephen Smith took charge of him.

A slave named Perry Wilkinson, a Baptist preacher, was brought by a guide from York to Samuel Mifflin's, arriving there and arousing the family about 10 o'clock at night. They went down stairs and prepared a bed for him. He would not accept anything to eat. After retiring again they heard him pacing the floor as long as they remained awake. He said in the morning he had not slept any on account of thinking of his wife and family, whom he had left behind. He had been the slave of Wilson Compton, of Anne Arundel county, Md., and had been hired out by his master for twenty years on a boat, which ran between his master's wharf and Baltimore. The master having recently died, and the widow being about to remove to Baltimore, she concluded she could do without Perry, and ordered the administrator of the estate to sell him. A friend of Perry's, who had a warm and pious regard for him, learning of this about a week before the sale was to take place, informed him of it, gave him five dollars, and advised him to escape. He went immediately to the boat, got on board of it for the last time, and as soon as he landed in Baltimore started on his journey north, travelling by night and hiding in the woods by day, until he reached York. Samuel Mifflin gave him into the care of Robert Loney.

During his residence at the old homestead from 1840 to 1846, Samuel Mifflin was active in the labor of assisting the liberty-seeking bondman on his way to freedom. In 1843 he married Elizabeth Brown Martin, daughter of W. A. Martin, and granddaughter of Thomas Brown, of Muncy, Pa., a member of the Society of Friends. His wife sympathized in his views and assisted him in his efforts for the freedom of the slaves. She was the mother of eight children, four of whom are living. She died in Columbia in 1858.

On leaving York county, Samuel resumed his profession of civil engineer, and was successively employed in Maine, New York and Pennsylvania. In 1848 he located the Mountain Division of the Pennsylvania Railroad from Huntingdon to Galitzin. He returned to Columbia in 1857.

It was during his residence in York county that he received a visit from the unfortunate Charles T. Torrey, on his way to Baltimore to rescue for a colored man, his wife, who was then held in slavery somewhere in Maryland. After staying with Samuel all night he started in the morning full of enthusiasm and hope in the success of his enterprise, but he never returned. He was apprehended and imprisoned in Baltimore and died of consumption in prison.

In 1861, Samuel Mifflin married Hannah Wright, eldest daughter of William and Phebe Wierman Wright, of Adams county, reminiscences of whose Underground Railroad work have already been given. She was an abolitionist from childhood, through family instruction and inherited principles. Her grandfather's uncle assisted in forming the " Pennsylvania Society for Promoting the Abolition of Slavery, and Protecting the Rights of the Free People of Color," of which Benjamin Franklin was President. Her father's two uncles set all the slaves free who came into their possession by marriage, although they were not Friends.

Samuel W. Mifflin and his wife now reside at Louella, Delaware county, where they own a large flower and vegetable garden and hothouses.

DANIEL GIBBONS.

CHAPTER III.

DANIEL AND HANNAH GIBBONS.—JAMES GIBBONS.—Incidents.—Daniel Gibbon's Method of Questioning Fugitives.—Other Incidents.

DANIEL GIBBONS.
(Born 1775—Died 1853.)

The first station east of Columbia, and the most important one in Lancaster county, was that of Daniel Gibbons. He was imbued from childhood with a repugnance to human slavery, and a sympathy for the downtrodden of the colored race.

His father, James Gibbons, was an anti-slavery advocate, and took a deep interest in everything pertaining to human freedom and human welfare.

JAMES GIBBONS was born in "Chester county, Province of Pennsylvania," in 1734. Although a Friend, he was such an ardent advocate of human rights that he was very much inclined to take part in the Revolutionary war. He was offered the position of a cavalry officer, partly on account of his large stature and commanding appearance, and partly on account of the great interest he took in the welfare of his country. He declined accepting the position, however, in deference to the earnest solicitation and prayers of his wife, who was devotedly attached to the "peace principles" of Friends.

He was married at Goshen meeting-house, Chester county, in 1756. There was a large gathering of Friends there, who came to bid farewell to the bride and groom, as they were going immediately after their marriage into the "far wilds" to settle. Some of the young women remarked that "not for the best man in the

RESIDENCE OF DANIEL MURRAY

Province would they go into the wilderness to live."
That "wilderness" was where the village of Bird-in-
Hand is now situated, in Lancaster county, 39 miles
west of Goshen meeting-house, and seven miles east of
Lancaster city.

About the year 1789, when a sitting magistrate in
Wilmington, Delaware, a colored man was brought
before him by a party of kidnappers. They attempted
as usual, to carry their case through by bluster. But
he told them peremptorily that "if they did not behave
themselves he would commit them." He then set the
man at liberty. He died in 1810.

Daniel Gibbons was a man of large firmness, independence of mind, clearness of perception, discreet
philanthrophy, conscientious, affectionate in his family,
and a devout member of the Society of Friends, in
which he was an elder for twenty-five years prior to his
death. His wife, Hannah, was eminently endowed with
fine intellectual capabilities, quick perception, excellent
judgment, affectionate and amiable in disposition, fond
of home and its endearments, and hence an earnest
sympathizer with the poor slaves, whose homes and
home-loves were so often severed by their being sold as
cattle in the mart. She was also a sincere Christian and
a consistent member of the Society of Friends, in which
she, like her husband, was an elder during the last
twenty-five years of her life. Thus were they adapted
by nature to fulfill the life-mission in which Providence
had called them to labor conjointly.

> "Oh happy they! the happiest of their kind
> Whom gentle stars unite, and in one fate
> Their hearts, their fortunes and their beings blend."

Her goodness of heart and self-sacrificing spirit were

pre-eminently manifested on one occasion when a fugitive, weary, sick and dirty called at their house. She administered to his wants, and in a few days there developed upon the surface of his body the unmistakable appearance of that loathsome disease small-pox. For six weeks, until he was restored, she attended to him faithfully herself, deeming it expedient that none other should have access to him. He remained with them afterwards eighteen months.

Daniel Gibbons was engaged in assisting fugitives from the time he arrived at manhood's estate until his death in 1853—a period of *fifty-six years*. He did not keep a record of the number he passed until 1824. But prior to that time it was supposed to have been over 200, and up to the time of his death he had aided about 1000. So wise and cautious was he in his management that out of the whole number that he succored, but one or two were taken from his house.

In the very early days, about 1818 or 1820, a colored man named Abraham Boston came to his place and remained. He was a very excellent man, and Daniel grew to love him as he would a brother. The kidnappers came one day and carried him off. Daniel, at great risk, went in search of him to Baltimore, Md., but for some reason could never get him back. This was the only person for whom he ever went to Maryland. He had a desease in his feet and legs, and could not, therefore, engage personally in going with, or after, colored people. But his wisdom and shrewdness were ever competent to devise plans which others with better power of locomotion could execute.

When a tap was heard on the window at night, all

HANNAH W. GIBBONS.

the family knew what it meant. The fugitives were taken to the barn; and in the morning were brought to the house separately, and each one was asked his name, age, the name of his master, what name he proposed to take, as Daniel gave them all new names, and from what part of the country he came. These questions with the answers to each were recorded in a book which gradually swelled to quite a large volume. After the passage of the Fugitive Slave Law he burned it.

When a company of colored people came to his house he asked what their situation was and whether they expected their masters soon. If not, they would get work in the neighborhood for awhile. If the masters were expected in a very short time, making it necessary for them to hasten on, they were made safe in the fields or the barn, or, if it was autumn, in the corn-shocks for a few hours, and then taken to the turnpike road that leads to Reading, and hurried on to the next station, which was the house of a Friend named Jackson who lived on the confines of what was then known as "The Forest," in Robinson township, Berks county. This was prior to 1827. After that he sent many to Thomas Bonsall, Lindley Coates and others.

He was very skillful in detecting the artifices of decoys or pretended runaways whom the kidnappers at times sent to his house, although he was occasionally puzzled if they came, or pretended to come, from parts in the South unknown to him. Yet every device of theirs to gain information relative to the management of the "road," or to impose upon him, was as readily foiled by his cunning as the stroke of the novice is parried by the experienced swordsman.

c*

A man came to his place at one time for the ostensible purpose of buying a horse. Daniel observed closely every look, motion, and the intonation of his voice, and suspected that his design was to look after slaves. He had one of them working for him whom the stranger happened to see. When he left, Daniel had the slave removed to a place of safety. Next day, a constable came from Lancaster to arrest him; but, like Paddy's flea, "he wasn't there."

It was his prime object to carry on every thing quietly, though expeditiously; and very few narrow escapes are to be recorded. Slave-hunters came one day after a slave who happened at the time to be in the house. While he detained them by talking and asking questions, his wife hastily slipped the fugitive out the back door and under an inverted rain hogshead. He then politely accompanied them through the house, and gave them free access to every apartment. They left satisfied that Daniel was not harboring their slave.

Dr. Joseph Gibbons assisted his father, doing most of the active work himself, owing to his father's physical infirmity, and then succeeded him—making three generations of earnest, zealous and successful Underground Railroad managers in one family.

A friend, describing the funeral of Daniel Gibbons, wrote as follows: "We turned and mingled our voices with the voices of the earth and air, and bade him 'Hail!' and 'Farewell!' Farewell, kind and brave old man; the voices of those whom thou hast redeemed welcome thee to the Eternal City."

DR. JOSEPH GIBBONS.

CHAPTER IV.

Dr. Joseph Gibbons.—Early Education.—Studies Medicine.—His Wife
Phebe Earle Gibbons, a Contributor to Literature.—Dr. Gibbons
Establishes *The Journal.*—Dr. J. K. Eshleman.—Incidents.

DR. JOSEPH GIBBONS.

(Born 1818.)

Joseph Gibbons, son of Daniel and Hannah Wierman Gibbons, was born at the family homestead, near
the village of Bird-in-Hand, Lancaster county, Pennsylvania, Eighth month 14th, 1818. He is the only one
of three children, all sons, that survived infancy. The
place where he was born is part of a tract of one thous-
and acres of land "and allowances" partly acquired by
purchase and partly deeded to his great-grandfather, for
whom he was named, by John and Richard Penn, in
the year 1715.

In his youth he was sent to boarding school for a
time, to Joshua Hoopes, in West Chester, and also to
the late Jonathan Gause, in West Bradford, Chester
county. At this time, too, Underground Railroad work
was carried on with great activity in Lancaster and
Chester counties, and Joseph Gibbons was his father's
faithful assistant, taking the active part that Daniel
Gibbons' ill health prevented his taking. To an exciting
midnight "run" with a party of fugitives, made when
he was about sixteen years old, the subject of this sketch
attributes a tenderness in the feet and difficulty in walking that have troubled him ever since.

At the age of twenty-one Joseph Gibbons joined a

temperance society, and from that time down to the
present he has been an earnest and active worker in the
temperance cause in his native county and State. He
was also one of the most steadfast advocates of the common school system in Pennsylvania. The system of
having county superintendents was at first very unpopular in Lancaster county. Joseph Gibbons went
around in his carriage with the first county superinten-
dent, giving him his countenance and support. One of
the first teachers' institutes in the county was held at
his house.

Joseph Gibbons early became a member of the Free
Soil or Liberty Party, voting for its presidential candidates from 1844 down to the time when it was merged
into the Republican Party. He attended the convention held in Pittsburg in 1844 that nominated Dr. F. J.
Lemoyne, as Liberty Party candidate for Governor of
Pennsylvania. He was one of the founders of the Republican Party in Pennsylvania. In 1856, when John C.
Fremont and William L. Dayton were nominated at Philadelphia by that Party as its candidates for President
and Vice President of the United States, Joseph Gibbons was not yet thirty-eight years of age. In the
prime of a vigorous manhood, he threw himself into
that "campaign," with all the ardor of a temperament
naturally sanguine and enthusiastic and a soul inspired
by love of freedom and "heart-hatred" of every form
of oppression. He distributed thousands of pamphlets
and documents, and rode night and day attending
meetings.

Although victory did not crown these efforts, they
were of the greatest benefit in arousing the people to re-

sist the encroachments of the slave power and preparing the way for the triumph that came four years later.

Going back a few years it is to be noted that Joseph Gibbons, after studying his profession in the office of the distinguished physician, Dr. Francis S. Burrowes, of Lancaster, took a long course at Jefferson Medical College, Philadelphia, and graduated there in 1845. In the autumn of 1845 he married Phebe, eldest daughter of Thomas and Mary Earle, of Philadelphia. Thomas Earle was a distinguished anti-slavery lawyer, candidate for vice-president on the Liberty Party ticket with James G. Birney, in 1840. Of the five children of Joseph and Phebe E. Gibbons, four survive.

In 1870, an article by Phebe E. Gibbons, entitled "Pennsylvania Dutch," appeared in the "Atlantic Monthly." It was followed by other articles that appeared in "Harper's Monthly" and other periodicals, and were gathered by their author into a volume a few years later, under the title of "Pennsylvania Dutch and Other Essays." A visit to Europe, made in the summer and autumn of 1878, resulted in the contributing of a number of articles to the magazines. These and others were collected, soon afterward, into a volume under the title of "French and Belgians." Both these works were published by J. B. Lippincott & Co., of Philadelphia.

Dr. Joseph Gibbons practiced his profession for about five years after his marriage. For four years, from the Eighth month of 1861 to about the close of 1865, he was an officer in the Custom House in Philadelphia. For some years prior to 1873 his attention had been directed to the lack of a literature in the Society of

Friends that would make its principles and testimonies familiar to the young by presenting them in an interesting form and combined with valuable reading of a general character. He felt that this lack of suitable literature, especially of a periodical kind, was one of the causes of the decline of interest seen in the Society and its failure to increase in numbers. These reflections resulted in the establishment, early in 1873, of *The Journal*, a weekly paper devoted to the interests of the Society of Friends and to the cultivation of literary taste, and the dissemination of general information of a useful character among its members. Its motto, " Friends, Mind the Light," shows the liberal spirit in which it is edited. Considering that it is an individual concern in which Joseph Gibbons and his family have labored with very little assistance from outside sources, it has enjoyed a considerable success and has aroused much interest in the Society of Friends. In the editing of *The Journal* he has been assisted by his daughters, especially the eldest, whose training and experience while connected with daily newspapers have fitted her for this work.

Two or three traits in the character of Joseph Gibbons may be worthy of mention in this connection. The first is his consistent carrying out of his early principles. Educated by his parents in an intense opposition to American slavery, he always advocated its extinction by political action, to which many of his friends were opposed. He did not, indeed, cast his first presidential vote in 1840 for the candidates of the Liberty Party, then first nominated, because he was not convinced of the expediency of forming a third political party, but, in the year 1844, his doubts having been removed, he voted for Birney and Morris. To his faithful adherence to the Liberty and Free Soil parties is due the fact that he never voted for a successful presidential candidate until the election of Abraham Lincoln.

He has also remained consistent in his opposition to intemperance, opposition to which he learned as soon as he was able to learn anything from hearing the subject discussed by his parents at home. He has participated in many debates on this subject, but has always felt that it would be unwise to attempt the founding of a separate temperance political party, the political organization that sustains the rights of his colored fellow-citizens being, in his opinion, worthy of his vote and continued confidence.

It may interest some to learn that, brought up by parents who were both elders in the Society of Friends, and with warm social feelings and no tinge of asçeticism, he has never drunk a glass of ardent spirits, never used tobacco in any form, never been within the walls of a theatre (even when a medical student and in four years of public office in Philadelphia), never played a game of cards and never read a novel.

DR. J. K. ESHLEMAN.
(Born March 2d, 1810.)

Dr. J. K. Eshleman, a warm sympathizer with the negro in bondage, and a willing assistant to those who were escaping, lived and practised his profession near Strasburg, Lancaster county. His Underground Railroad work began in 1840. He was physician in the family of Thomas Whitson, whose labors in that line of travel began about the same time. They were warm personal friends, and frequently visited each other socially. Yet, as Thomas Whitson was extremely reticent upon Underground Railroad matters, the subject was rarely, if ever alluded to in any of their conversations, although it was to him the doctor sent fugitives. He received them from Daniel Gibbons.

The neighborhood in which he lived contained many bitter opponents of the anti-slavery cause who sought opportunity to annoy and persecute abolitionists in any way which could gratify their animosity, even to the extent of burning their barns. A rich field for the enjoyment of their coarse and lawless propensities was in the disturbing and breaking up of these anti-slavery meetings. On one occasion when Lindley Coates took Charles C. Burleigh to lecture in that vicinity a number of this clan pelted them with decayed eggs and threw stones through the curtains of their carriage on their way home.

The doctor rarely ever asked fugitives any questions. He cared to know nothing about them, further than to ascertain who sent them. If they were men, they generally came on foot, with a slip of paper containing directions and telling where they came from. If women and children, they were brought always in close carriages, if danger was immediate, and were conveyed from his place to other stations by the same means.

In 1848 he relinquished practice and moved near to Downingtown, in Chester county. Here he received fugitives from agents in both Chester and Lancaster counties, and invariably sent them to John Vickers, either on the night they arrived or the following night.

Like all others who assisted the fleeing slave, he

passed through many exciting and dangerous scenes, but discretion and promptness of action carried him safely through the perils even of Scylla and Charybdis, where, epecially in later times, the Fugitive-slave Law on one side, and close pursuit on the other, required skilful piloting.

At one time after moving to Chester county, he had occasion to drive to Belle Ayer in Maryland. He overtook a young man near the Brick Meeting-house, and inquired of him the way. The man said he was going near there, and if not encroaching on his kindness he would be glad to ride. The doctor took him in. On the way the subject of slavery was alluded to. The young man said "it was a nuisance and that slaveholders were better off without their slaves," in which opinion the doctor heartily concurred. He said it was only recently that the last of theirs ran away; they did not pursue them; they were satisfied to let them go. It happened to be the very lot the doctor had helped a short time before.

A colored man in the western portion of Chester county was in the practice of going into Maryland to sell salves. While there he obtained from slaveholders a description of all their runaway slaves. On his return, if he saw persons along the northern routes corresponding to the descriptions given, he informed the owners, who sent a constable, had them taken legally and sold to go South. He followed this for a number of years. Finally his treachery was discovered, and a number of colored people assembled and gave him a terrible beating, from the effects of which he never fully recovered. His last illness was supposed to have been the result of this severe punishment.

After the Christiana riot three men who had been engaged in it came to Dr. Eshleman's place, were kept in the barn until next night, and then sent further on.

A whole family came in a four-horse wagon just after the battle of Gettysburg. They had formerly been slaves, but at that time owned a farm between York and Gettysburg. They were very much frightened, and thought if they remained at home they might be killed, or if the rebels gained Pennsylvania they might all be made slaves again. They proceeded as far as Norristown; and hearing there that the rebels had been repulsed, they returned.

After Dr. Eshleman moved to Chester county, Thomas Whitson moved to near Christiana, and their former visits were continued.

His house was ever open to the Burleighs and all other lecturers on anti-slavery and temperance.

THOMAS WHITSON.

CHAPTER V.

THOMAS WHITSON.—Member of First National Anti-Slavery Convention.—Incidents.—JACOB BUSHONG.—Incidents.—JEREMIAH MOORE.
—Incidents.

THOMAS WHITSON.

(Born Seventh mo. 2d, 1796—Died Eleventh mo. 24th, 1864.)

Thomas Whitson, of Bart, Lancaster county, was one
of the most prominent and respected champions of the
anti-slavery cause. His connection with the Underground Railroad began about, or prior to, 1841. Although he passed great numbers of slaves, it was quietly
done, and but few reminiscences are to be gleaned of his
wo k in that direction. His greatest labors were accomplished *above* ground. A minister once said, speaking of the life of Jesus Christ, " It can be given in a
few words ' He went about doing good.' " The life of
Thomas Whitson might be condensed in a similar
manner.

He attended and spoke at anti-slavery meetings
throughout the country ; was eloquent and cogent in
thought, sound in logic, wise in counsel, and his broad
and advanced humanitarian views commanded for him
the respect of all, and placed him in the foremost rank
of the earnest and able opponents of negro slavery. He
was decidedly original, witty, jocose, one of the most
apposite in thought and expression, and had a great
faculty for "splitting hairs" in a close argument. When
he and Lindley Coates, who was also remarkable for

this talent, were engaged on opposite sides in debate, their fine drawn distinctions, close questions, terse answers, and clear ratiocination from irrefragable facts adduced, were at once amusing, edifying and exalting.

At a convention where he, William Lloyd Garrison and others spoke, his speech was characterized by such a flow of wit, good humor, clear logic, sententious expressions, and sometimes sarcasm when the subject evoked it, that Garrison arose at the close of the meeting and said "*the speech of the day* must decidedly be accorded to Whitson."

He had not the advantage in early life of acquiring more than the rudiments of an education. Arriving at manhood's estate, he studied the principles and objects pertaining to the higher welfare of man, as presented to him in his daily observations and intercourse with men, developing his own faculty for originating thought, instead of directing his time and attention to the study of written lore. One amusing feature of his speeches was that his *grammar* was exclusively his own. *It knew no rules*, nor did he care for any.

Benjamin S. Jones said of him in a little volume of word-pictures of the prominent anti-slavery leaders :

Friend Whitson, Friend Whitson,
Like " dunder and blitzen,"
Thy fists and thy words both come down ;
A diamond thou art,
Tho' unpolished each part,
Yet worthy a place in the crown,
          Friend Whitson !
Yet worthy a place in the crown.

He gave freely of his means whenever needed, regarding neither time nor cost. He attended the first convention of the American Anti-Slavery Society, held in

Philadelphia on the 4th, 5th and 6th of December, 1833, of which Arthur Tappan was president. As soon as the "Declaration of Principles" were adopted he stepped up to the desk and affixed his signature, as he had to withdraw from the convention immediately to return home. He thus became the first signer to those "Principles" adopted by the national organization of the earnest, able and indefatigable advocates of universal liberty—principles which gained warm moral adherents and steadfast friends, but which met with the staunchest opposition throughout the entire North, as well as in the South, until the mandate of God, "Let my people go free," went forth and was obeyed by a nation then deluging its soil in fratricidal blood.

As an Underground Railroad agent Thomas Whitson was remarkably reticent. Hundreds of fugitives were taken care of and assisted on their way, but no record was kept. The children saw colored people there frequently, but they were not permitted to ask any questions, or to know anything about them. He spoke of his management to but very few friends.

The fugitives who came to his place at night were chiefly sent by Daniel Gibbons, in care of a trusty colored man, who knew how to awaken Thomas without arousing others of the family. Those who came in daytime from Daniel Gibbons had a slip of paper upon which was written, "Friend Thomas, some of my friends will be with thee to-night," or words varying, but of similar import. No name was signed. The general advice of Daniel Gibbons to the colored people was to "be civil to all, and answer no questions of strangers who seemed eager to get information."

Thomas frequently procured places for them to work
in the neighborhood. Although widely known as an
anti-slavery man his premises were never searched by
slave-hunters. Even the notorious William Baer, who
hunted up and reported fugitives in the neighborhood,
never approached the premises of Thomas Whitson.
After the Christiana riot, when "special constables,"
furnished with warrants and piloted by pro-slavery
men of that section, were scouting the country and
ransacking the houses of abolitionists and negroes, his
house was not molested. On hearing that a party of
these deputized officials were carrying off a colored
man who had worked for him, he pursued and overtook
them, and asked for the man's release. They refused to
grant it. One of them on being told who he was advanced toward him with a volley of Billingsgate, and
flourishing a revolver asked if he were not one of the
abolitionists of that neighborhood.

"I am," said Thomas, "and I am not afraid of thy
shooting me. So thee may as well put thy pistol down."

The officer continued his invective, and turning to
another, said: "Shall I shoot him?"

"No," was the immediate response, "let the old
Quaker go;" and they left him, convinced that he was
not a man to be frightened by bluster or to renounce
a principle in the face of an enemy. He went next
morning to a neighbor who had seen the colored man at
the hour the riot was going on, several miles distant
from the scene of the tragedy, and in company with
him went to where the officers had the man under guard,
proved that he had no connection with the riot and obtained his release.

JACOB BUSHONG.

(Born Seventh mo. 7th, 1813.—Died Fifth mo. 28th, 1880.)

Jacob Bushong, of Bart, Lancaster county, a quiet but devoted laborer in the cause of freedom, relates the case of one Hamilton Moore who settled in his neighborhood. He was peaceable and respected, and to all appearances a white man. Not a tinge of African blood was discernible in his complexion, nor had any one the least suspicion that there was any. He married a white woman and became the father of three children. After the lapse of several years a number of men came to his dwelling and claimed him as a runaway slave; the leader of this gang being Hamilton Moore's father.

Although that was a pro-slavery community, the man's purely Anglo-Saxon appearance and good character had so won the esteem of his neighbors that they would not submit to what they termed an outrage upon him, but arose en masse and rescued him from his captors. He was then taken to the house of Henry Bushong, · Jacob's father, in Adams county, who assisted him to a place of greater security.

About the year 1831, a person calling himself William Wallace, but whose slave name was "Snow," came to Wm. Kirk's in West Lampeter township, Lancaster county. Here he worked for some time, then went to Joshua Gilbert's in Bart township, and afterwards was employed by Henry Bushong, who had now removed to Bart township, and whose place became one of the Underground Railroad stations. After remaining there two years, his wife and child were brought to him from one of the Carolinas. He then took a tenant house on the place, in which he and his family resided two years longer. While there another child was born to them.

In the summer of 1835 while he and Jacob Bushong were at work in the barn they observed four men in a two-horse wagon drive into the lane, accompanied by two men on horse-back. Jacob thought them a "suspicious looking crowd," and told Wallace to keep out of sight while he went out to meet them. They inquired if Mr. Wallace lived there. Jacob replied in the negative, satisfying his conscience by means of the fact that William lived at the tenement house, but worked for him. Pointing towards Wallace's house they asked if his family lived there; to which he made no reply. Leaving their horses in charge of two of the men, they went to the house, tied his wife, brought her and the oldest child to the wagon, loaded them in, took them to the Lancaster county jail, and lodged them there. The youngest child being born on free soil was left with a colored woman who happened to be in the house at the time. From there they went to John Urick's, a colored man, whose wife had escaped from slavery with Wallace's wife. They bound her, took her to jail also, and had the two women placed in the same cell while they started out on another hunt.

The startling news soon spread throughout the country, and was immediately carried to that foremost friend of the slave, Daniel Gibbons. Very early next morning the two women came to his house. The family would not have been more surprised had an apparition come suddenly into their midst. When asked how they came, one of them said, " I broke jail."

"How did you do it?"

" I found a case-knife, and got up from one room to another until I got next the roof, when I cut the lath and shingles and broke through ; got out and down to the roof of an adjoining house, and thence from one house to another until I came to one that was low enough, and then I jumped from it to the ground." They were taken to the wheat field and provided with blankets and food, and next night were taken by Dr. Joseph Gibbons, Daniel's son, and Thomas Peart, several miles to the house of Jesse Webster. From there they were taken to Thomas Bonsall's, thence to John Vicker's, and thus on to other stations.

The account given by the women seemed so strange and incredible that Dr. Gibbons interviewed that eccentric character " Devil-Dave" Miller, who was then sheriff, and lived in the jail. When asked how it happened that he allowed two negro women to slip through his fingers, he winked and laughed. It was afterwards discovered that he opened the jail door and let them walk out. This was the only black woman known to Daniel and his son who persisted in keeping her own secret.

In 1832, a colored woman and her daughter came to Henry Bushong's. The back of this poor woman was a most revolting spectacle for Christian eyes to behold. It had been cut into gashes with the master's whip until it was a mass of lacerated flesh and running sores. Her owner was exasperated to this deed of cruelty on account of one of her children having successfully escaped, and she, knowing its whereabouts, refused to tell. To compel her to reveal this secret, they bound her down in a bent position, and five hundred lashes with a cat-o-

D

nine-tails were inflicted upon her naked back. Yet
with the faithfulness and devotion of a mother's love
she endured it all. Seeing that no amount of whipping
could induce her to betray her child and thus return it
from freedom to slavery, and fearing her own life might
be lost by further infliction, they ceased plying the lash
upon that quivering back, which was now a mass of
mangled flesh and jellied blood. As soon as she had
sufficiently recovered she determined to risk her life in
an attempt to free herself from the cruelty and tortures
of a slavery like this. After being kindly and tenderly
cared for in the home of Henry Bushong she was taken
to a station further east.

About the same year there came two slaves, named
Green Staunton and Moses Johnson, belonging to different masters. They had been sold to slave-traders and
lodged in the jail at Frederick, Md., for safe-keeping
during the night; their owners sleeping in an apartment
above them. With pocket-knives and other small imple-
ments they commenced at once picking out mortar and
removing stones, determined if possible to escape before
morning. They succeeded, and both men ran to the
plantation of Staunton's father, who had been his master.
Mr. Staunton had not intended to sell him, but being
on the brink of insolvency was compelled to do it.
Having compassion for him he gave them both victuals
and assisted them on their way to Daniel Gibbons.
From there Johnson went to Allen Smith's, and Staunton to George Webster's, both in Bart township. After
some time Johnson removed to Thomas Jackson's, at
the "Forest," in the northern part of Lancaster county,
and Staunton, remaining in the neighborhood, sent to

Maryland for his wife, who was a free woman. In 1835 he removed to the tenement of Jacob Bushong. Just at daylight on the morning of August 31st, 1837, six men entered his house, tied and gagged him. His wife infuriated at this assault, seized an axe and was about to deal a blow upon the head of one of the assailants, when she was caught, thrown to the floor, and held there until her husband was borne away. He was placed in Lancaster county jail to await further action.

The news of his arrest was conveyed at once throughout the neighborhood. Several of his friends who had long known him as an honest, peaceable and industrious man, could not allow him to be carried back into slavery, deprived of the rights of manhood, to be sold and driven to work like beasts of the field, if any effort of theirs could prevent it. Accordingly Lindley Coates, George Webster, George Webster, Jr., William Rakestraw, Henry Bushong, Jacob Bushong, John Bushong, Samuel Mickle, Gainer Moore and John Kidd, Esq., agreed to contribute whatever sum might be needed to purchase his freedom. They went to Lancaster, had an interview with his master, and secured his manumission upon the payment of six hundred and seventy-five dollars. He returned to his home, and resolved to compensate his friends as far as possible for the amount they had paid for him. Shortly after this, his wife died. He married again. He remained at that place several years and then removed to Conada, and died. Before he left, he had reinbursed his friends to the amount of one hundred and forty dollars.

Moses Johnson returned from the "forest" in the spring of 1836, and was working for Henry Bushong at the time of Staunton's capture. Hearing of it, and knowing the party was searching for him, he requested some friends to negotiate with them for his freedom. An interview was had with the slaveholders, and as he was not yet in their possession, and there was a doubt lingering in their minds as to whether or not he would be, they agreed to accept $400, which was paid. In a few years, by industry and economy, he returned the full amount, and then acquired sufficient capital to purchase a small farm with good buildings. He died in 1873.

About the year 1848 there lived in "Wolf Hollow," near Pine Grove Forge, Lancaster county, a free colored man, who had married a slave woman. They had several children. Early one morning, after he had gone to a neighbor's to work, some men drove up in a covered wagon, entered the house, dragged the wife and children out of bed, bound them, loaded them in the wagon with others they had kidnapped, some of whom were free, and drove off at a rapid rate toward Maryland, eight miles distant. Their actions were witnessed by a person near by, who immediately informed the neighbors, and Joseph C. Taylor, James Woodrow, Joseph Peirce and others mounted their horses and gave chase. Overtaking them near the Maryland line, Taylor dashed by, then wheeling his horse and facing them, he raised to his shoulder an old musket without a lock, and ordered them to surrender. Not liking the appearance of the deadly looking weapon pointed at them, they halted, and the others of the party just then coming up took the kidnappers, with the colored people they had stolen, prisoners. They locked them up in Lowe's tavern and went to Lancaster to procure legal authority to arrest them for kidnapping free negroes. Before they returned the kidnappers had escaped, carrying with them their load of human plunder.

John Russell, Micah Whitson, Henry Carter, and Ellwood Brown are also mentioned as friends of the fugitive, whose assistance was always freely given.

JEREMIAH MOORE.

(Born Fifth mo. 12th, 1803.)

Many slaves were sent from Daniel Gibbons to Jeremiah Moore's at Christiana. They were to know his residence by its being "the first house over the bridge where the public road crossed the railroad." He secreted them in one of the upper rooms in his house, and when they were brought down to meals the doors were bolted. He not unfrequently noticed parties whom he knew to be pro-slavery in principle and unscrupulous in character, loitering a long time in the adjacent woods under pretence of gunning, or coming to the house ostensibly on other business, when their scrutinizing looks and other actions led to a strong suspicion, and even conviction, that their object was to ascertain if slaves were there, and if so to inform on them.

From Moore's the fugitives were sent in a furniture wagon in care of a trusty colored man to James Fulton's, Ercildoun, eight miles distant.

Abraham Johnson, a young slave, belonging to a Mr. Wheeler, of Cecil county, Md., hearing that he was to be sold next day, told his mother. Early in the night they, with his sister and her child, fled to that well known colored man, on the Susquehanna, Robert Loney, who ferried fugitives across the river in the night at various places below Columbia, and gave them into the care of William Wright, who distributed them to other agents. These came to Jeremiah Moore's. The lad hired with him five and a half years. The mother lived with Lindley Coates, and the sister with Thomas Bonsall for awhile, when she removed to Reading, and married. At the time of the Christiana riot they all went to Canada.

Some of the slave women told of their having been stripped naked to be examined upon the auction-block, and to show their muscular development and activity. Some told of their having been sold in the Northern Slave States and sent into the planting States to pick cotton. Not being accustomed to this work they could not accomplish their daily task with others, in consequence of which they were whipped. To escape this treatment they ran away. Some had been caught, returned, severely flogged, and were then escaping again. Their backs bore the marks where the whip lash had been plied.

This account of the shameful treatment of women at the public sales of slaves for the purpose of stimulating lively bidding and securing higher prices, was corroborated by the uniform testimony of fugitives from various States of the South.

Pro-slavery men in Moore's section were wont to speak of abolitionists as "no better than horse-thieves." One Quaker preacher, sincere in his own way of thinking, asked Jeremiah the direct question which he thought covered the whole moral ground against abolitionism—" What would thee think if thee had a horse stolen and taken to Maryland, and the persons having him, and knowing him to be stolen, would refuse to give him up?"

Jeremiah simply responded by adverting to the unjust and un-Christian comparison between a man and a brute.

Clothing was furnished by himself and his antislavery neighbors for such fugitives as were in need of it, and if they came to his house sick they were attended to with the same care as were members of his own family.

CHAPTER VI.

JOSEPH AND CALEB C. HOOD.—Women Aided by Rev. Charles T.
Torrey on His Last Trip to Maryland.—Sketch of the Life of
TORREY.—Three Men Who Had Been Engaged in the Christiana
Riot.—Other Incidents.—LINDLEY COATES.—Incidents.—JOSHUA
BRINTON.—Incidents.

JOSEPH AND CALEB C. HOOD.

Joseph Hood (Born Twelfth month 5th, 1812.—Died
Ninth month 27th, 1866), and his brother Caleb C.
(Born Fourth month 6th, 1817), of Bart township, Lancaster county, gave assistance to fugitives at all times
when called upon.

Eight, whom it was necessary to hurry along with
great speed, were sent to the home of Joseph and Caleb
C. Hood, one night in the spring of 1843, by Joseph
Smith, of Drumore township. They were given something to eat, and taken by Caleb the same night to
Lindley Coates, where they were secreted until the following night, and then taken further on.

On another occasion, Joseph Smith sent to their
place an elderly colored woman with her son and
daughter. Caleb took them to James Fulton's.

On their way, the woman told him they had been
brought from Baltimore to a place on the Susquehanna
by Rev. Charles T. Torrey. The slaveholders got on
their track and nearly overtook them when they reached
the river. They crossed, however, in safety, but Torrey
on his return for another load, fell into the hands of his
pursuers, was taken to Baltimore, tried, sentenced to

CALEB C. HOOD.

confinement in the penitentiary, and died during his imprisonment. He was a good sincere man, a most earnest and indefatigable worker. He was a native of Massachusetts, a graduate of Yale College, and a minister of the gospel. His sympathy for the oppressed slave impelled him to give up his pulpit and give his entire time and labor to the cause of anti-slavery. While full of ardor, bold and daring, he was so indiscreet and rash in his designs and movements as to keep many of the Underground Railroad agents, who received fugitives sent by him, in constant fear lest he would get himself or them into trouble. His outfit when he started on this last journey, was furnished him in Kennet, Chester county, although it was done with extreme trepidation and reluctance by most of the anti-slavery people, as his plan of going among slaves and encouraging them to leave their masters was not in accord with the general views and wishes of abolitionists, and they endeavored to dissuade him from it. But he believed that by so doing, property in slaves would be rendered so insecure that it would hasten emancipation, or the introduction of hired or free labor. So confident was he that his views were correct, that no argument could move him, and he died a martyr to his cherished scheme of obtaining freedom for others.

After the Christiana riot, three men who had been engaged in it, William Howard, Charles Long, and James Dawsey, formerly slaves, who were acquainted with Caleb C. Hood, came to his place about midnight to ask his advice about the best course for them to pursue. A good supper was given them, and after consultation it was decided that they shoud take shelter in the woods, as

D*

the premises might be searched. They wanted to proceed at once to Canada; but their clothes were at their homes, and the money due them in the hands of their employers, and they dare not return for them lest they might be captured. At their desire, Caleb went next day, collected their money and clothing and delivered it to them that night. Howard's wife sent especial request for them not to attempt to leave the country then, as every place was closely watched. Taking a woman's advice, proverbial for being best in emergencies, they gave up their plans of risking an attempt to escape in the midst of so much danger. The family gave them victuals, and saw no more of them for two weeks, when they returned one dark and rainy night at 12 o'clock, and called them up. They had been secreted during that time under the floor of a colored man's house in Drumore township, and now felt the time had come for them to "strike for liberty." Caleb took them that night to Eli Hambleton's. On the following night Eli took them ten miles to the next station. In ten days they reached Canada. Howard then wrote to his wife, who immediately sold their household goods and went to him.

There was a this time a colored woman named Maria living at C. C. Hood's, who one day, when a slave, heard her master selling her to a slave-trader to go South. Horrified at the prospective change, she lost no time making her escape, and through agencies on the Underground Railroad got to William Howard's, thence to C. C. Hood's, where she had been living but a week when the Christiana riot occurred. She was the mother of nine children, eight of whom she left in slavery. One, a son, had preceded her, and was living with Moses Whitson. In the following winter he went to Massachusetts. Obtaining employment there by which he could support his mother, he wrote for her to come. Cyrus Burleigh was at that time at Hood's, and proposed, that if she would remain a few weeks until he was ready to return to Massachusetts, near where her son was living, he would see her safely to the place. She assented, and at the appointed time she met him in Philadelphia, and was taken care of to the end of her journey.

In 1828 or 1829 a fugitive slave was living with Truman Cooper, in Sadsbury, Lancaster county. One day two slaveholders who had received information of him, accompanied by a guide, entered the field where he was at work, and watching the opportunity to seize him when he could not resist, bound his hands behind him and carried him off. A boy living with Cooper saw the transaction and immediately carried word to Thomas Hood's tannery, near by, when John Hood and Allen Smith started in pursuit of them. Overtaking them at John Smoker's they engaged in a kind of easy familiar conversation until they ascertained that the party was going to put up for the night at Quigg's tavern, Georgetown. Then riding in advance they notified the colored people of that vicinity, who assembled with arms after dark, and surrounded the house in ambush. While the party were at supper, Hannah Quiggs, the landlady, secretly loosened the slave's handcuffs, when, with the bound of a liberated hare, he opened the door and fled. The slaveholders and their guide rushed out to pursue him, but a dusky phalanx

of resolute men arose before their eyes, and presented a
solid front, which they knew it was death to encounter.
Reaching a grove some distance off, he remained there
until the following night, when by some means his pursuers got on his track and gave chase. He, however,
eluded them and found a safe retreat in a wood near
the residence of Jeremiah Cooper, Sadsbury, Lancaster
county, whose wife carried him victuals for a week. He
was then furnished with a suit of Jeremiah's plain
clothes, and sent to one of the Underground stations in
Chester county, whence he made good his escape from
danger.

LINDLEY COATES.
(Born 3d mo. (March) 3d, 1794.—Died 6th mo. (June) 3d, 1856.)

Lindley Coates, of Sadsbury, Lancaster county, was
one of the earliest of the active abolitionists. Possessing more than ordinary intellectual ability, earnest in
the cause of the slave, conscientious in all his purposes,
and a clear and forcible speaker, he inspired others
with the same sincerity and zeal that actuated him in
the anti-slavery movement. Though modest in his ambi-
tions, he was a man adapted by nature to rule over
men, and made a masterly presiding officer. He was
noted for his clearness of thought, soundness of judgment, and steadiness of nerve, and marked executive
ability. Hence his counsel was sought in all matters of
enterprise in the community in which he resided. By
his neighbors he was called " long-headed."

He was not voluble in speech, but being a clear
reasoner, very sagacious, terse and apposite in his remarks, he was considered a sharp contestant in debate,
and never failed to adduce irrefragable argument in all

LINDLEY COATES.

discussions upon moral reform in which he felt an active interest. One noted characteristic he possessed was a remarkable astuteness in so cross-questioning an opponent as to elicit answers confuting his own argument.

Benjamin Jones, the humorous poet who portrayed the characteristics of leading abolitionists in amusing rhymes, thus pays his compliments to Lindley Coates:

> Pray Lindley, don't vex one,
> By asking a question,
> That answered, upsets his own side;
> 'Tis very perplexing,
> And shamefully vexing,
> For one's self to prove he has lied:
> 'Tis, Friend Coates!
> For one's self to prove he has lied.

He was opposed to avarice, and considered it one of the greatest evils instigating men to impose one upon another.

Slaves came to his place from Maryland and contiguous States, from Daniel Gibbons, Thomas Whitson and others, and were taken to James Williams, Joseph Fulton, Mordecai Hayes, Emmor Kimber and to other stations, as seemed best, according to circumstances or exigences at the time. Some who were very intelligent were taken a considerable distance and then directed how and where to go. Some called who were steering for Canada, taking the North Star as their guide. These would obtain the names of the Underground Railroad agents along the route, and then proceed by themselves, taking their own chances.

Connected with the vast numbers who passed through his hands there were many exciting incidents and narrow escapes, the particulars of which are not now remembered. It was a custom with the family to make very few inquiries beyond what they felt needful to satisfy themselves that the applicants were *bona fide* fugitives from the South.

Extra precautionary measures were taken after the Christiana riot to prevent the arrest of any negroes about their premises. All who came at that time were taken to the cornfield and secreted under the shocks, as Lindley and his wife were expecting their house to be searched by deputized officials who were then scouting the country, searching the houses of abolitionists to see if negroes were in them, and arresting every colored person upon whom they could in any way cast a glimmer of suspicion of having been connected with the tragedy at Christiana.

In a few days six or seven of these "special constables," or persons representing themselves as such, came during the absence of Lindley and his son Simmons, (Born March 5th, 1821.—Died October 2d, 1862,) and examined every apartment of the house from cellar to garret, notwithstanding they were told by the women that no colored persons were in it.

Isaac Slack, a carpenter, who was then working at the barn, heard that these men were at the house. He went there immediately, but they had finished their search. He asked if they had a warrant. They replied they had not. Incensed at the outrage of their going through the house in that manner without legal authority he told them in most emphatic language that had he known in the beginning of their being on the premises he would have prevented their unlawful search.

A colored girl living at that time with Simmons and Emmeline Coates who occupied a part of the house, was engaged to be married to one of the slaves whom Gorsuch was after.   He made his escape to Toronto, Canada, and wrote to the girl to meet him there.

On the night of the tragedy, Simmons told her and another colored girl living in the house, to go to the cornfield and remain under the shocks till morning, as it was not improbable that their house might be searched.   They did so, and as soon as practicable started for Toronto, where the affianced couple met and were married.

Although deprecating the condition of the enslaved negroes whose dearest rights were witheld from them Lindley Coates never encouraged secret means to entice them to leave their masters.   But when they had left, and sought aid at his hands in their effort to be free, he assisted them with all his earnestness and ability as he claimed to be the duty of a Christian in behalf of a brother in need.

From Deborah S., widow of Lindley Coates, the editors of this history have received the following sketch, which appeared in an anti-slavery newspaper a few days after his death: .

"Under our obituary head this week a death is recorded which calls for something more than a passing notice.   Lindley Coates, of Lancaster county, Pennsylvania, whose death on the 3d inst., is there announced, was no common man, and his past relations to the cause were such as to make his departure from our midst no ordinary occurrence.   He was one of the earliest, ablest and most devoted friends of freedom of the State of Pennsylvania. He aided in forming the Clarkson Anti-Slavery Association before the American Society had an existence and was an advocate of immediate emancipation when the name of William Lloyd Garrison was comparatively little known. He was a man of great simplicity of character and of inflexible moral honesty, and was endowed with a mind of unusual vigor and of the strictest logical accuracy. On all the great questions of the day his views were clear and decided. He was quick to see and prompt to embrace the truth, and few had more skill than he in detecting and exposing the fallacies of error. Though not a man of liberal education, he was moderately well read and more than commonly well informed; and, although not a fluent speaker, his high order of reasoning powers gave him a strength in debate which made him a formidable opponent and secured for him an enviable distinction among the early champions of the anti-slavery cause. His reputation was not confined to Pennsylvania; he was known and appreciated by the friends of the cause throughout all the country.

"In 1840, when the new organization schism took place at New York, he was chosen president of the American Anti-Slavery Society, and filled, creditably and satisfactorily, the duties of that office till, upon his resignation, William Lloyd Garrison, its present incumbent, was appointed to take his place. For the last few years, owing to ill health, he has taken but little part in the anti-slavery conflict; but his heart beat true to the cause.

"If he was less confident and more apprehensive as to immediate results, it was because disease had impaired his natural hopefulness; his principles had undergone no change and his faith in their final triumph " knew no shadow of turning."

"He died as he had lived, a true friend of freedom, and his name will be preserved in the history of the anti-slavery enterprise as one of its ablest and most worthy champions."

Lindley Coates was a member of the Constitutional Convention of 1837, and made the most strenuous efforts to prevent the insertion of the word "white" into the organic law of the State of Pennsylvania, whereby the suffrage was restricted to members of the Caucasian race. Thomas Earle and Thaddeus Stevens, also prominent members of the convention, worked hard against this change, but all without avail.

JOSHUA BRINTON.
(Born February 28th, 1811.)

The house of Joshua Brinton, Salisbury, Lancaster county, was not on any of the direct routes, and was therefore not one of the regular stations. Yet as he was well known for his kindness, and his sympathy for the condition of the colored race, fugitives were frequently directed to his place which was called by many "a home for colored people."

He often hired those whom he strongly suspected to have come from the South. But when he saw they were not disposed to talk much in reference to themselves, he deemed it best to know as little as possible of their history. He directed many to safe places where they found employment. They had implicit confidence in all he said and did for them, and that confidence was not misplaced.

CHAPTER VII.

JOSEPH FULTON.—Incidents.—Assists Wives of Parker and Pinkney.—
MOSES WHITSON.—Colored Man Betrayed by Fortune-Teller.—Inci-
dents.—William Baer Assists in Capturing a Slave at Marsh Cham-
berlain's.—ABRAHAM BONSALL.—Elisha Tyson.—THOMAS BONSALL.
Meeting of Abolitionists.—Clarkson Anti-Slavery Society Formed.
—Incidents.—Marriage to Susan P. Johnson.

JOSEPH FULTON.

(Born Second mo. 2d, 1782—Died Fourth mo. 11th, 1852.)

Joseph Fulton, of Sadsbury township, Chester county,
began his anti-slavery labors in the days of Benjamin
Lundy. He was an enthusiastic admirer of Lundy
and a constant reader of his paper, *The Genius of
Universal Emancipation*. So ardent was he in the cause
that he subscribed for all the anti-slavery papers, and
refused to give his patronage to the political papers of
other parties "because," as he said, "they feared to
speak out against the crying sin of the nation."

Slaves came to his place chiefly through the hands of
Thomas Whitson, Lindley Coates, and Daniel Gibbons,
and were sent to the Pierces and Fultons, at Ercildoun,
and to others.

They generally came between dusk and 10 o'clock at
night. It was the policy of Joseph's family to ask but
few questions, but to give them supper and comfortable
lodging, either at the house or the barn.

A family of seven came from Daniel Gibbons.
Among them was a fine little girl named Julia, six
years of age, whom Joseph's family took quite a liking

to, and kept until she was eighteen. The others were passed on by way of Ercildoun.

A big, strong, resolute, and rather rough man came at one time. He had an implacable hatred for his master, and would sleep nowhere except in the garret, with an axe near his hand; he declared "if marser came he would knock his brains out." He was a vindictive specimen of humanity, but was probably made so by the injustice and cruelty that he had suffered.

The enactment of the Fugitive Slave Law, in 1850, made it doubly imperative upon the Fulton family to be cautious in their proceedings, as their place, with those of many other anti-slavery people, was closely watched by those who would have gladly seen the talons of the law fixed in every abolitianist. Aside from these there was a gang of negro-informers, headed by a well-known character near the "Gap," who scoured the country with Argus eyes and Briarean arms, ready to seize upon any fugitive and remand him to the chains of a life-long slavery.

In the midst of this dangerous environment, when all was excitement in consequence of this recently passed law, a slave man came to Joseph Fulton's house and was hidden under the hay in one of their barns for nearly a week before they felt it safe for him to venture on the roads. Joseph's daughter, Mary Ann, carried food to him after dark. She was afraid to speak, lest some one might be lurking around and hear. After tapping three times on the partition, she left a basket of food for him, enough to last until next evening, and returned. Before his leaving she drew him a chart of the route to Binghampton, N. Y., and gave him a compass, with directions to travel only at night. Some time afterward she received a letter from him stating that he had arrived there and had found employment.

About 7 o'clock on the morning after the Christiana riot two women, one carrying a child, called at the door, much excited and in great distress, and asked if "something could not be done for them; they didn't know what to do, nor where to go to." On being asked who they were, they replied they were the wives of Parker and Pinkney: that they had got away from their masters the afternoon before, and were endeavoring to escape to some place of safety. As soon as it was dark in the evening they started out, but getting bewildered they had wandered about all night, while the home they left was but five miles distant. They were asked why they came there, and replied that on the road they inquired who lived at that house, and when told, they thought they would have friends there who would do something for them. Mary Ann, with a woman's sympathy and that inspiration and impulse that come in the hour of need, took the case into her own hands at once, and ordered "Julia" to run out the carriage while she went to the field to ask her brother for one of their fleetest young horses.

"What for?" he asked.

She told him. He remonstrated with her against such a dangerous adventure, and refused her the horse, saying she would have all their property confiscated. But she persisted, and would not be put off. He told her then she might take "old blind Nance," thinking possibly she would not risk going with her. But she did. And when ready to start, the question arose in her mind, Where shall I take them? She thought of some persons near Caln Friends' Meeting-house who were wanting help, and went there, thinking she could secure places for them until the officers had left their neighborhood. But all in vain. Every one she called upon refused to take them. Evening now came on; and as they drove through a wood, the darkness of approaching night, with their want of success thus far, began to bring a shade of gloom over their spirits, and they halted to consider what they should do next. While thus deliberating in silence, they saw a little colored woman coming toward them, carrying a tub on her head. Mary Ann asked her some questions and then began to explain their situation, when the colored woman interrupted her by saying, "You need not tell me. I knows, I knows all about it. I've helped in many a scrape this. Just drive down the hill there, you'll see my house. Just go in an' set them down; I'll be back in a little bit." They did as she directed. What this little colored woman did with them, we have not been able to find out. The last account received of them was, that they had got to Edwin H. Coates, who took them to Thomas Hopkins, and he conveyed them to Norristown on the eve of the Governor's election. They were then placed on board the cars at Bridgeport, in care of Benjamin Johnson, colored, who accompanied them to Canada where they joined their husbands. Political excitement being intense that evening in Norristown, their escape was effected without much suspicion.

The editors have received the following additional reminiscences from a son of Joseph Fulton:

"Among my recollections of father's connection with

the Underground Railroad, the case of a mother and her four daughters, slaves of a man named Hall, of Maryland, is, I think, worthy of mention. The mother and children were almost white. They ran away to escape sale and were brought to my father's place by Lindley Coates. As soon as the woman saw father she recognized him, having seen him at her master's in Maryland, he having been employed by Hall to build a barn. The woman, as might be expected, was much pleased to see him, knowing him to be a friend. It not being safe for them to remain at father's, he directed me to take them at night to the house of widow Marsh of Caln. I hesitated to do so, knowing the severity of the law, but father's answer was: 'We'll risk it.' I arrived at my destination about twelve o'clock at night. The widow Marsh took them, the same night, to Micajah Speakman's; thence they made their way to Canada.

"Another family were brought to father's place under a load of corn-fodder in broad daylight. They were forwarded north that night. After the Christiana riot, father sheltered a great many, one of whom was secreted in the barn." * * *

MOSES WHITSON.

(Born 8th mo. (August) 24th, 1789.—Died 2d mo. (Feb.) 14th, 1853.)

Moses Whitson, Sadsbury, Chester county, was in sympathy with the Underground Railroad management, and gave assistance when it was practicable for him to do so. Being a surveyor and civil engineer, of whom there were few then in his section, he was from home much of the time. Hence his place could not conveniently nor with safety be made a station. He frequently employed fugitives.

A young man, named Henry Harris, lived with him several years, was an excellent hand and trustworthy. While at work in the wheat-field one day during the absence of Moses Whitson, his master and master's brother-in-law, accompanied by the constable of Sadsbury, came suddenly upon him, caught and handcuffed him while the master held two pistols pointed at him, bore him to Penningtonville, placed him on the cars, took him as far as Downingtown, and thence to West Chester by stage. Another man, who was at work in the field, ran to the house and gave the alarm. Moses' wife despatched a messenger for him immediately, then ran to the field just as they were taking Henry away. She asked if they expected to take him without proving that he was their property. The master said he would take him to West Chester, prove him to be his, and then take him home with him. She followed them to Penningtonville in the hope of detaining them until Moses arrived. As soon as he received information he and Caleb Brinton, of Pequea, Lancaster county, went to Penningtonville; but too late to see them. Being on horseback they rode rapidly to West Chester, reaching there just after the party had arrived at the White Hall hotel. Moses was not satisfied with the proof they gave, as Henry said he did not know the men. He consulted a lawyer and had Henry detained until the master could furnish satifactory proof. With the means of conveyance then furnished throughout the South, this required a month.

The slave was then confined in jail in heavy irons. Moses visited him while in prison. He then acknowledged that one of the men was his master, and that he had been betrayed by persons of his own color who persuaded him to go to a colored man who professed to tell fortunes. This fortune-teller told him if he would tell his master's name, his own name when in slavery, and where he came from, he would put a spell upon his master so that he couldn't touch him if he did see him. For this blessed immunity Henry paid him ten dollars. The man of "rare gift" then wrote to the master telling where Henry was. In a short time there burst upon him the sad realization that for—not *thirty*, but *ten* pieces of silver, he had been betrayed by this colored Judas into the hands of his master, to be carried back to his former home, and in all probability to suffer the fate of the majority of remanded slaves—to be "*sold to go far South.*"

In about a month the master returned, bringing with him a number of witnesses who proved Henry to be his property. Moses Whitson was present at the examination. He offered to buy Henry, but the master would not sell him; saying that "when he lost Jack" (which was Henry's slave name) "he lost his best nigger."

In a few weeks these same men returned to take another fugitive from the same neighborhood. The owner, on this visit, told Lindley Coates, he had sold Henry to a man in Natchez, for $1,800.

A colored woman named Elizabeth was sent by Daniel Gibbons to Moses Whitson's. Needing help in the house at that time, they employed her. Her master received information of where she was, and taking a man with him in a two-horse wagon started out for his property. They arrived at Mount Vernon tavern, Lancaster county, in the evening and remained over night.

Early in the morning they went to Moses Whitson's, entered the kitchen, seized the woman, testified to her belonging to one of the men, and took her with them to the tavern. Then ordering their breakfast, they sat down to it with a hearty relish and cheerful serenity after the morning's triumph. Benjamin Whipper, a colored man living with Whitson, saw the transaction, and without a moment's delay notified William Parker and other colored people in the neighborhood who at once assembled and devised means for her rescue. Four or five of the men concealed themselves by the roadside below the tavern, while Whipper watched the departure of the slave-hunters, and then, mounted on a *white horse* of Whitson's, rode behind the wagon containing the woman, to designate it from other wagons. As soon as the party approached these men they bounded like lions from their covert, seized the horses and turned them in the road. The slaveholder drew his pistol, but before he could fire, one of the colored men struck him upon the arm, breaking it. The other man fired, but without effect. The negroes then fell upon the slave-catchers, pummelled them severely, and then let them proceed on their way to reflect that fugitive slaves are dangerous people for negro hunters to encounter in a Free State while in the attempt to carry one of their number back to the condition of chattel property.

Not thinking it safe to return the woman to Moses Whitson's, she was taken to one of the neighbors, and thence sent to Emmor Kimber with whom she lived two years.

Some slaves belonging to a widow in Elkton, Md., ran away, and coming into Lancaster county, one hired
E

with Marsh Chamberlain, near the Gap. The widow married, and her husband at once instituted search for the absconded property, and advertised them in the newspapers. Wm. Baer, of that section, whose bent of mind was known to be in the interest of slaveholders, and who was not known to reject emoluments offered for returning slaves, saw that the description of one of the fugitives coincided with that of the man at Chamberlain's. He corresponded with the husband who offered $200 for the colored man's return. Baer with two others went to the house of Chamberlain one evening after dusk, knocked at the door of the basement kitchen, entered, and seeing the man, made an onslaught upon him at once to secure his arrest before he could resist. He, however, made a vigorous effort to repulse them and escape, but was overpowered, knocked down, badly bruised and cut about the head and had his ankle dislocated. During the melee the light was put out, and they continued the struggle in the dark. Chamberlain was away, the other members of the family were up-stairs, but being frightened by the sudden commotion, and knowing they could do nothing to rescue him, they did not go down. He was bound, carried to a wagon and driven off. The blood flowed so freely from his wounds, that by it the party was tracked next morning through Penningtonville, Russelville and to Elkton. As the man was so badly injured, the husband refused to pay the stipulated reward. He succeeded, however, in selling the negro, and Baer received his portion of the price of that flesh and blood he had so ingloriously remanded back to the sad and weary life of a chattel laborer.

The consternation and shock of the occasion so prostrated Chamberlain's wife that it was a long while before she recovered from it.

As soon as information of the affair was reported in the neighborhood, Moses Whitson, Samuel Whitson, Samuel Brinton, John Cain and Dr. Augustus W. Cain, held a private meeting at the house of Lindley Coates to consider the propriety of taking some action in reference to the case. They believed that the manner in which the man was taken would be clearly defined by law as kidnapping. Samuel Whitson and Dr. Cain were appointed a committee to visit Elkton, ascertain the particulars of the case, and if sufficient evidence could be adduced to commit Baer, they would commence prosecution against him. On consulting Lawyer Earle of that place, he told them nothing could be done as the slave had been delivered to his legal master, although he admitted the man was not arrested precisely according to law.

Threats were now made that the barns of Samuel Whitson, Lindley Coates, and Dr. Cain would be burned. The two former fell a sacrifice to the flames, but whether in consequence of the threat or not was never ascertained. Dr. Cain kept a guard around his barn for two months and it escaped.

ABRAHAM BONSALL.

(Born 1764.—Died 1840.)

About the year 1805, John Clark, a fugitive, hired with Abraham Bonsall, then living on the farm now occupied by Benjamin Johnson, in East Bradford. While in West Chester one day he became intoxicated, and was arrested by Constable Thomas Mason and lodged in jail. His owner at that time being in the neighborhood in search of him, heard of his arrest, proceeded to the jail, identified him and was about taking legal measures to remove him, when he deliberately walked up to his coat which was hanging in his cell, drew from it a razor and cut his throat, rather than be returned to his revolting experience in slavery.

The owner of a fugitive slave girl living with Abraham Bonsall came there one day and seeing her, at once identified her and proceeded to carry her off. She ran to Abraham's wife Mary, and with piteous cries and screams clung to her, but was forcibly dragged from her side and borne away. Mary's sympathy for the poor girl, and the rough manner in which she was taken produced a shock upon her nervous system from which she never recovered.

During and subsequent to the year 1810 Elisha Tyson, of Baltimore, Md., forwarded colored people to Jacob Lindley, near Avondale, Chester county. He sent them to Philip Price, East Bradford, north of Strode's mill, and he to Abram Bonsall, who by this time had removed near to Valley creek bridge, on the Pennsylvania Railroad. Abram sent them to Isaiah Kirk, near Pughtown, or to Enoch Walker's at Moore Hall Mill, east of Valley Forge.

THOMAS BONSALL.
(Born 1797.—Died 1882.)

Thomas Bonsall, son of Abraham, settled on a property near Wagontown, in West Caln, since owned by Steele, Worth and Gibbons. Fugitives were frequently sent to him by Daniel Gibbons, with a piece of paper containing his name. Pro-slavery men in the neighborhood were never approached by the fugitives, but they knew who Thomas was, and that his place was one of the stations on the road. They frequently asked: "How is it that fugitives never come to us and tell of their running away, but somehow they always get to you abolitionists?" "Oh," Thomas replied, "I suppose we look at them differently." He lived on this farm thirty-three years, during the whole of which period he was an active agent, but kept no notes of the number he passed along. His hired men frequently tried to find if any were hidden in the barn, by running a pitchfork into the hay and straw mows, hoping to plunge it into the body of a negro. But they were safely placed in the granary of his double-decker barn, and his daughter carried them food. Well did they know the approach of her footsteps, and the kind hand that gently tapped at their door as a signal that she was there. But when others were about all was quiet.

Thirteen were secreted in his barn at one time during the period of the Fugitive Slave Law when the pro-slavery men of the North were exasperated to the highest pitch of passion against the "detested abolitionists" who opposed this law as antagonistic to humanity, and a blemish upon the escutcheon of a republic assuming to he free, and to be based upon the principle of equal rights to man.

The majority of those who stopped at Thomas Bonsall's were passed to John Vickers, Lionville, until after his death, when they were sent to Gravner Marsh, East Caln.

At one time Lindley Coates or Thomas Whitson asked Thomas Bonsall if there could not be some means devised by which they could meet together and form a society for mutual consultation. Accordingly, Thomas Bonsall, Lindley Coates, Thomas Whitson, Amos Gilbert and Moses Whitson, met in Sadsbury school-house, just over the line in Lancaster county. They could not reconcile themselves to the idea that man had any right to hold as property his fellow-man. Nor could they conscientiously sustain a law which gave him this prerogative.

At this meeting they prepared a bill to abolish the use of the jail in Washington, D. C., as a slave-pen. It was signed by Lindley Coates, as president of the meeting, and sent to John Quincy Adams, member of the House of Representatives, asking him to present it to Congress. He answered that he would introduce the bill but would not advocate it, as he thought we ought not to meddle with the subject.

This meeting was followed by others, and very soon a dozen or more anti-slavery people, among whom were Asa Walton, Thomas and Eli Hambleton and others, assembled and held meetings in a school-house where Homeville is now situated, and a general interest soon began to extend itself. They then formed a more thorough organization under the name of the *Clarkson Anti-Slavery Society*.

Some of the fugitives coming to Thomas Bonsall's wished to hire with him, "because he was an abolitionist." All whom he did employ proved honest and faithful laborers. One man sent to him by Daniel Gibbons said his master died, and a dealer coming along purchased him from his mistress for $700, and started him with a drove of others from Norfolk. The men were handcuffed, two abreast, to a long rope to prevent their running away, and were thus driven along, while the women and children were conveyed in a wagon. They were kept thus uncomfortably pinioned together, both while they ate and when they slept. They travelled several weeks to some place unknown to him, and here he was sold for $2,100. Taking sick shortly afterwards he was left behind until the second lot came along, when he was sent on horseback to return to Virginia. Here he chanced to see his wife and children. Joy sprang up again in his bosom, and visions of them floated before his mind in sleep. He was permitted to talk and be with them, and was put to work at blacksmithing. Soon, however, he was again sold, handcuffed as before, separated from his wife and children, placed in another gang and driven off. They travelled several days, and were then put in a jail for safe keeping. A free negro in there suggested to him that they try to escape. He devised a plan, and told one of the women outside if she would get him a knife he would make her a corset-board. It was furnished him. With it he nicked his razor and used it to saw one of the bars of the prison window sufficiently deep to enable them to bend and break it, and the five men escaped. They travelled by night. It being moonlight and the freeman able to read, the others hoisted him up to read the directions on the handboards along the way. At one time he read a notice of $1,000 reward offered for their detection. They came to York county, and crossing the river at Wrightsville to Columbia were told by a Methodist to go down to Chester county, there were Quakers there. They got to Daniel Gibbons, from there to Lindley Coates, and thence to Thomas Bonsall's who hired this man. One of the others hired a few miles distant; but none of them would ever reveal, except to these "agents" that they had ever been in slavery, lest they might be informed upon.

Two women from Alabama narrated the wretched and degrading treatment imposed upon them and others in the rice swamps and cotton plantations of the far South. During the very busy season in time of cotton picking they were compelled to work all day, and during moonlight nights until nearly morning, not being allowed time to rest, nor to eat, but had to carry a small bag of corn around their neck from which they might pick the grains and eat while at work, while the driver with his whip kept them continually going to the utmost limit of their strength. The field hands were kept in a state of nudity, and when allowed to sleep at nights they were huddled together in a pen; and, with ball and chain attached to each to prevent their running off, were thus left to lie down and sleep together like so many brute beasts. These two women were assisted by a sea captain to make their escape.

This treatment of slaves in the most Southern Slave States by *some only*, we can hope, of the planters, might seem incredible to us of the North who were unaccustomed to seeing such treatment of laborers, were the accounts not corroborated by others who were successful enough to escape from that section. It was a knowledge of this usage which gave the slaves of the more Northern States such a horror of being "sold to go South."

The two women and a boy spoken of in the account of Jacob Bushong, who were arrested in his house and taken to Lancaster county jail from which they escaped, and through Daniel Gibbons and others were taken to Thomas Bonsall's, were secreted by him until next night when he took them to John Vickers. The night being dark, he rode on horseback a short distance in advance of the wagon containing them. This was a hazardous ride, as their pursuers were searching the country around for them, ready not only to fasten again upon them the chains of an ignominious servitude, but to fasten upon every abolitionist who aided them the inexorable chains of the Fugitive Slave Law. But He who said " Whatsoever ye do unto the least of one of these my brethren ye do unto me," seemed to guide them through the darkness of night, through the perils of opposition to this law, and cheered the hearts of these pilots in their mission of love and mercy to the unfortunate ones of a race whose burden was heavy, and whose yoke was grievous to be borne.

Not only were those early anti-slavery advocates reviled by the pro-slavery portion of the community, but abusive epithets were heaped upon their children, who, even at school, were taunted on account of their parents being " *abolitionists*," a term they contumeliously applied as a stigma of reproach and disgrace.

When the colored people in the vicinity of Christiana first celebrated the Emancipation proclamation the captain of the company meeting Thomas Bonsall, and knowing him to be one of the old Underground Railroad agents, ordered three cheers for him, which were given with a zest and exuberance of spirit such as they only can feel who have known and experienced the rapture of a sudden transition from the degrading thraldom of a slave to the enobling rights of a man.

E*

He has on various occasions since the war met colored people who recognized him, and reminded him of the time he helped them to freedom, when to do so imperiled the safety of his own property and his own person.

He is still residing at Christiana, and is now, Fifth month (May), 1882, in his 86th year. He is a member of the Society of Friends, has held the position of Clerk of the Preparative, Monthly and Quarterly Meetings in his section for a number of years, and that of overseer, elder and member of the Representative Committee between forty and fifty years. He still occupies the position of overseer and elder.

On Tenth month 16th, 1823, he married Susan P. Johnson, of London Grove. She passed from life First month 9th, 1847, in her 53d year. She was an earnest sympathizer and co-worker in the anti-slavery cause. When fugitives came, and her kind hands portioned out to them a bountiful repast as she gave them words of counsel and encouragement on their road to freedom, the large tear of gratitude were ofttimes seen to trickle down their dusky cheeks.

CHAPTER VIII.

THE CHRISTIANA TRAGEDY.—Sketch of Life of William Parker.—Dickerson Gorsuch Lay Wounded, and was Cared for at the House of Levi Pownall.—Caster Hanway Tried for Treason.—Other Cases Removed to Lancaster.—Acquittal.

THE CHRISTIANA TRAGEDY.

It is not my design to give a full and detailed account of the tragedy at Christiana. An account of it was published at the time, when the whole country was in a state of excitement over this first great defense of the negroes against an armed force to capture and carry back to slavery a portion of their number, under the recently enacted Fugitive Slave Law, and has already become a part of history. Reference will only be made to some of the causes which led to it, and some of the incidents connected with it, as they come within the scope of this work, are related by private individuals in the neighborhood, and gleaned from published statements.

Nearly all the laboring class around Christiana at that time were negroes, many of whom had formerly been slaves. Some of these were occasionally betrayed and informed upon by persons who received a pecuniary reward for the same, kidnapped, and carried back, bound or hand-cuffed, to their masters.

There was a band of "Land Pirates" known under the familiar name of the "Gap Gang," scattered throughout a section of that country, who frequently gave descriptions of these colored people to southerners

which led to their capture; and when opportunity
offered, they assisted in kidnapping free negroes, and
carrying them into the Border States to be sold. This exasperated the colored people against all slave-hunters,
and they held meetings, assisted by their white friends, to
consider and adopt means for self-protection. The man
who stood prominent among their race in that vicinity
as one of acknowledged intelligence and indomitable
will, was William Parker. He possessed a strong social
nature, and would at any time put his own body in danger to protect a friend. These qualities gained for him
the respect of a very large class in that community: for

> " Kindness by secret sympathy is tied ;
> And noble souls in nature are allied."

He had repeatedly foiled the kidnappers in their un-
dertakings, rushed upon them in defiance of their
weapons, beaten and driven them before him out of the
neighborhood, as one man may put a herd of buffaloes
to flight. He was therefore the one above all others
whom they wished to get rid of.

Before entering upon even a brief narrative of that
tragedy, it may be due the general reader to advert to
some of the earlier and the later incidents in the life of
Parker, as it was to him the colored people looked up
in his neighborhood as their head and leader, and
around whom they gathered when armed slaveholders
and their aids, headed by Edward Gorsuch, attempted
to capture some of his slaves and carry them back into
slavery; the resistance to which resulted in a fight,
made national by a trial for treason instituted by the
slaveholders, and in the death of Edward Gorsuch.

WILLIAM PARKER was born a slave in Anne Arundel

county, Maryland. His master, who was somewhat easy with his slaves, neither very harsh nor very indulgent, died before Parker grew to know much about him. His mother also died while he was quite young; and to his grandmother, he said, he was indebted for the little kindness he received in his early childhood. No mention is made as to who was his father.

After his mother's death he was sent to the "Quarters," which consisted of a number of low buildings in which slaves of both sexes were lodged and fed. One of these buildings was set apart for single people and for children whose parents had been sold or otherwise disposed of. This building was 100 feet long and 30 wide, with a fireplace at each end and a row of small rooms on each side. In this place all were huddled together. The larger and stronger children would push forward and occupy the best and warmest places, and make the smaller and weaker stand back and occupy the less desirable positions. This principle, however, is not peculiar to these little parentless negro children thrown together in one room like animals in a stock-pen, but manifests itself among far too many of the intelligent and even professedly religious class of white people whose love for lucre prompts to individual oppression, that by pushing another aside they may gain the coveted object of their desire. Alas for the injunction, "Bear ye one another's burdens!"

Young Parker's grandmother being cook at the "great house," could only do him her little acts of kindness when she had the opportunity of going to the "Quarters."

As he grew older, "his rights at the fire-place," he remarked, "were won by his childish fists. And this experience in his boyhood," he adds, "has since been repeated in his manhood, when his rights as a freeman were, under God, secured by his own right arm."

Neither of his young masters would allow his slaves to be beaten or abused, as many slaveholders did, although the overseers sometimes whipped or struck them; but every year a number of them were sold—sometimes as many as six or seven at a time.

One day the slaves were told they need not go to work, but come to the "great house." As they were preparing to go, a number of strange white men drove up. They proved to be slave-traders. Parker and a companion of his about the same age, became alarmed, ran away and climbed a pine tree where they remained all day listening to the cries and wailings of men, women, and children as one by one they were being sold, and family connections and ties were being sundered. These slave sales were more solemn occasions in reality to the blacks than the funerals of loved ones among the whites. Families separated, not by deaths, but by sales; and those who remained seldom ever knew the fate of those who were driven off to be sold again in other markets.

It was while in the pine tree that day, that the idea first entered his mind of running away to the Free States to escape being sold. He was then about ten or eleven years of age. He proposed it to his companion, Levi. But he thought if they got clear this time, perhaps they would not be sold.

Night came on. Its darkness added to the solemnity of the day's sadness. Levi wanted to go back to see if

they had sold his mother; but Parker, in speaking of
that occasion some years after, said, "I did not care
about going back, as I had no mother to be sold. How
desolate I was! No home, no protector, no mother, no
attachments. As we turned our faces toward the quarter
where we might at any moment be sold to satisfy a debt,
or to replenish a failing purse, I felt myself to be what
I really was—a poor friendless slave-boy."

On seeing his mother, Levi ran to her and asked—
"Mother, were you sold?"

"No, child."

She then told the boys who of their uncles and
aunts had been sold.

About a year after this Levi was sold. Parker remained on the plantation until he was about seventeen;
still harboring in his mind thoughts of and desire for
freedom; yet not for once thinking that it was a possible thing for him to leave without some exciting provocation. So one day when his master was going to whip
him with an ox-gad for refusing to go out in the rain to
work, young Parker thought that was his opportunity,
and seizing the stick, whipped his master and bade him
good-bye. On his way past a field he beckoned to his
brother, who joined him, and they pursued their way
northward. Once having started, the fires of liberty
glowed in his bosom; he had cast off the shackles of
slavery, and never more would he submit to a return to
them.

The fugitives' liberty was not always secured without
a struggle, and thus these two boys found it. When
near to the town of York they were interrupted by
three white men. After some conversation one of them,

a very large man, said: "You are the fellows this advertisement calls for," at the same time reading to them out of a paper. It was their description exactly. The man continued:

"You must go back."

Parker signified that they would not.

"I have taken many a runaway and I can take you," replied the man as he put one hand in his pocket as if to draw a pistol, and reached the other toward Parker, who struck him across the arm with a heavy stick. The arm fell as if broken. Battle commenced. The men ran. The boys gave chase, determined to inflict still greater injuries, but the men outran them.

When nearing Columbia, in the darkness of night, they heard men coming behind them; they dropped into a fence-corner to let them pass. They recognized the voice of one as that of their master.

They both arrived safely in Lancaster county and hired with farmers. Kidnapping and rumors of kidnappers were of frequent occurrence and kept the colored people in a constant state of apprehension. They formed an organization for self-protection, and to prevent any of their number from being carried into slavery. In that part of Lancaster county the majority of white people were very hostile to negroes; and if slaveholders or kidnappers wished to enter a house they did not hesitate to break open doors and forcibly make their entrance.

This unwelcome intrusion was made at the house of one of Parker's friends while he was there visiting and discussing the dangers to which they were subjected from these parties of white men. About three or four came and knocked. Upon refusing to tell who they were, admittance was denied them. They opened the door and walked in. The leader drew a pistol on Parker who seized a pair of heavy tongs, struck him a severe blow in the face which knocked him senseless for a few moments; the others did not dare to risk an encounter, but lifting up their injured comrade, walked sullenly away. This began to give Parker a reputation among both the colored people and the kidnapping fraternity for undaunted boldness and remarkable power. He had resolved that "no slaveholder or kidnapper should take back a fugitive if he could but get his eye on him." And they had abundant testimony of how faithfully he kept his word. Neither unequal numbers, nor pistols pointed at him could impress him with a thought of fear. It was a remark of Lindley Coates that "he was bold as a lion, the kindest of men, and the warmest and most steadfast of friends."

He led a few colored men against far superior numbers at the Court-house in Lancaster to rescue a man whom the slave-owner had proved to be his property. Pistols were fired, stones and brick-bats thrown at him, but he heeded them not. They unbound the man, but he was so bewildered by the sudden struggle that he stood still and allowed himself to be bound again and taken back to the jail. During this time the slave-owners and their posse, with a number of pro-slavery co-adjutors were trying to arrest the blacks. Three times they had Parker, but they were to him as the green withes to Samson. One after another fell before the heavy blows dealt by his strong arm, until the others turned and fled. The friends of the recaptured man then raised a sufficient amount of money to purchase his freedom—the master undoubtedly thinking it better to sell him then than to attempt again to take him back.

At another time kidnappers seized a man and were hastening with him to Maryland. Parker with six others pursued, and on coming up to them pistols and guns were freely used on both sides. Parker received a shot in the leg, which brought him to the ground. He quickly rose; the kidnappers called for quarter; the man was released and the victors returned. Arriving home Parker cut the ball out of his leg with a pen-knife and kept the secret of his being wounded to himself.

These are but a few of the many incidents in which he was the leading spirit, and chief instrument in preventing the colored people of his section, both free and slave, from being bound and carried off. How many more might have been swept away from their homes without legal warrants, by those mercenary negro-stealers who infested that party of Lancaster county, had they not been afraid of, and measurably held at bay by the the powerful and dauntless Parker, it would be impossible to tell. So frequently did colored men go to work in the fields and never return, and were colored girls snatched from the homes of their employers, or whole families carried off in the night and never again heard from, that it was an almost daily question with them, "Whose turn will come next?" No law threw its guards around the free negroes to prevent their being stolen; and there was no law to protect the fugitives, who loved even the imperfect freedom they possessed better than the bondage in which they once lived.

Such was the condition of things in that section of country adjacent to Christiana for some time prior to the riot, and which prepared the colored people for, and incited them to the resolute stand which they took in self-defence on that occasion.

For some days before this conflict two or three men were travelling through the neighborhood peddling goods. Their looks and actions aroused suspicion that they were spies, and this feeling was impressed still more upon the colored people by reports afloat that an attack was soon to be made on Parker's house. He gave but little thought to the rumors, although he did not question the probability of their truthfulness. He and his two brothers-in-law, Alexander Pinkney and Abraham Johnson, lived in a tenement belonging to Levi Pownall, one and three-fourths miles southwest from Christiana. Sarah Pownall, wife of Levi, had a conversation with him the night before the riot, and urged him, if slaveholders should come, not to lead the colored people to resist the Fugitive Slave Law by force of arms, but to escape to Canada. He replied that if the laws protected colored men as they did white men, he too would be non-resistant and not fight, but would appeal to the laws. "But," said he, "the laws for personal protection are not made for us, and we are not bound to obey them. If a fight occurs I want the whites to keep away. They have a country and may obey the laws. But we have no country."

When Parker went home that evening he found two of his colored neighbors there very much excited over a report that slaveholders with a United States officer were on their way to that place to capture slaves. The

Managers of the Underground Railroad depot in Philadelphia, who were in close communication and knew everything of importance that was transpiring, learned that Edward Gorsuch, of Maryland, with several others, was in the city arranging plans for the capturing of some of Gorsuch's slaves at Christiana. So adroitly and successfully did these managers, or Vigilance Committee, carry out their part of the work, that they ascertained the whole plan of the slaveholders and their allies, and sent one of their trusty agents, Samuel Williams, a colored man, to accompany the party, and when he had the most favorable opportunity, to notify the colored inhabitants of that section of the approaching danger. He left the cars at Penningtonville (now Atglen), and proceeded hastily to Christiana and gave the information before the party, who had separated and taken different routes, had met at the place they had designated.

Parker's friends remained in the house all night. In the morning before daylight, (September 11th, 1851), when one of them started out, he was met by two men, while others came up simultaneously on either side. He ran back to the house, and up stairs where Parker and his wife were sleeping, and shouted "Kidnappers! Kidnappers!" He was followed by the men, one of whom, Henry H. Kline, started up stairs after him. He was met by Parker who asked, "Who are you?"

"I am the United States Marshal," answered Kline.

Parker cautioned him against advancing further.

"I am United States Marshal," bawled Kline again with the evident assurance that the announcement of his legal authority would intimidate the negroes.

" I don't care for you nor the United States," replied Parker with an emphasis that convinced Kline it was not an ordinary " nigger" he was encountering.

Pinkney then spoke, and said "they might as well give up."

Parker rebuked him. A colloquy then ensued between Kline and Parker, when Edward Gorsuch advanced, and with some remarks began ascending the stairs.

Parker told him he might come, but warned him of the consequences.

Kline told Gorsuch to stop and he would read the warrant to Parker. He did so. But he might as well have read it to the Rock of Gibralter and commanded it to come down and crumble at his feet. Gorsuch then told Kline to go up as he was marshal. He started again, saying, " I am coming."

" Come on," said Parker.

But Kline's vaunted interpidity failed him. He went back and urged the negroes to "give up without any more fuss, that he was bound to take them anyhow."

But all talk availed nothing. Kline then threatened to burn the house, and ordered his men to bring straw.

"Burn us," said Parker, " but you can't take us. None but a coward would talk like that."

By this time daylight was appearing. Parker's wife asked if she should blow the horn. He assented. She blew it from a garret window. Kline wanted to know what it meant. Parker made no answer. It was an understanding among the colored people that when a horn was blown they were to run to the spot. Kline

told his men to shoot any one they saw blowing a horn.
When Parker's wife went to the window a second time and
commenced blowing, two men fired at her, but missed her.
She dropped below the window, and blew continuously,
and the men kept firing, but without effect. The colored
people of the neighborhood were now aroused, and came
in from different directions, armed with guns, clubs, etc.
About twenty or more white men came out of the woods
close by, whom Parker supposed to be members of the
Gap gang in collusion with the slaveholders, and whose
object was, after Gorsuch should discover that he and
his brothers-in-law were not his slaves, to take advantage of the occasion to kidnap them.   These men were
immediately enrolled by Kline as "Special Constables."

When Pinkney saw the white men there in superior
numbers, he thought there was no use in fighting them ;
they might as well give up, and started down stairs.
Parker threatened to turn his battery on him if he
showed any more such pusillanimity. "Yes," remarked
Kline, "they would give up if it was not for you."
There was a lull in the firing. The blacks had not yet
returned a shot. Elijah Lewis and Castner Hanway
now came up, the latter on horseback. Kline read his
warrants to them and demanded their assistance. They
refused, and told the slaveholders if they attempted to
take those men they would get hurt. They paid no heed
to the admonition. While they were talking, Parker,
followed by the four men in his house, came to the door.
Gorsuch thought they intended to escape. He drew out
his revolver and signalled his men into line. They
numbered about three or four times as many as the
blacks. Parker stepped up immediately in front of

him, and placing his hand upon his shoulder, said,
"Look here, old man, I have seen pistols before to-day."
Turning to Kline, he said, "you said you would take us;
now you have a chance." Dickerson Gorsuch entreated
his father to come away, but he asserted with an oath
that he would have his property. Parker still maintaining his position said, "We don't want to hurt you,
but you ought to be ashamed of yourself to be in this
business, and you a class-leader at home."

Dickerson's face flushed, and he said, "father, I
would not take that insult from a d——d nigger;" at
the same time he raised his revolver and fired, the ball
passing close to Parker's head, cutting the hair. Before he
could fire another, Parker knocked the pistol out of his
hand. Fighting then commenced in earnest. Dickerson fell wounded. He arose and was shot again. The
old man, after fighting valiantly, was killed. The
others of the slaveholders with the United States Marshal and his aids fled, pursued by the negroes. While
Dickerson lay bleeding in the edge of the woods, Joseph
P. Scarlett, a Quaker, came up and protected him from
the infuriated negroes, who pressed forward to take his
life. One was in the act of shooting, when Joseph
pushed him aside, saying: "Don't kill him."

Dickerson remarked: "I did not think our boys
(meaning the slaves), would have treated us in this way."

Joseph asked if he had seen any of them.

"Yes," he replied, "I have seen four."

When the fight had ended Parker returned to his
house. There lay Edward Gorsuch near by dead.
Dickerson, he heard, was dying, and others were
wounded. The victor viewed the field of his contest,

but he possessed too much of the noble spirit of manhood to feel a pride in the death of his adversary. He offered the use of anything in his house that might be needed for the comfort of the wounded.

He then went to Levi Pownall's and asked if Dickerson could not be brought there and cared for, remarking that one death was enough. He regretted the killing, and said it was not he who had done it.

He then inquired of Levi Pownall, Jr., what he thought best for him and Pinkney and Johnson to do.

Levi advised them to start for Canada that night.

Dr. A. P. Patterson was sent for and examined Dickerson's wounds. He pronounced them serious, but not fatal. Levi Pownall put a soft bed in a wagon and had Dickerson conveyed upon it to his house, where for three weeks he received as assiduous care and attention as though he had been one of their own household. He did not expect this from Quakers, whom he had learned to despise as abolitionists. As each became acquainted with the other during his stay, they grew to esteem him for the noble characteristics which he possessed, and he manifested gratitude for the kind and home-like nursing he received at their hands. They told him they had no sympathy with the institution of slavery, but that should not deter them from giving him the kind care and sympathy due from man to man.

In the afternoon Levi Pownall, Jr., went to the house of Parker to look after clothing, etc. To his surprise he found a great number of letters put away in safe places. He carried them home, and on examination they proved to be from escaped fugitives, many of whom Parker had assisted. Had these letters been found by the slaveholders or the United States Marshall they would have led to the detection of the slaves, and would have divulged the means by which they had escaped. He destroyed them all.

When night came Levi Pownall's house was crowded with friends of the wounded man, together with commissioners, deputy marshalls, lawyers, etc., all of whom were there entertained. A police force filled the front porch and yard, as the party feared they might be attacked by colored people and abolitionists.

After dark, Parker, Pinkney and Johnson, who were unaware of what was going on at the house, were observed by the family cautiously approaching the kitchen part of the dwelling. One of the women went out, quickly brought them in at that door, which fortunately was not guarded, and apprised them of their danger. On entering, they had to pass so near to one of the guards at a partly open door that the lady's dress rubbed against them.

A counsel was held in a whisper, in a dark room. It was decided to dress the men in good clothes, especially hats, and let them walk boldly out the front door, accompanied by some of the ladies. Sarah Pownall, wife of Levi, with her characteristic thoughtfulness and motherly kindness inquired of them if they had eaten anything during the day. They said they had not. She . filled a pillow case with provisions and gave it to one of the younger children who put it under a tree at some distance from the house, and returning, told the men where to find it. All things being in readiness, and the men admonished to silence, they walked out past the guards, accompanied by E. B. Pownall and her sister,

F

who conversed with them upon some ordinary topic as
though they had been friendly callers, and bade them
good-bye at the gate. The darkness of the night prevented the guards from discovering the color of the men.

As they were about to start out of the house, Pinkney
and Johnson appeared in a thoughtful mood, as if
weighing in their minds the chances before them. The
one was leaving behind him a mother, the other a wife
and child. Tears came to their eyes. But their faltering
appeared to arise from a feeling of fear and a wavering
of resolution at the critical step they were about to
take. But not so with Parker. His was a resolution
as fixed as the law of gravitation. He had determined
years before that no slaveholder should ever again
fasten upon him the inexorable chains of a degrading
and inhuman bondage. He compressed his lips, and with
a look and tone of Roman firmness, commanded them
to "follow him and not to flinch." Obeying him, and
accompanied by the women, they passed out of the house.

After leaving this family, with whom they had lived
for several years, they truly were, as Parker remarked
the evening before, "without a country"—homeless
wanderers in a "Land of Freedom," soon to be hunted
by men as eager as bloodhounds to seize them and carry
them back into the possession of incensed slaveholders,
to be sold or treated according as their feelings or passions should dictate—and this hunting ground was the
soil of free Pennsylvania.

> " Where all Europe with amazement saw
> The soul's high freedom trammelled by no law ;
> Here where the fierce and warlike forest men
> Gathered, in peace, around the home of *Penn,*
> Where Nature's voice against the bondsman's wrong,
> First found an earnest and indignant tongue."

When vague rumors came floating in to the Pownall's that Parker had been killed, or that he had been fatally wounded, Dickerson invariably ejaculated, "I hope that is not true," adding in his Southern vernacular "he's a noble nigger."

It might here be remarked, that when Edward Gorsuch resolved to come North to capture his slaves, Dickerson endeavored to prevail with him against it. But the old man was "determined to have his property," and would not be counselled. Dickerson then accompanied him as a filial duty. In the fight he was the bravest of them all, refusing to leave when the others fled, and his son remained with him until the one received his fatal blow and the other his almost mortal wound.

A few days after the riot a lawyer came to Pownall's, read a paper to them giving notice of a suit, and claiming damages for harboring the slaves of Edward Gorsuch. The names of Gorsuch's slaves with alleged *aliases* were given. Among the aliases were the names of Parker, Pinkney and Johnson. The date of the escape of Gorsuch's slaves was given correctly, but Parker, Pinkney and Johnson had been in the neighborhood several years before. Sarah Pownall noticed this error, and when the lawyer finished reading, she asked to see the paper. It was given to her. She handed it to a friend who was present, and called his attention to the date. He read it, and testified that Parker had worked for him and for others two years before that time. Seeing the clearness of this error the lawyer took the paper again in his hands. Sarah remarked to him, "We are witnesses to the date in that paper, and it cannot be changed. It proves that there was no warrant for the arrest of the men living in our house, but for other men; and *we* have a legal claim for damages against those who entered our house and destroyed property. Thee has no legal claim against us." Nothing further was ever said about a suit for damages.

This action of Parker, Pinkney, and Johnson in self-defense against slaveholders who had no legal claim to them, nor any warrant, actually, for their arrest, who fired the first shot in the affray, and the refusal of Castner Hanway, Elijah Lewis and others to assist in arresting these colored men, under the Fugitive Slave Act, was considered by Southerners as *Treason*, which means, in the language of the Constitution, "levying war against the United States, or in adhering to their enemies, giving them aid and comfort." Hanway was the first, and only one tried under that charge. Theodore Cuyler, Esq., in his speech for the defense said; " Do the facts of the case sustain the charge?

"Sir—Did you hear it? That three harmless, non-resisting Quakers, and eight and thirty wretched, miserable, penniless negroes, armed with corn-cutters, clubs, and a few muskets, and headed by a miller, in a felt hat, without a coat, without arms, and mounted on a sorrel nag, levied war against the United States? Blessed be God that our Union has survived the shock."

When the Southern men with the United States Marshal and his aids fled from the fight, a gentleman from Baltimore, whose name we withold, ran precipitately across a field to the house of Thomas Pownall, and without stopping at the door to knock, or to ask permission to enter, rushed in, got under a bed, and begged one of the women to bring him a razor to shave off his beard, that the negroes might not recognize him. His beard was dark and very heavy. He removed it, wrapped it in a paper, and left it under the bed. The paper was discovered next morning and opened, and lo! the beard was white!

In the evening he went to Levi Pownall's, He was very nervous, and apprehensive of every noise. During the night he became alarmed. He thought the negroes were marshalling near by to attack them. He could hear the toot of horns and the answer. He aroused those who were sleeping in the room with him, and his fears could not be quieted until it was discovered that the noise he heard was the sound of water dropping down a spout from the corner of the house.

The wives of Parker and Pinkney, who had formerly been slaves, went to the home of their mother. They were there captured and taken back to the town.

Pinkney's wife asked permission to return and get her baby to take with her. Her request was granted, and the man having the two women in custody took both with him in a dearborne. When arriving opposite the house, which stood across a field, with no lane to it, he allowed the women to go for the child while he remained in the vehicle. As they staid an unusual length of time, his suspicions became aroused. He hitched the horse and went to the house. Entering it he saw no one. An empty cradle first greeted his eye. Baby and women had gone; and he was left alone to ponder over the "vicissitude of earthly things."

By some means unknown, the slaveholders got the mother, who, it is said, gave herself up, and expressed a wish to return with them as a slave again. Whether this expression was voluntary, or extorted from her, was never known, as she went with them, and was not heard from afterward.

A further account of the two women's escape is given in the reminiscences of Joseph Fulton.

Henry C. Hopkins, colored, lived with Dr. Augustus W. Cain (born 1820), Sadsbury, Chester county, near to Christiana. On the morning of the tragedy he did not come to his work. About six o'clock the doctor saw him walking rapidly down the turnpike road with an iron rod or cane in his hand. Meeting the doctor he said hurriedly "Kidnappers at Parker's!" He was very much excited, and his usual calm, peaceable, inoffensive disposition was at once aroused to the ferocity of an enraged lion. After the lapse of about two hours he came to the doctor's holding one arm, and said he was shot. The doctor found a bullet lodged in the flesh of the forearm, removed it and dressed his wound. He was extremely anxious to tell all about the riot, but the doctor declined hearing him. He knew the event would create intense excitement, and he did not want to learn of it through any of the participants. He would then have no knowledge to convey from them to a court in case there should be a trial; but he told the colored man that unless he made his escape he would certainly be arrested. So anxious was he to tell the result of the riot, that when he was refused permission to do so he shed tears freely.

About an hour after, another colored man, John Long, came with a bullet in his thigh. The doctor extracted it and dressed the limb, He then went to

Christiana to see and hear for himself the extent of the riot. A great number of the neighbors had already collected, and the roughs and rowdies of Philadelphia and Baltimore were sweeping the country, searching barns and houses, and behaving quite rudely at some places.

Immediately after the riot, the United States Government ordered a portion of the Marine Corps from Philadelphia, to be stationed at Christiana "to keep the peace;" while about eighty police and other officers under the government's employ, piloted by pro-slavery men of the neighborhood, scoured the country for miles around, searched the houses of abolitionists and all colored people, arrested every person, white or black, whom they suspected to have been in the fight, or to have encouraged it. William Baer was now on hand, elated with the opportunity of legally rendering his professional services to the government, and was notably in the height of his importance. Many of the fugitives who had long resided in the neighborhood fled through fear of being arrested. One colored man who had been taken up as a witness to the affair, and placed in Moyamensing prison, by some means made his escape, returned, dug a cave in the woods, in which he lived for a long while, and was fed by the neighbors. His only object in thus escaping was to avoid being called upon to testify at the trial.

A colored man living near Penningtonville (now Atglen), was arrested with some others on suspicion of being connected with the riot, and incarcerated in Moyamensing prison. Here he was identified by some slaveholders as being a slave. After the trial of Castner Hanway for treason he was removed to Lancaster prison to await a trial upon charge of complicity in the riot. No bill being found against any of them, they were discharged. He was then taken in custody by the slaveholders, driven to Penningtonville in the night, hand-cuffed and placed in charge of two men in the bar-room of a hotel until morning. Before daylight, the hostler seeing the men were drowsy, went to the door, quietly unfastened it and beckoned to the slave who, seeing the opportunity offered him to escape, quickly left and ran across the fields to the house of William Williams, a colored Methodist minister living in a tene-ment of Diller Ferree's, near Parkesburg. The preacher filed off his fetters, which the slave put in his pocket as a memento of the occasion, and then started for Phila-delphia, accompanied by Williams, taking the ridge on north valley hill to avoid the public highway. As they were crossing a stream near Parkesburg they met some men, when Williams, feeling apprehensive of detection, told the colored man he would better get rid of the cuffs. Accepting the suggestion, he dropped them in the stream. He arrived safely in Philadelphia, and from there was forwarded to Canada. Joseph P. Scarlett, learning where he had left those interesting (?) relics went to the place, found them, and kept them in his pos-session for several years.

The wife of this slave went to Lindley Coates', and from there was sent through other agents to Canada.

One of the colored prisoners, a pious man, who was arrested and put in Moyamensing jail, was heard by Anthony E. Roberts, United States Marshal, praying to the Lord to "shake Kline over Hell," but in the fulness of his charity he ejaculated, "*but Lord, don't drop him in.*"

A letter was found in the hat of Edward Gorsuch, giving information of his slaves with names, aliases, etc. A description of some colored people in the vicinity of Christiana, the locality of Parker's house, etc. The writing corresponded with that of a white man in the neighborhood who professed to be an abolitionist, and who had frequently endeavored to elicit from them such knowledge as he supposed they possessed in reference to certain colored persons whom he suspected to be slaves. Among the negroes he assumed to be their faithful friend. The letter was signed with his initials. After the fear of the colored people had somewhat abated, their feeling of indignation toward him for this treacherous act became so intense, that, apprehending revenge from them, he disappeared from that section, and has not been known to return there since.

Parker came back to Pennsylvania in the summer of 1872. In August he spoke at a political meeting in Christiana, and spent several days there visiting friends.

Castner Hanway and Elijah Lewis, who refused to assist the slaveholders in capturing their slaves when the warrant was read to them, were arrested upon charge of Treason, and Joseph P. Scarlett and thirty-five negroes were arrested with them. They were all taken to Philadelphia, and confined in Moyamensing prison 97 days. Castner Hanway was tried in the Circuit Court of the United States, for the Eastern District of Pennsylvania, held in Philadelphia in November and December, 1851, before Judges Grier and Kane. The jury, after being out about fifteen minutes, returned a verdict of NOT

F*

GUILTY. After this J. W. Ashmead, District Attorney for the United States, addressing the Court said: "*May it please your Honor.* It is not my intention to try the cases of the other defendants who are in custody, charged with having committed High Treason against the United States. Judge Grier has decided, that taking the whole of the evidence given on the part of the government in the trial of Hanway to be true, it does not constitute the crime charged in the indictment. He does say, however, that the facts proved make out the offenses of riot and murder, and that they are cognizable only in a State court. Under these circumstances, it is my design to enter a *nolle prosequi* on all the untried bills for treason, and to transfer the custody of the prisoners to the county of Lancaster, to await the result of such proceedings as the State authorities may deem it necessary to institute."

They were therefore transferred to the Lancaster county jail. When their cases were brought up at the next term of court in that county, to answer to the charge of riot and murder, the grand jury ignored the bills, and the prisoners were all released.

Thus ended the prosecutions which grew out of the Christiana tragedy. No one was convicted upon either the charge of " Treason," or of " Riot and Murder."

CHAPTER IX.

J. WILLIAMS THORNE.—Incidents.—Kidnapping at Michael Myers.— SEYMOUR C. WILLIAMSON.—JAMES FULTON, JR. AND GIDEON PIERCE.—Incidents.—GRAVNER AND HANNAH MARSH.—Incidents.— Sarah Marsh marries Eusebius Barnard.—Work of Station Closes.

J. WILLIAMS THORNE.

(Born December 25th, 1816.)

Anti-slavery advocates, like all other thinking men and women, entertained different views as to their duty in relation to the system of holding human beings as chattel property. In a political discussion upon this subject in Christiana, J. Williams Thorne on the part of the "Liberty Party," the purpose of which was to abolish slavery through voting and legislation, and which had for its advocates such prominent men as John G. Whittier, William A. Goodell and Gerrit Smith, maintained that political action was essential to the success of their object. Thomas Whitson, who was among the non-voting abolitionists with William Lloyd Garrison and others, believed that we could not take political action under existing circumstances without compromising the principles of liberty by endorsing the pro-slavery clauses in the Constitution of the United States, and remarked interrogatingly to Williams, " would thee be willing, against the pro-slavery clauses of the Constitution to assist fugitives in escaping from bondage ?"

" Yes," replied Thorne promptly, " there is nothing in the Constitution to prevent it. The very spirit of the preamble commands that I shall do it."

"Thee shall have the opportunity," said Whitson.

"I will be glad of it," said Thorne emphatically; and he had abundant opportunities after that, and gave assistance to all who came to this newly established station. This was in 1850, after the passage of the "Fugitive Slave Law."

Many were sent to him by Thomas Whitson and many others by Lindley Coates, Joshua Brinton, Joseph Moore, Joseph Fulton and James Williams. He sent them in the night to other stations—generally Bonsall's —in a covered wagon in care of trusty colored men. Some remained a few weeks and worked for him, for which he paid them the full customary wages. No case was ever proved to his knowledge of any anti-slavery men employing fugitives for weeks, and then startling them with a report that slaveholders were in the vicinity, and hurrying them off under plea of security, giving them two or three dollars when they owed them much more. This was an accusation commonly and falsely made against the Underground Railroad men by their pro-slavery neighbors.

A negro called "Tom-up-in-the-barn," living near the Gap, started early one morning to Caleb Brinton's to assist in threshing, and was never heard from afterwards. As there were kidnappers known to be lurking in the neighborhood at that time, the supposition was that he had been captured.

MICHAEL MYERS.

Michael Myers, two miles east of Coatesville, frequently hired fugitives who came to him from James Williamson's. One of them, Thomas Hall, living in his tenant house was aroused at daylight one morning by four men who proved to be kidnappers. The early call made him suspicious that something was wrong. Arming himself with an axe he approached the door and opened it. The men rushed in. He struck at one, but failed to hit him. A pistol was then fired at him, but the ball missing him, entered the shoulder of one of their own party. They then seized him, dragged him out upon a platform, bound and handcuffed him. The man who was to appear at this juncture missed the road, and did not arrive on time. The firing of the pistol and the noise aroused Michael, and he went to the scene of action. So much were the colored people in that neighborhood incensed against kidnappers, or even the lawfully authorized slave-hunters, and so much were they always on the alert for them, that in one-half hour from the firing of that pistol about thirty of them had assembled armed with clubs, hoes, pitchforks, etc., and it was with difficulty they were restrained by neighbors who had then arrived, from murdering the whole party of slave-catchers. They seemed utterly regardless, or destitute, of fear, even when the threatening pistol was pointed at their heads. During the detention Isaac Preston went to 'Squire Robert Miller's, for a warrant to arrest the kidnappers. It was obtained and they were arrested. The handcuffs were then filed off Hall's wrists, the slave-hunters refusing to remove them. During the detention and arrest on one side of the house, Hall was allowed to escape from the other side. He afterwards acknowledged that he belonged to one of the party, but they had come without a warrant, and had attempted to take him without legal authority. After giving bail they returned home, but came back at the time for trial. When the case came before Court the grand jury ignored the bill. A colored man, well-known in West Chester, was suspected of having given the owner information of Hall. Two men named Windle and Cooke were professionally engaged in hunting up fugitives, but were never known, in Chester county, at least, to claim any others.

Not long after this another colored man living with Michael Myers went to a colored Quarterly Meeting at New Garden, and was never heard of afterwards. It was supposed he was kidnapped.

SEYMOUR C. WILLIAMSON.
(1813—Eighth month 23d, 1880.)

The residence of Seymour C. Williamson, in Caln, Chester county, was a branch station. He assisted many, and some of his experiences were quite exciting. Those who arrived there came chiefly through the hands of Thomas Hambleton and James Fulton, and were taken to William A. and Micajah Speakman's.

He was emphatic in his denunciation of slavery with its concomitant evils, earnest in the work of assisting fugitives, and rejoiced in passing them further on their way from the land of chains and masters to that of freedom. When about to give the author some reminiscences of his labors, he was suddenly removed by death, shortly after leaving Chester county for a residence in Kansas.

JAMES FULTON, JR.
(Born Fourth mo. (April) 8th, 1813.—Died Eighth mo. (Aug.) 25th, 1850.)

One of the most noted stations on the slaves' route to freedom was Ercildoun, Chester county. The families of James Fulton and Gideon Pierce, living near each other in the same village, worked together on all occasions, so that the homes of the two families were, in reality, as one station, and it mattered not to which place fugitives were sent. James Fulton, jr., being from his youth a peacemaker, and being earnest, able and active in all moral and educational reforms, a clear writer and a cogent and logical speaker, became widely known and highly respected. It was as natural then for him to assist the slave in gaining freedom as for a stream to flow from its fountain.

The greater number of slaves who arrived at this station crossed the Susquehanna at Wrightsville, and came by way of Daniel Gibbons and Lindley Coates. Many crossed at Havre-de-Grace, and came by way of Hambleton's, in Penn township.

The men generally came on foot, but the women and children were brought in wagons. At one time twenty-five men, women and children arrived, and were kept two or three nights. They were taken to Nathan Evans by Lukens Pierce, son of Gideon (born July 29th, 1821.—Died April 25th, 1872), in a large covered wagon with four horses. To provide for such a family must necessarily draw heavily upon the resources of charity. But it was freely and cheerfully given. No stinginess cramped their souls. No thought arose in their minds, except, that the greater number they thus assisted, the greater amount of good they were doing for a suffering people. Upon the arrival of these, supper had to be prepared. One item of this meal was a washboiler of potatoes. Add to this the amount of bread and other things required, and we must naturally conclude that no one but a kind-hearted, benevolent spirit could, in those times, be an abolitionist, and especially an Underground Railroad agent. People may assume goodness when it costs nothing, or in a business point of view when a money-making object is the underlying motive, or give to a public charity, however, grudgingly, for reputation's sake; but these people, in the secret of their homes, without a thought or hope of compensation, gave of their time, labor and money, to the oppressed of a down-trodden race who sought their aid, while the public reviled them, society ostracized them, and the spirit of denunciation was manifested toward them by individuals of all ranks, from a scavenger to a President.

Sixteen fine looking intelligent men, all waiters and coachmen from Washington and the District of Columbia, came at one time, were provided for, and taken to Nathan Evans. And thus for many years, until the abolition of slavery, they were coming and going, in large and in small numbers. Some remained and worked in the neighborhood.

Three brothers, Jacob, Joseph and Richard Carter, from Leesburg, Va., arrived there in the autumn of Buchanan's election (1856). Jacob and Joseph had been sold and sent to Richmond where they were put in a slave pen with a lot of others to be sold again. In the meantime they were hired out temporarily; and taking advantage of the occasion, they left, returned "home," got their brother Richard, and all started for the North. They came to Dr. Joseph Gibbons; he sent them to Lindley Coates, and he to Ercildoun. On their way through the slave section they encountered the usual difficulties and dangers of fugitives. They were pursued by their overseer, who came so close to them as

SARAH MARSH BARNARD.

to be on one side of a stream, or river as they called it, while they were on the opposite. They challenged him to come across. But he, no doubt doubting the feasibility of such a step, declined the invitation. Quickly gathering reinforcements he renewed the chase and arrived in sight of them as they reached and entered a dense thicket

> "Where hardly a human foot could pass,
>   Or a human heart would dare:
>   On the quaking turf of the green morass,
>   Each crouched in the rank and tangled grass,
>   Like a wild beast in his lair."

Here they successfully eluded all pursuit. After remaining until they considered all danger past they came out and made the rest of the journey in safety.

Joseph and Richard hired in the neighborhood. Jacob remained in Ercildoun, was industrious and saving, purchased a property on which he still resides, is a minister and much respected.

GRAVNER AND HANNAH MARSH.

Gravner (1777—1848), and Hannah Marsh (1789—1864), were among the early abolitionists whose home became one of the first "regular stations" on the fugitives' route through Chester county. They resided in Caln township, five miles west of Downington. The husband felt it a duty to encourage political action against the national evil of holding the descendants of one country as chattel slaves for no other cause than that of being black; while the government threw open its doors and invited the white inhabitants of all other countries to come, settle on our lands and become free citizens under the ægis of our laws. He therefore united himself with the Free-soil Party who considered that—

> " Man is one,
> And he hath one great heart. It is thus we feel
> With a gigantic throb athwart the sea
> Each other's rights and wrongs."

Hannah was also an active worker in the cause, and attended all anti-slavery meetings in the neighborhood when the public denounced them as not respectable gatherings. She was known as being a very kind woman —a real mother to all.

Slaves came to their place from Daniel Gibbons, Joseph Haines, James Fulton, Lindley Coates, Mordecai Hayes, Thomas Bonsall, and others.

When sent on foot they were generally given a slip of paper with writing which the family would recognize. James Fulton frequently wrote but the single word " Ercildoun," or " Fallowfield." They were to know the place by its having large stone buildings with extensive white-washed stone walls around them. These came in daytime. When brought, it was chiefly at night, or after dusk. The barking of the watch-dog, announced their coming and aroused the family who would raise a window and call. A known voice would reply "Thomas Bonsall's carriage;" or similar replies would be given by conductors from other places.

These fugitives were always provided with food; the women were secreted in the house, the men in a hay-mow at the barn. Sarah Marsh, daughter of Gravner and Hannah, took them to Allen Wills, John Vickers, Grace Anna Lewis, Micajah Speakman, and occasionally, when she could not go so far, to Dr. Eshleman. These journeys were made in day-time until after the passage of the Fugitive Slave Law—the women riding with her while the men went on foot. Sometimes her

dearborn was so full that she rode in front with her feet
on the shafts. This attracted no attention, as she attended Philadelphia markets and was frequently compelled to ride in that way when her wagon was packed
with marketing.

When danger was apprehended, the women were
dressed in plain attire, to make them look like Friends,
with large bonnets and veils as was the custom in those
days.

After the passage of that punitive law they felt it necessary to be even more wary and careful than before,
and she seldom ventured with them in day-time. If
they came in the early part of night, a supper was given
them and she took them to the stations mentioned, and
returned before morning, regardless of the condition of
roads, darkness or the weather.

She took nine, men, women and children, one night,
to John Vicker's, a distance of nine miles. She paid
toll on the turnpike road, as if going to market. The
men walked, and when arriving at the toll gates, went
around them through the fields. They arrived at 11
o'clock, and she returned by morning.

Their neighbors were pro-slavery, and knew that they
assisted fugitives, but yet bore a respectful regard for
them, and manifested no disposition to inform upon them.
The curiosity, however, of one woman to know how
many slaves passed through their hands in one year was
aroused to such a degree that she watched the road for
twelve months, and counted sixty; and "*she knew* that
they and James Fulton and others didn't do all that
for nothing. They wouldn't harbor and feed that
many in a year without getting paid for it in some way."

But of the number that may have passed when she was
"off guard," at meals or otherwise, and of the number
that were brought at nights, she had no conception. The
idea of pecuniary compensation for services rendered
these poor human beings never entered the minds of their
Christian benefactors. A purer, loftier, nobler purpose
actuated their hearts than that of doing mercenary work
under the semblance of charity and benevolence.

> "Hast thou power? the weak defend;
> Light?—give light; thy knowledge lend;
> Rich?—remember Him who gave;
> Free?—be brother to the slave."

While Richard Gibbs, a colored man, was at work
after harvest in the barnyard of Gravner Marsh, a slave
master drove up in his "sulkey," followed by his drivers
in another vehicle. So intent was the colored man
upon his work that he did not notice any one coming
until he was accosted with "Well, Gibbs, you are hard
at it." There was something alarmingly familiar in
the sound of that voice. He raised his eyes, and there,
behold! was his old master close upon him. He did
not stop to parley about matters, but dropping his fork,
he put his hands upon a fence close by, leaped it and
ran down a hill toward a grove along side of which was
Beaver creek. The men jumped from their carriage
and pursued, gaining on him, as he wore heavy boots.
The master was a cripple and could not run. When he
reached the fence at the foot of the hill the men were
but a few feet behind him; but he sprang for the top
rail, tumbled over it with a somersault, ran through a
a creek and into a thicket of grape vines and briers
where he disappeared from their sight while they halted
on the swampy bank of the stream as if reluctant to

pursue him through that mud, water and tangled fen. He went to Thomas Spackman's, where he was safely ensconced, and sent for his wife. Gravner Marsh was also informed. He went there and consulted with Thomas as to the best means for their escape. They deemed it expedient for him and his wife to go entirely out of the neighborhood into some distant parts, and to change their names, and then gave them the necessary amount of money to go with. After some time they wrote back stating that they had arrived at their destination, and were safe.

Gravner Marsh died in 1848. His widow continued to aid fugitives as before, assisted by her ever earnest and energetic daughter, Sarah, (Born First month 30th, 1819), who still made her journeys at night. No thought of its being a trouble ever marred the pleasure that filled her heart in thus forwarding slaves to liberty. No sombre clouds of selfishness could ever bedim the rays of happiness that fell upon, and lightened her spirit in those nightly missions of love to the oppressed of God's creatures, although, undoubtedly she heartily wished at all times that the *cause* for this draft on benevolence had no longer an existence.

In 1854 she married Eusebius Barnard, (1802—1865), a minister in the Society of Friends, an earnest abolitionist, an enthusiastic reformer, and an active agent on the Underground Railroad. In her new capacity she rendered as valuable services to her husband in aiding fugitives as she did to her father and mother.

The main props of the Gravner Marsh station being now removed, the extensive accommodations it had furnished could be supplied no longer.

In 1864, on the 23d of 7th month (July), Hannah Marsh passed from a life she had nobly filled with good works, to one, we have every reason to believe, as replete with glorious rewards. The announcement of her death was accompanied by the following tribute to her memory:

"The reformed and the oppressed, have lost in her a firm coadjutor and substantial friend. She resided with her husband, Gravner Marsh, for about forty years in Caln township, and was always recognized as a rock of adamant, to whom reformers and the friendless ever flocked and in whose shelter they took refuge. Her house was emphatically a refuge to the weary pilgrim fleeing for his freedom, and hundreds of these were kindly received by her, fed and assisted on their way. Her motto was, "All should give proof of religion by works of practical righteousness and beneficence to men."

JOHN VICKERS.

CHAPTER X.

John Vickers, Early Education and Domestic Life.—Incidents.—Abner Landrum.—Other Incidents.—Paxson Vickers.—Charles Moore. Micajah and William A. Speakman.—Sarah A., daughter of Micajah, marries J. Miller McKim.

JOHN VICKERS.

(Born Eighth mo., (Aug.) 8th, 1780.—Died Fourth mo., (Apr.) 28th, 1860.)

John Vickers was born of Quaker parentage, in Caln township, 8th mo., (Aug.) 8th, 1780. His father, Thomas Vickers, was a prominent abolitionist, and one of the earliest and most active agents on the Underground Railroad. He was one of the original members of the Pennsylvania Anti-Slavery Society, formed in Philadelphia in 1777 with Isaac T. Hopper, Anthony Benezet and others, of which Benjamin Franklin was the first President.

His grandfather, Thomas Vickers, was an earnest and indefatigable laborer in the Friends' Ministry, and traveled much in his religious calling.

It was around the hearthstone of home, from his earliest youth, that John Vickers, whose name was afterwards known throughout North and South, as one of the most active, cautious, conscientious, and skillful managers of the "Underground" transit of the bondman to liberty, learned a deep sympathy for the wrongs and oppressions of the enslaved negro.

In 1803 he married Abigail Paxson and remained on the place in partnership with his father in the manufacture of pottery; they having an extensive reputation for their superior skill in making a fine variety of ware.

RESIDENCE OF JOHN VICKERS.

In 1813 he purchased a farm in Whiteland, erected pottery buildings and carried on the business until 1823, when he purchased a property in Uwchlan, near Lionville, where he continued the manufacturing of ware until his death, when he was succeeded by his son, Paxson.

In his domestic life he was devotedly attached to his family. Their physical comfort, moral and intellectual culture, and spiritual growth were a part of his daily thoughts and care. The regular family reading of the scriptures, when all were collected around the table for that purpose, was not the cold formality of a religious duty, but a season of true, sincere enjoyment in which he felt the warm flow of a devoted, cheerful, religious spirit.

In business transactions, or in the social sphere, he was wholly unselfish, ever considering what would advance the practical welfare and conduce to the happiness of others. In the words of Charles G. Ames, in a eulogy upon President Garfield, " He never shoved another aside that he might have the better place, nor sought to secure for himself emolulents, or gains in any thing, to which strict justice to others did not entitle him."

" For other aims his heart had learned to prize,
More bent to raise the wretched than to rise."

His benevolence was universal, regarding neither sect, race nor color. No one ever came to him with heart oppressed with sorrow and went away without receiving words of cheer and comfort, and the unmistakable evidences of his tender sympathy. No one in need ever appealed to him in vain for kindly assistance. In integrity he was as strict as in morals he was just and benevolent.

G

"He never broke his freedom faith
And never broke his word;
He lived an upright, steadfast life,
And quietude preferred."

He was a man of few words, of modest pretensions, clear perceptions, calm and profound in thought, and deliberate in forming and expressing his judgment. Yet in cases of sudden emergencies, demanding immediate action, his mind would at once take in the situation, grasp the means imperatively required at the moment, and adapt them to the end to be achieved with surprising promptness and without apparent effort.

He was clerk of Caln Monthly and Caln Quarterly Meetings for several years prior to his removing to Uwchlan and uniting with that Monthly Meeting. Later he served as elder and overseer, resigning the office of elder a few years before his death which occurred 4th mo. (April 28th,) 1860.

About 1818 two fugitives were sent to John Vickers' place from his father's, and were hidden in an attic over the garret. All through that forenoon things went on in the house in the usual quiet way, the women busied themselves about their domestic duties, feeling an inward satisfaction that they were throwing their mantle of protection over two human beings who were endeavoring to escape from the slavemaster's lash to manhood's freedom. And quietly did these negroes repose under their roof, confiding their lives and their liberties in the hands of these their northern friends, drinking in the sweet anticipations of a newer, nobler life, when suddenly the kitchen door burst open and in rushed John, pale and trembling with anxiety and said, "The owners of these slaves are at my father's searching the house and they

will soon be here. We must get the men away at once."
With almost the swiftness of an arrow he sped up
stairs, mounted a ladder, removed the attic door, told
the men of their danger, hurried them down to the
backyard, bade them flee across the field to a wood and
make good their escape. This was barely done when
the pursuers, like hounds in close chase of the deer,
rode up to the opposite side of the house and demanded
entrance. " It will be of no use to search my house,"
said John, " for I know there are no fugitives in it."

" We'll soon see about that," was the tart response.
" They were seen coming this way." Forthwith they
began search from cellar to garret, under beds and in
closets, and in every nook or box where they thought a
man could be doubled up. John accompanied them
with the utmost placidity. He knew the negroes were
fast lengthening the distance between themselves and
their pursuers.

Reaching the garret and yet finding no one, they were
about to give up in despair when one of them espied the
trap-door in the ceiling leading to the attic. Elated
with this timely discovery he shouted in his hoarse
voice, " There they are ; they are up in that attic ; we'll
search there."

" They are not there," said John, " we never use that
place."

" But you have a way to get there, and we must see
into it."

" It will be of no use," " for there is no one there I
know."

" We must see," was the laconic and mandatory reply.

A ladder was procured and they ascended and groped

around in the dark, over uncovered joists until fully satisfied that the objects of their search were not there. Incensed at their disappointment and chagrin at their utter failure, they abandoned all further efforts there. On leaving the house, one of them caustically remarked, "We might as well look for a needle in a haystack as for a nigger among Quakers."

They however, continued their search in the neighborhood for a day or two, but with no better success. The slaves got safely to Canada.

Mary, daughter of John, five years of age, had so indelibly stamped upon her mind the whole transaction—the appearance of her father as he entered the house, his hurried movements, the flight of the fugitives, the looks and demeanor of the masters—that ever afterwards her feelings revolted with horror at the thought of such treatment of human beings, and she became a sympathising worker in the anti-slavery cause.

At one time two fugitives were concealed at Thomas Vickers'. While there, the owner accompanied by a slave-catcher who had obtained information of the course they had taken, arrived at the house and began search. While these men were engaged in one part of the house, the slaves were assisted out the other part and fled toward John Vickers'. The hunters seeing them, started in close pursuit. Arriving there, bewildered with fear, the slaves ran into the house, when John, who fortunately saw the chase, immediately hurried them through the house and bade them speed to a woods in the opposite direction, and then very calmly met the hunters at the door. They told their business, described the negroes, and at once proceed to enter. John told them there were no colored men of that description in his house.

"There are," said the men impatiently, "for we saw them go in, and your place smells of niggers."

"Have you a warrant?"

"No."

"You cannot enter my house without one. Get it and you shall have perfect liberty to search, and I will assist you. But I can assure you there are no such persons here to my knowledge."

He kept them parleying for awhile, thus giving the men time to escape. Finding no threat or entreaty could move him, one of them proceeded to a Justice of the Peace to obtain the requisite papers, while the other kept guard around the house. After considerable time the warrant was produced, and a thorough search made. Of course it was fruitless. They were dumb-founded at the complete failure. How it was that two men could enter the house immediately before their eyes, the family standing around cool and unconcerned, and a guard stationed to keep watch, and yet no trace of them be discoverable was something beyond their comprehension. There was certainly a mysterious *Underground* Railroad somewhere about.

A planter from Georgia visited Philadelphia on business in the early part of winter. He brought with him Cuffy, a young man about 24 years of age, as his body servant. This slave was well dressed, gentlemanly, dignified, and carried a gold watch and chain. His bright intelligent look, his easy manners and lofty carriage attracted toward him the abolitionists of the place, who sought and obtained a favored opportunity to decoy him from his master, when they proposed to secure for him his freedom. He was more than delighted with the proposition and the opportunity to escape; said he had been treated well, and if he were sure his master would never sell him he would not leave. But he dreaded being sold, which he said he was liable to be at any time if a good price should be offered for him. For this reason, and seeing the treatment of the farm hands, he hated slavery and longed to be free.

He was stolen from Africa when about 11 years of age; was the son of a Prince, and was about being sent to this country to be educated by the abolitionists, when he, with several others, was kidnapped by gang of pirates, put on board their vessel, and taken to Georgia and sold.

He told the friends in Philadelphia that he preferred not being sent further north if they could so arrange matters that he could be under their protection during the winter, go to school, and then in the spring, if possible, return to his home near Cape Town in Africa.

Isaac T. Hopper and others, knowing the very good character of Thomas Vickers, sent him there. Thomas placed him under the care of his son, John, with whom he remained during the winter, assisted in the work and went to school. He was very obliging and very kind to the children. His teacher, Sarah Vickers, cousin of John, who afterwards married William Trimble, and is still living, said that he was an apt scholar and made good progress.

In the spring the abolitionists contributed money enough to pay his passage back to Africa. He corresponded with them frequently afterwards.

Soon after Cuffy left, two men came, one a farm-hand, the other a house-hand or body servant. The former John Vickers named Ben. Jones, the latter John Ridgway. Ben remained with him several years, married and settled in the neighborhood. His descendants are living there still. Ridgway remained a short time only. He was very gentlemanly, dignified, pleasant and kind to the children. As his inclination was to "go West," John sent him to some of his relatives in Ohio. After a time he married, lived well, bought a property and was prosperous. Both men said they had been treated kindly, their masters never were harsh to them, but they saw the treatment others received, and like Cuffy, "they could not bear to be slaves."

A young man named Abner Landrum, son of a wealthy planter in Georgia, found a species of clay on their plantation, which it was thought would make very fine porcelain ware. He came north to learn more of its quality, and of the manner of making it into fine ware. He was directed to John Vickers, as one of the most extensive and reliable manufacturers in the country. It was early in the morning when he arrived. The family had finished breakfast. As he had not yet eaten they prepared a table for him. Sarah Vickers, then about sixteen, waited on him. She noticed as she moved around that his eyes followed her rather unusually, and after eating he turned pleasantly toward her and asked, "Do you ladies here North wait on the table?" "Oh, yes!" she replied, "we have no slaves here."

During the early part of his visit he remarked that he saw a nigger boy going out of their lane with a basket, and a book under his arm, as if he was going to school. "Is my surmise correct?" he asked.

"It is," replied John, "we think colored people *need education*, and *are entitled to it* as well as white people."

He raised his hands and turned up his eyes for a moment as if struck with astonishment; then with a look of thoughtfulness he slowly remarked, "Well, that is a new idea to me entirely. I never thought of such a thing as educating the colored race. It takes me by utter surprise. But, I declare, the idea pleases me."

There was something more than ordinarily good, congenial and kind in the heart of this young Southerner that pleased John, who was himself a young man at this time, and a warm mutual friendship was thereby established. He made the Vickers' house his home while visiting other places of interest in the vicinity, and a correspondence was kept up between them for many years. During his stay with this intelligent and benevolent abolition family, he became so imbued with the just and noble principle of liberty to all, and with a sense of the injustice and degradation of human slavery, that he would never afterwards own a slave, but was instrumental in many instances in modifying to some extent the harshness and cruelty with which the slaves were generally treated in his section of the South.

A slave named Tom Jones was sent to John Vickers. He remained there several years, worked in summer and went to school in winter. He married a girl who had been reared at Richard Thomas' in the valley, and who went to the same school that he did. They had a large family of children. Soon after his marriage he purchased a small property, about twenty or thirty acres, near John Vickers. He never neglected the improvement of his mind even after marriage when accumulating cares and labors devolved upon him. One time in conversation in the store at Lionville he said he wanted to understand grammar, and thought he would ask Miss Mary Vickers if she would instruct him. The white men who were always fond of hearing him talk, for he was intelligent, jokingly remarked, " What's the use in that ? A thick skull like yours could never take in grammar." He, however, asked Mary, who promised to instruct him. He purchased Comly's Grammar, studied it while at work, and recited to her two nights in the week, and became quite proficient in it.

Having so large a family he occasionally got into straitened circumstances temporarily. He then made known his wants to John Vickers, who always assisted him, and he never failed to return the money, except on the last occasion. Tom wanted to lime his place, which would cost $50. He had not the money. John lent it to him, and took his note. Soon after this, when John was taken seriously ill, which illness finally resulted in his death, he called one of his executors to his bedside and said to him, " I have a note of $50 against Tom Jones. He is now becoming an old man. If I die, I request you to destroy that note, and never require its payment." His apprehension of an early change proved too true. He died suddenly, and the executors destroyed the note as requested.

Tom was a constant subscriber to the *Liberator*, and a warm admirer of those early earnest abolitionists who labored unremittingly for the freedom of his race. He named one of his daughters Angelina Grimke Wells,

G*

after an Orthodox Friend from South Carolina, who was one of the first women in this country to take the platform and speak publicly against slavery. One of his sons he named Aaron Vickers, after a son of John, who was the youngest signer of the "Declaration of Principles of the American Anti-Slavery Society," at their first convention, held in Philadelphia in December, 1833.

A fugitive, very scantily dressed, arrived at John Vickers' house one very cold day in mid-winter. He had journeyed thus far without any Underground Railroad assistance. He asked for work. The women requested him to come in and they would call the man of the house. But he seemed shy, and would not enter. When John Vickers arrived he still persistently refused to go inside the house and asked for nothing but work. John perceived there was a wildness in his look, his motions were nervous and betrayed apprehension.

"Come in," said John in a kind sympathizing tone intended to allay his fears, "don't be afraid; I am an abolitionist and will do thee no hurt. I am thy friend."

At the sound of "*abolitionist*" he started with increased fear. The whites of his large eyes stood out aghast—a complete circle of pearl set in ebony, and he was on the point of dashing away as if his life depended upon an instantaneous flight, when John partially calmed his fears by a few well chosen words. He was laboring under the delusion so often inculcated into the minds of the slaves, that "the abolitionists of the North were their worst enemies—wicked people who would torture and destroy them."

"Thee is not to leave me," said John in his firm but

kind manner, after obtaining in a measure the negro's confidence. "Thee can come into the shop, sit by the fire, and I will have some victuals brought to thee, for thee is perishing with hunger and cold." These kind words fell upon his soul, as refreshing as was the manna to the Israelites. His fears departed, and he went in.

"Sit there now," continued John, "and the women will soon bring thee something to eat. Then thee must rest awhile and I will bring thee some water, and thee must wash all over here by the stove, and I will give thee good clothes to put on."

In a few minutes, Mary, daughter of John, brought him a large plate piled up with food, enough she thought for three ordinary men. But the cravings of hunger seemed not to be appeased until the whole pile had disappeared. Nor need we be much astonished at this when he said that during the several weeks he had been on his way from Carolina he had subsisted entirely upon nuts which he gathered from the frozen ground, with the exception of a few meals given him by some colored families he chanced to see, and whose houses he thought he might venture to approach. But this, he said, was the first white man's house he had dared to enter.

After his ablutions he was attired in a full suit of good warm clothes. But it was found that his feet were of such unusual dimensions that no boots or shoes about the place were large enough to accommodate them.

John went to the store of John McKinley, at Lionville, who had become an abolitionist through his convincing arguments upon the subject, and related to him the circumstance. "If there are any in the store large enough," said McKinley, "take them; I will do that much for him."

A pair of the required size was found and given him. So pleased was he with this entire outfit of clothing, so changed his feelings from those of a short time before, when, cold, hungry and dirty, he stood in terror before that dreaded abolitionist, so thoroughly astonished and bewildered was he at this unexpected manifestation of disinterested kindness, that the poor fellow could scarcely realize whether he was still on earth, or whether he had been suddenly been translated to some sphere above it. Language was not at his command to express his gratitude; but his looks and gestures were eloquent with his emotions. He never knew before, he said, what kindness was, and never imagined it was possible for any beings on earth to be so kind. His lot had been cast with the most cruel of masters, and the lash, the curses of slave-drivers, the labor and suffering of hard-wrought slaves, were the only surroundings he had ever known.

He was told to remain there awhile and they would try to find him employment. In a few days, Jacob Peirce, from near Kennett, called on a visit. The history of the slave were related to him. Knowing that one of his neighbors was needing help, he took the man home and next day obtained for him the situation. In the summer, when he received his first wages—the first money that was ever his—he put thirty dollars in his pocket and went immediately to his old friend, John Vickers, and offered it all to him for the clothing he had given him in the winter.

"Does thee think I would take pay for what I gave thee?" asked John. "All the compensation I wish is that when thee sees any one needing assistance, give it, and I will feel myself amply repaid."

Instances were so numerous of fugitives coming and and going, that no record of them was kept. Loads of six, seven, or more were very frequently brought in at the mid-hours of night from other stations, when the women, always cheerfully ready, arose and prepared a good meal for them; after which they were secreted in the house or about the premises; or if it was known their pursuers were close upon them they were scattered around in various places and provided for until next night, when the colored man was sent with them to one of the next stations. When a dozen or more were to be taken, the farm wagon was used to convey them.

After the passage of the "Fugitive Slave Law," John Vickers did not keep fugitives about the premises, but sent them to a tenant-house in the woods, occupied by a colored man named Joshua Robinson, with provisions, which he paid the wife to cook for them. Here they were kept in a back room until preparations were made to take them further on.

Although this was the great central station in that part of the county, and the arrival of fugitives was very frequent, he never quailed before the authority of that wicked law, was as brave as he was cautious, and no slave that came into his hands was ever captured.

On one occasion two women from Virginia, one very light colored, left their master to seek freedom in a northern home. They were pursued, captured, and placed in jail. During the night, by the assistance of

some abolitionists and the jailor, they were enabled to
escape through the roof. A reward of one thousand
dollars was offered for them. They were brought in the
night to John Vickers. On account of this reward, and
the recent enactment of the Fugitive Slave Law im-
posing a penalty of $1,000 fine for each negro found in
the hands of one who was assisting them, the utmost
care had to be taken for their successful transportation.
They were taken to William Hall's, a retired place
about one and a-half miles from the public road, and
there secreted three days and nights until arrangements
could be made at headquarters in Philadelphia to receive and forward them without delay. J. Miller Mc-
Kim and James Mott agreed to receive them at the latter's house, at 8 o'clock on a specified morning. John
Vickers and daughter, Abbie, supplied them with provisions, and then starting with them in the night to
Philadelphia, a distance of thirty miles. The night was
very dark and stormy and when going through a wood
about half way to the city, they drove too near the side
of the turnpike road and upset. The dearborn was
broken, the horse kicked and disengaged himself from
the harness, but was firmly held by the lines and prevented from getting away. The first concern of the two
women was to know if "Missus was hurt." Fortunately all ascaped injury. Hiding the slave woman in the
woods, John and his daughter went back a mile and a
half to a tavern and procured another wagon. To avoid
even a suspicion of his having fugitives in case any one
should come to his assistance, he ordered the women to
remain quiet until he gave a particular sound of voice,
as a signal that he was ready for them. This precau-

tion proved as fortunate as it was wary. For the tavern-keeper kindly proffered his aid, took a horse, returned with them, assisted in gathering up the debris and took the broken dearborn back to his place to have it repaired by the time John should return from Philadelphia. After the tavern-keeper drove off the signal was given, and the two women emerged from their wet covert lively and laughing at " Massa's " artfulness and success.

With this delay they did not arrive at James Mott's until 10 o'clock—and two hours after the appointed time. James had gone to meeting, and Miller McKim was waiting, tremulous with anxiety lest the party had been captured. Agents immediately took charge of the women. The one who was so white and good looking was at once dressed up in different attire with false curls, and Isaac T. Hopper taking her by the arm went with them to the wharf, registered their names on the boat as Isaac T. Hopper, lady, and servant, accompanied them to New York, where other agents received them and forwarded them to Canada.

" Black Pete," a one-eyed slave, lived a short time with John Vickers, in 1824. He had had a hard master, and showed the stripes upon his back where he had been whipped, and salt and pepper rubbed into the wounds. One day while breaking stone on the turnpike-road, three men came along—his master, overseer and a constable, and attempted to arrest him. Being a powerful man, he seized one of them, raised him up and with terrible force dashed him upon the solid ground. Then with the apparent ferocity and intrepidity of a tiger which dazed his antagonists he sprang upon each of the others, and with seemingly superhuman strength, and after a short but decisive struggle hurled them with a stunning thud upon the hard macadamized road. Leaving them bruised and almost senseless upon the ground, he ran to the house and told of his encounter. The family then secreted him in the house until night, when, with money and provisions, which they gave him, he started for Canada. He wrote them afterwards that he had arrived there safely. The slave-catchers however did not pursue him further, nor were they heard of again in that neighborhood, except that all were more or less crippled from the rough handling he gave them.

> " What are fifty, what a thousand slaves,
> Match'd to the sinew of a single arm
> That strikes for liberty ? "

"Black Charles and Jane," were two "runaways" who came to John Vickers' in 1820. The family needing help, they remained two or three months and seemed perfectly happy. This was a characteristic condition of all the fugitives while under their care. They felt they were safe while in the hands of friends who were interested in securing their liberty. Charles was kidnapped in Africa, and was as black as pigment-cells could make him. He still longed for the home of his birth, and intended when he could save sufficient means to return to the dear native spot from which he was stolen. His wife, by that Southern custom and social abomination of relationship between slave and master, was several shades lighter than he. From John Vickers they were passed on to Canada.

A number of slaves were purchased in one of the Northern Slaves States and put on board a vessel to be

taken to Louisiana. Among them was the wife of
James Cummichael, a slave quite affable in his demean-
or and possessing an unusual degree of cunning and sagacity. He resolved that his wife should not be taken
to those Southern plantations of rice and cotton to work
under the lash of brutal drivers. The slaves always
had a horror of being "sold to go South." It was this
great dread which impelled hundreds to leave their
masters, and especially when they had an intimation
that such sales were about to be made. Cummichael in
the shrewdness of his device took money with him
which he had earned by overwork, went to the men who
had the vessel and cargo of slaves in charge, talked
pleasantly with them about the prospects of his wife and
others having a happy time "down in de souf," and said
he thought he would like to go along. He pleased them
with his conversation, played games with them, and like
a liberal good fellow, paid for the liquor of which they
drank largely at his expense until they grew stupid,
when he took advantage of the besotted condition into
which he had seduced them, took his wife and several
others off the boat, fled to a grove, and there esconced
himself and his companions until night when they
started on their hazardous but determined journey
northward to that section of country which had an existence in reality, and not simply in song, as

"The land of the free and the home of the brave."

Having successfully made their escape, they reached
Pennsylvania and were conducted along the Underground Railroad to John Vickers. Here they remained
awhile and assisted on the farm. So grateful was James
for the release of himself and wife from Southern bond-

age, that the very utmost he could do for the family seemed in his mind but a meagre compensation for their manifold acts of kindness and generosity.

Two men came one morning in a wagon of peculiar make belonging to their master. The horse and wagon were put in the barn, and the men sent to the tenant-house in the woods, occupied by the colored family, Robinson. Next day about noon the owners arrived at Lionville, having tracked their slaves so far. The tavern-keeper said the most probable place to hear of them would be at John Vickers', and he accompanied them to the place. The wife of Paxson Vickers, son of John, who now did most of the active work for his father, as the latter was advanced in years, told them to be seated in the house and she would send to the field for her husband who would know about them, for she had heard him say that two men drove there that morning in a peculiar-looking wagon. She entertained them by talking, and treating them to apples, nuts, etc., until Paxson arrived. Before going to the house he sent the colored man home to take the two men to a cornfield and put them under the shocks. On meeting the slaveholders he told them there was a horse and wagon at the barn which had been driven there by two men, but they left, and if they were about his buildings they were hidden unknown to him. But he would help *look* for them, being careful to not say he would help *find* them. He then accompanied them through his buildings and to the tenant-house—but the men were not found. The owners then returned with the horse and wagon.

Paxson Vickers was a man of sound thought, a clear

profound analytical and synthetical reasoner, and well versed in science. He enjoyed debates upon subjects involving a wide latitude of thought, embracing scientific facts and political economy. He spoke upon various subjects at public meetings as occasions demanded, and his grove in which he erected a stand for speakers, was a well-known place in that part of the county for the holding of temperance, anti-slavery and political meetings.

He fulfilled various duties of a public character to which he was frequently appointed. In the fall of 1856 he was elected a member of the State Legislature and took an active interest in all important bills that came before that body at its regular session in 1857, among which was an Act authorizing the sale of the Pennsylvania Railroad. He also took an active part in analyzing, and in considering the best means for adjusting the financial difficulties for which the Legislature was convened in extra session during the fall of that year.

At the following election, the opposite political party having obtained a majority in Chester county, he failed to be re-elected.

He died after a brief illness on the 22d of 10th mo. (Oct.) 1865, aged 48 years.

CHARLES MOORE.

Charles Moore lived near Lionville, but at such distance from the main route along which slaves were generally moved without much delay, that they were not very frequently sent to his place. Yet his " latch-string hung outside the door" at all times, and he was ever

willing to give assistance when called upon. He was a
remarkably quiet, modest person, humane and benevolent, true to his convictions, a devoted member of the
Society of Friends, and moved but little outside of that
society and his immediate associations.

MICAJAH AND WILLIAM A. SPEAKMAN.

Of the hundreds of fugitives who passed through the
hands of Micajah (1781—May 22d, 1852) and William
A. Speakman (Born 1810) in Wallace township, Chester county, as in the instance of many other agents, no
record was kept nor any effort made to learn of them
concerning their bondage and escape. Should any
that they had assisted ever be captured and they be
colled upon to testify, they wished to have as little
knowledge as possible to disclose. This was the policy
of many others. They aided all who came, clothed those
who needed, and gave especial care to the sick. Their
place for sheltering them was at the barn. When they
sent them to other stations on foot, specific directions
were given. When it was required to take them in a
vehicle, William accompanied them.

Slaves came to their place from Maryland and Virginia, through the hands of Thomas Garrett, Lindley
Coates, Daniel Gibbons, Thomas Whitson, Gravner
Marsh and others, and were either taken or directed,
chiefly to the house of Jacob Haynes.

Many were sent on branch routes to Benjamin Schofield, Richard Janney and Dr. Fell, in Bucks county.

Three came at one time from Maryland. One hired
with Micajah; the others found places in the neighborhood. In about six weeks some person betrayed two of

them. The slave-hunters came precipitately upon one, captured him, then drove to the barn of Micajah, about daylight, where the other was at work, and immediately took possession of him. They showed their warrants, which testified to their legal claim upon the man. These were the only fugitives ever known to have been captured in that neighborhood.

A man and woman with an infant came there in February, almost barefoot. The woman's feet were frozen. Micajah hired both man and wife. They proved to be good servants, and remained until next August, when they man heard a huckster, who drove up, say, that he brought these fish from Chester. This alarmed the negro, and when the huckster left, he asked, " Did dat man bring dem fish from Chester, and dey not spile ? "

" Yes."

" Well, den, I am not as far from Maryland as I thought I was."

Nothing could induce him to stay longer. He wanted to go to Canada " right away." Micajah gave him a note to an agent in Bucks county, asking him to pass the man and his family on to Canada. A letter from them afterwards stated that they had arrived there safely.

Some selfish and unscrupulous individuals who were neither abolitionists nor directly opposed to them, and had not the manhood or character to be honest in their expression on either side, professed to be friends of the fugitives, and occasionally hired them in busy seasons. When the work was finished, they frightened them by a startling announcement that their masters were in rapid pursuit, and nearly there; paid them *a part of their wages*, and under that contemptible mask of pretended kindness and sympathy, either directed them northward to distant friends, or took them part way and bade them God-speed in safety.

> "O serpent heart, hid with a flow'ring face!
> —— —— fiend angelical!
> Dove-feather'd raven! wolfish-ravening lamb!
> Despised substance of divinest show!
> Just opposite to what thou justly seem'st."

Some of the neighbors, after the Fugitive State Law was enacted, were very determined that its requirements should be fully enforced. One of them, however, became so relenting as to say he would help a woman to escape, but not a man.

Another said, "the law should be enforced, and he would fight for it against the nigger."

There was then living in an adjacent town a very fine, genial, upright colored man named Bill, who kept a barber shop. Everybody liked him. One morning before daylight, a noted abolitionist of the place was summoned to "come down quickly and save Bill; a gang of men are there in search of him." He hastily arose, got some apparel with which to disguise him, ran to where he was, and hurried him off to a place of safety. On his return, which was just after daylight, he met that pro-slavery man who "would fight for the Fugitive Slave Law against the nigger," and inquired of him, "Where are you going?"

"Going to get shaved."

"You needn't go. He's not there. His master is after him. I want you to give us some money to help send him to Canada."

This sudden and startling announcement touched the

finer feelings of the proslavery man's nature. He could not think of the good, honest, kind-hearted Bill being seized and carried back into slavery by a band of rough and heartless negro-hunters, if means of his would assist in preventing it. Nor did he want it known, from the position he had always assumed, that his sympathies were ever moved in that direction. He did not hesitate to ask a question, but drew from his pocket book ten dollars, and said: "Take that; but for God's sake don't tell anyone that I gave it."

In October, 1840, Sarah A. (Born March 1st, 1813); daughter of Micajah and Phebe Speakman, (Born August 27th, 1785.—Died March 25th, 1832), was married to James Miller McKim, of Philadelphia, one of the ablest and most prominent of the anti-slavery leaders, who was born November 14th, 1810, and died June 13th, 1874. He was connected with the Underground Railroad depot at the Anti-Slavery office in Philadelphia, and his writings in the *Anti-Slavery Standard* and other papers, wielded a powerful influence throughout the entire country in advancing public sentiment in favor of abolishing human slavery. He accompanied the wife of John Brown on her sad trip to Harper's Ferry, to take final leave of her husband before his execution; and returned with the distressed widow, bearing the body of her husband to North Elba, where, joined by Wendell Phillips and others, the remains of the martyr hero were with fitting ceremonies, consigned to the earth.

Lucy McKim, daughter of J. Miller and Sarah, is married to a son of William Lloyd Garrison.

CHAPTER XI.

THE LEWIS FAMILY.—Descent.—Labors for the Slave.—Clothing Furnished Fugitives by Friends.—Incidents.—DR. EDWIN FUSSELL.—Experience and Incidents.

THE LEWIS FAMILY.

An English writer has called the period during which opposition to the slave power arose and flourished, "the martyr age of America." In all history there is to be found no other conflict in which the motives of those who fought were so entirely unselfish. Even martyrdom, when it came, was so quietly suffered, that those who witnessed it scarcely realized its sublimity, and the present generation, which is reaping where the fathers sowed, will soon, if careful record is not speedily made, lose sight of their heroic labors.

Among the little flock of heroes whose whole lives were devoted to obeying the sublime command of the Hebrew prophet: "Prepare ye the way of the Lord, make straight in the desert a highway for our God," none is more deserving of gratitude and eternal remembrance than the Lewis family of West Vincent, Chester county. John Lewis, Jr., the husband and father, was born in Vincent (now West Vincent), Third month (March) 29th, 1781. He was fourth in descent from Henry and Margaret Lewis, who, with their father, Evan Lewis, came from Narbeth, Pembrokeshire, South Wales, about the year 1682. Hon. J. J. Lewis, late of West Chester, Eli K. Price, of Philadelphia, and Bayard Taylor are descended from the same stock. The mother

of John Lewis, Jr., was Grace Meredith Lewis. The
name Meredith occurs very early, in the eleventh or
twelfth century, in the history of Siluria, as Wales was
then called. It will thus be seen that his ancestry were
mainly Welsh, but it was said of him by the late Hon.
J. J. Lewis, of West Chester, who remembered him,
that his face was Saxon, not Celtic. His immediate ancestry were all Friends or Quakers. He was a member
of Pikeland Preparative, Uwchlan Monthly and Caln
Quarterly Meetings. Beside being a consistent Friend,
he was a man far in advance of the age in which he
lived, as was shown not only in his active opposition to
slavery, rare at that early time, but also in his arranging of his affairs, of which something will be told further on.

In the year 1818, John Lewis married Esther Fussell, (Born Third month 18th, 1782.—Died Second
month 8th, 1848), daughter of Bartholomew and Rebecca (Bond) Fussell, and sister of the distinguished
abolitionist, Dr. Bartholomew Fussell, a sketch of whom
appears elsewhere in this work. Among her ancestors
were the Bond, Jeanes, Dawson, Brewer and Long-
streth families, well known in the history of Chester County and Philadelphia. When only sixteen
years old, being the eldest of a large family,
she opened a little school for her brothers and
sisters. She was so successful that her neighbors
and friends were glad to place their children under
her care and instruction, and she taught for many
years. A person who knew her very well, writes of her
as follows: " She was the source and inspiration of all
contained in the home of the Lewis family.   *   *   *
H

She was a very remarkable woman. She belonged
to the type of which Phebe Wright (wife of William Wright, of Adams county), was one. Her
business ability was of the first order and was so recognized by all with whom she came in contact. In her own
neighborhood she wielded almost unbounded influence
by her force of her character. As a peace-maker, coun-
sellor and friend, she stood first, not only in her own
family but in the community, before the hatred of abolitionists began to be rife. As the head of an unusually
hospitable family, she always held the position freely
accorded her by all—leading as long as she lived. Her
broad and capacious mind sought and retained the
knowledge of the day, keeping her well informed concerning what was going on in foreign countries as well
as in our own. Nothing of note escaped her earnest attention. I do not see many women of the present day
who, with all their advantages, I can consider as her
equal. She was the product of an age which *aspired*
but had not *obtained*. The effort required developed the
individual to a wonderful degree. I should like to see
one such example of the age to which she belonged,
pictured with fidelity. They were grand women, those
mothers!"

It was believed by many that knew Esther Lewis
well, that she was peculiarly fitted to be a physician.
The thought of her abilities and of the utter want of
opportunity for their development stimulated her
brother, Dr. Bartholomew Fussell, in his labors in
founding the Women's Medical College of Philadelphia.

To John and Esther Fussell Lewis were born the following children: Mariann Lewis, born Sixth month

GRACE ANNE LEWIS.

(June) 1st, 1819, died Ninth month (September) 3d, 1866; Rebecca Lewis Fussell, born Sixth month 10th, 1820; Graceanna Lewis, born Eighth month (August) 3d, 1821; Charles Lewis died in infancy; Elizabeth R. Lewis, born First month (January) 15th, 1824, died Tenth month (October) 10th, 1863.

In 1823 and 1824 there lived near the home of the Lewis family, two colored people, who were so utterly worthless—physically, intellectually and morally—that, even had the prejudice against their race been much less violent than it was, none of their neighbors would have cared to have anything to do with them. During the winter (1823–24) they were taken with typhus fever. No one cared even to take them to the alms-house. John Lewis went to them, "ministered unto" them, nursed them carefully, even tenderly, and so constantly that he contracted the disease from them, and, despite all efforts made to save him, died—a martyr to Christian philanthropy—Second month (February) 5th, 1824. He showed his appreciation of his wife by making her sole executrix of his will. This was such an entirely unheard-of thing in Chester county at that time that several of Esther Lewis's neighbors instituted legal proceedings to set aside the will. Before she had risen from her sick bed, her infant being but three weeks old when her husband died, the law suit began and the troubles connected with it did not end until that infant was two and a-half years old. The mother was compelled to leave her child for a week at a time, when it was so young that its grief at such ill usage poured itself out in inarticulate sounds for an hour at a time, as the tears poured down its cheeks. Esther Lewis came to forgive her persecutors, but it was a terrible ordeal through which to pass, and her family's sympathy for her knew no bounds.

From 1824 to her death in 1848, Esther Lewis held the place as head of her family that has been heretofore described. With their father's example and her training it is not strange that her daughters went heart and soul into the anti-slavery cause. They were taught not only by example but by constant precept. Anti-slavery poems and other writings were read to them and their abhorrence of the enslaving of human beings " grew with their growth " as the mighty and magnificent oak grows from its tender germ, the acorn, deposited in good soil.

Their home was not merely a station where the dusky fugitive was received, fed, concealed and forwarded to other Friends, but it was a *home* where the sick and over-fatigued were kept and nursed with unsparing kindness until able to proceed again on their journey. This was being almost continually done for many years, and especially in the case of women and children who were often so weary and sick as to require assiduous care and tender nursing for days and even weeks before they were able to resume their travel. Yet with all this attention the little ones occasionally succumbed to death in the arms of these kind northern strangers.

When quite young children the sisters saw two colored men bound with ropes and carried off to slavery. The terror of the scene and the agony depicted in the men's faces, made an ineffaceable impression on their minds and henceforward through life, their sympathies and their labors were enlisted for the unfortunate and suffering slaves. In this instance the betrayal came through a white woman living in the family. The two men were hired with Solomon Fussell, a brother of Esther Lewis, and an excellent man, who at that time had the charge of her farm. The incident occurred in 1827, and at that period, there lived in the neighborhood a well known "kidnapper," Abel Richardson by name, who was greatly dreaded by the colored people, detested by their employers, and both feared and abhorred by all children, black and white. This man, accompanied by the masters of the two slaves, appeared at the old farm house, and at a preconcerted signal, the arrest was attempted. One of the men, named Henry, raised an axe, but with worse than death before him, he paused, and in tones of mortal anguish, cried out, "Solomon, shall I strike?" The kind, genial man, the Quaker and non-resistant was compelled in an instant to decide. The awful solemnity of the struggle brought a look into his face impossible even for these children to forget. It imprinted itself forever, but he answered in accordance with his life-long principles, "No." The upraised axe dropped and Henry and his friend went, passive victims, into the abyss of slavery. They were never heard of more on earth. Henry was a very kind and affectionate man, and the children of both families were greatly attached to him.

After the death of their mother, the sisters continued their work of benevolence as before: and so skillfully did they manage the affairs of that station, that so far as was ever learned, not one of the vast numbers who passed directly through their hands, or who were kept for weeks and nursed, was ever retaken, although they

were surrounded by persons adverse to the cause, and
eager to find some proof by which they could persecute
the "detested abolitionists." And some of those men
were especially vindictive toward these sisters on account of their additional offense of giving aid to temperance.

On one occasion when they had, within a week,
passed forty fugitives on the road to freedom, they were
amused at hearing the remark of one of their pro-slavery
neighbors, that "there used to be a pretty brisk trade
of running off niggers at that place, but there was not
much of it done now."

They frequently employed fugitives to labor on the
farm and in the house. Some of these remained with
them a long time, and were industrious, trust-worthy
and economical. One carried away with him to Canada
the sum of five hundred dollars, and others smaller sums
in proportion to the length of their stay.

Quite recently, after the lapse of many years, while
Graceanna Lewis was walking along Walnut street,
Philadelphia, a colored woman who was scrubbing the
front steps of a house recognized her, and, dropping the
brush, ran to her as if forgetful of surroundings, and
throwing her arms around her exclaimed, "Oh Miss
Lewis, I'se glad to see you. Don't you know me? It
was my baby that died in your arms one time."

When the sick and weary were sufficiently restored
to leave, Norris Maris or others took them to E. F.
Pennypacker's, Lewis Peart's, or to places more remote;
sometimes to different stations on the Reading Railroad.
All who took the trains at the Reading Railroad stations, went directly through to Canada. These had to

be well dressed to give them the appearance of "through passengers," and to enable them more readily to elude the searching eyes of slaveholders who might be on their track. For this purpose a great amount of clothing had to be furnished by the friends of these fugitives. They were always good clothes that had been partly worn. Rebecca, wife of Dr. Edwin Fussel, late of Media, who was one of the Lewis sisters, contributed largely, as did William Fussell and his two sons, Joseph and Milton, and a few other anti-slavery persons in the region, whose opportunities did not admit of their assisting in other ways.

Large quantities of exquisitely clean and nicely mended clothing were frequently sent by the many descendants of John Price, a Dunkard minister belonging to an earlier generation. He and his wife were strongly opposed to slavery, and opposition to it became hereditary in the family. These friends, living in Pottstown, Lawrenceville, and a great portion of the region around, could at all times be relied upon for aid in any especial emergency. Occasionally, as circumstances required, the women of the neighborhood, being willing and even desirious to give assistance in this way, would meet at one of their houses, on an afternoon and make up such articles of wear as were most frequently needed. In this manner an ample supply was constantly kept on hand, even for the many changes required. Articles of Southern manufacture were wholly unlike those made at the North, those designed for the use of slaves being of the coarsest material. Occasionally women would come with only one garment, fashioned in the rudest manner of cloth less fine than our bagging. This uncleanly article had to be disposed of as a means of safety, and the speediest and best way was to burn it, and with it as many of the old slave habits as possible. Their exhibition anywhere was fraught with danger as evidence of Southern origin.

At one time a company of eleven men, women and children left the South in a body, willing to peril everything for liberty. The owners immediately started out men in pursuit of them, sending large advertisements, with careful descriptions, in advance. These advertisements, printed in the interests of slavery, served the argus-eyes of Northern Underground Railroad agents and put them on the alert. The company, having reached the home of the Lewis sisters, were resting awhile from their dangers, but speedily a messenger arrived from William Still who had learned of their danger and also of their place ot halting, by means known only to those engaged in the work. The request from the anti-slavery headquarters in Philadelphia, was to scatter the body of fugitives as widely as possible. The first requirement was an entire change of clothing—not a thread of Southern tow was to be left unburned to tell the story. C. C. Burleigh with his wife and children was visiting the house at the time and entered heartily into the work of rehabilitation. A few other friends who could be relied upon, were hastily called together— dresses were fashioned, bonnets trimmed, veils bestowed, and in a few hours, all was in readiness. It was judged best to send the women and children immediately to Canada by the Reading Railroad, funds for the purpose having been sent by the messenger from Philadelphia.

These passengers must be so attired as not to excite suspicion and as much change of identity be made as possible. One little boy was dressed as a girl, his pretty little face and laughing eyes, looking very becoming in a bonnet wreathed with artificial flowers, given for the purpose by Lydia P. Jacobs. The bonnets of the mothers were decorated in a similar way, and these, by the addition of veils, completed the disguises which had been wrought by nimble fingers. That very evening they were distributed at different stations on the Reading Railroad so as not to call attention by their number at any one point. They reached Canada and were in safety before there was time for the slaveholders to ascertain their route. The men were sent in different directions among farmers who could be trusted—and worked in corn-fields and elsewhere in rural districts until they had earned sufficient to pay their own way, when they, one by one, joined their wives in Canada, and the whole party were secure.

In taking passengers to the railroad, the twilight of evening was generally chosen, night being the least dangerous time for recognition. At one station at least, the railroad officials did not feel they were placed there in the interests of Southern masters. They gave tickets to whomever paid for them, and asked no questions.

A woman with her child arrived one winter and remained as an assistant in the house for over two years. She was remarkable for the warmth of her affection, and for her unusual degree of mental ability, proving a sincere and valuable friend in seasons of sickness and death. She mourned almost as did her own daughters, when Esther Lewis, the head of the house, was removed.

H*

After a time she married and went to Canada, where she gave birth to a daughter and died. On her death-bed she requested her two children to be sent to her friends, the Lewis sisters, to be brought up under their guardianship. The youngest child died after its return to Pennsylvania, the other was placed in the family of Isaac Lewis, of Brandywine township, and is at present living in Philadelphia.

Another woman reached this home who was the daughter of her master, having with her a daughter who bore the same relation to her master's son. This condition of morals under the "sacred"(?) institution of slavery, was so extensive throughout the South, that a mere allusion to this case is sufficient to characterize what was general.

At one time, a man having been injured by jumping from a train while in motion, because he thought he saw his master, was brought to the Lewis' by Samuel Pennock, in the early winter, and being unable to be removed, had to be cared for until spring. He could not be sent to a hospital or other public institution since it was known the slave-hunters were in waiting, and he was therefore necessarily dependant on private nursing. During all the time of his stay, no neighbor suspected his presence. When able to be removed, he was sent to William Still, in Philadelphia, and thence to Boston, where his injured limb was amputated, and an artificial leg provided for him by kind friends there. One day he surprised the Sunnyside family by his reappearance. This time it was as a consumptive whose days were numbered, the waste from his injuries having induced that disease. He was sent, with a number of other immigrants, to the milder climate of Jamaica, where he finally died.

As the war approached, the bitterness of Southern feeling and the hatred of their Northern allies began to express itself more freely even than in the days of mobs and burnings. " That nest of niggers and traitors was to be broken up." Those disposed to be malignant never knew just when there were any " niggers" there, who ought to be sent home to slavery; and to do them justice, many of them were kind enough to those whom they supposed to be free, but who were in reality fugitives long resident at the North, but who had been cared for at first in one of those very " nests" of traitors.

When an invasion from the South was expected at one period of the war, the home of every abolitionist, was on the list for destruction, and there were those who vaunted their purpose to point them out to an invading army. No harm came to any, and their days passed on, saddened by anxiety for friends and relatives in the Union Army, or busily employed for their aid and comfort.

When the duties which called him to the field were over, a soldier returned to his wife at the Lewis home. For months he battled with a fever whose seeds were planted in the South, but finally he was prostrated. Then in feeble health, each morning Elizabeth R. Lewis visited the room where he was nursed by his faithful wife. He recovered, but Elizabeth contracted the same fever, and in a very short time her life on earth was ended. This was the true breaking up of the Sunnyside Home. It was never again what it had been. The three had trebled the power of each, but the charmed

unity was broken. In a few years Mariann followed
her sister, and now only one of the three is left, and the
home is possessed by strangers.

That one, Graceanna Lewis, now lives in Philadelphia, is a member of the Academy of Natural Sciences,
and a lecturer upon ornithology and kindred subjects.
Edward D. Cope, the distinguished scientist of Philadelphia, recently said of her: "She is the only woman
in Pennsylvania that has done any original work in
natural science."

SUNNYSIDE.

[The following tribute to the home influence of the
Lewis family is considered worthy of a place in this
work.—EDITORS.]

Who that has shared the hospitality of that home can
fail to remember the genuine courtesy, the refinement
and spiritual grace that reigned there? It was the
home, not only of its own proper inmates, but rich and
poor found there a welcome—the fortunate and cultivated seeking its congenial atmosphere and the poor
receiving its bounty. There the fugitive from bondage found a safe harbor or was helped onward to at-
tain to his uncontested freedom in Canada.

Happy the children that were brought under the influence of this home! They are men and women now,
yet in the tangled skein of circumstances out of which
their lives have been woven, will be found one shining
thread leading back to Sunnyside, taking its hue perhaps from some golden precept learned there, or, better
still, from the example of noble lives.

For the benefit of the children of the neighborhood,
a little library association was formed at Sunnyside.

One evening of each week was devoted by the sisters to reading aloud to the assembled children whose wrapt attention bore evidence of the interest kindled. Here a first delightful acquaintance was made with Mary Howitt, Miss Edgeworth, Miss Sedgwick, Lydia Maria Child, and other excellent writers for children. Not unfrequently the wrongs of the slave were impressed upon our young minds by the reading of some touching story of bondage. One evening I remember so well when the Life of Frederick Douglass was read, and we cried till our little hearts were ready to break!

Among those whose presence and influence were felt at Sunnyside was Mary Townsend, daughter of Charles and Priscilla Townsend, of Philadelphia, who once spent sixteen months with the Lewis family. She was the author of "Life in the Insect World," a sister of John K. Townsend, the well-known naturalist, and was the lovely invalid to whom Grace Greenwood addressed one of her finest poems which she sent with a picture of St. Catharine, borne by the angels. Mary Townsend exercised a wonderful influence upon the children by whom she was surrounded at Sunnyside. They regarded her as the impersonation of all that was pure and lovely, and, in childlike faith, adored her as their saint. Her chamber in Philadelphia, where she lived with her parents, was the place toward which the footsteps of many turned who looked up to her with a faith as sincere and devoted as that of those children. Mature life and business cares only deepened their sense of the ministry of one so elevated and ennobled by patiently and cheerfully borne suffering—one whose soul bloomed into extraordinary beauty under its discipline.

DR. EDWIN FUSSELL.

(Born Sixth month 14th, 1813.—Died Third month 10th, 1882.)

Dr. Edwin Fussell, son of William and Jane Fussell and nephew of Dr. Bartholomew Fussell, was a member of the Society of Friends, an earnest advocate for the abolition of slavery, and an able lecturer upon that subject. He personally aided fugitives in their escape from bondage, and contributed his means for that purpose.

While not seeking to be aggressive through a fondness for aggression, he was fearless in his encounters with the opponents of justice and of human progress.

After graduating in 1835 at the University of Pennsylvania, and practicing one year in Chester county, he removed to Indiana. His anti-slavery labors continued there as here. After remaining seven years he returned.

He was a warm advocate of temperance and of the liberal education and suffrage of women, in behalf of which causes he gave much heart-felt and efficient labor. He was one of the founders of the Woman's Medical College of Philadelphia, and in connection with Dr. Ellwood Harvey, of Chester, Pa., almost alone for some time kept the institution on its feet. He was professor in two departments successively for a number of years. It was with him purely a labor of love, no salary commensurate with the duties of his position being attached to it.

The following letter from Dr. Fussel describes certain phases of the anti-slavery work so well that it is given entire:

MEDIA, 2d Mo. 26th, 1880.

DEAR FRIEND: I will endeavor to give a few of the

facts in relation to the operations of the Underground Railroad in Chester county, so far as they fell within my knowledge. Although I am a Chester county man by birth, I only lived in that county for a few years of the time when the Underground Railroad was in full operation, but knew of its workings in the West and also in Philadelphia.

I do not think there were signs, grips, signals or passes, by which the fugitives were known, or by which they reached in safety the various friends of freedom and agents on the route of the Underground Railroad. They were generally too well marked by the unerring signs of slavery not to be distinguished at once by any one that should see them on their way or hear them speak three sentences. The trains on this remarkable road nearly always ran in the night, and its success was owing to the darkness, the guidance of the North Star and to the earnest souls of the men and women who loved freedom, and who recognized the rights of every man to be free, and the duty of every one " to remember those in bonds as bound with them."

Those were stirring times in Chester county as elsewhere. We were surrounded by enemies; contumely and persecution were our portion; danger beset us at every step in the dark, yet there were few who bore the despised name of abolitionist that did not take up the work bravely, counting it for gain that they were able at any risk, danger, or sacrifice "to open the prison doors to them that are bound." My heart leaps at the recollection of those earnest souls who were the fearless workers in those days and nights of peril; guiding the stricken and hunted out of Egypt into the promised land.

The movements were almost always made in the night, and the fugitives were taken from one station to another by wagon and sometimes on foot; they consisted of old men and young, women, children and nursing babes. Sometimes they came singly, sometimes by the dozen. In the middle of the night there came a low knock on

the door, a window was raised softly—" Who is there?"
a low, well known voice in reply—" How many?" The
matter is soon arranged. Hidden away in garrets,
barn, cellar, or bedroom during the next day, (or sometimes many days) and then on an auspicious night forwarded to the next station. Clothing is changed where
possible, fetters removed when necessary; wounds are
dressed, hungry bodies fed; weary limbs are rested,
fainting hearts strengthened and then up again and
away for Canada. Some were brave and willing to
take risks and, having found friends and a home, would
remain, to be undisturbed and still live in Chester
county, where they found shelter thirty-five years ago.
Some were hunted and traced to be moved on again ;
some, alas, to be overtaken and carried back from
Chester county in chains !

One of the earliest cases that I saw was an old man,
moving in pain and evidently very sore. It was at the
house of Esther Lewis, my wife's mother. I took him
into the house and helped him remove his clothing to
his hips. His back from his neck to his thighs was
gridironed with seams from a recent whipping with a
raw-hide, the cruel instrument of torture cutting deep
into the flesh with every blow. Pressure upon the back
with the end of the finger almost anywhere would cause
pus to flow in a stream. His back was also scarred all
over with seams and protuberances, the results of former
whippings of different dates, from which one could read
the history of his life of suffering as plainly as we read
the Earth's history by its convoluted strata, burnt out
craters, and scars on mountains of upheaval. The offense for which this poor man had received this terrible
whipping, was *going to see his wife*, who belonged to another master; he was detected in the *crime*, suspended
by his wrists to an apple tree limb, his feet tied together, and the end of a rail placed between to keep his
body steady, and then the fiendish raw-hide fell with
brute force for a hundred times. This man secured his
escape to freedom.

Sometimes the slaves would escape with iron fetters upon them placed there to keep them from running away, but these were generally removed by "friends by the way" before they reached Chester county. I once had in my possession a neck ornament taken from a fugitive, an iron band an inch wide, and more than a quarter of an inch thick with three branches each nine inches long, turned up at the end. This trinket was riveted around the man's neck, and the prongs made it impossible for him to lie down except upon a block of wood or other hard substance. Ankle ornaments, made of heavy iron bands, riveted around the legs, were a common device, and often had prongs or chains and balls attached. These were so heavy as to wear into the living flesh, and yet, thus equipped, men set off on their journey to the North Star of freedom.

While living in Philadelphia, we had one day a visit from a young lady of our acquaintance. She was not accounted an abolitionist, was the daughter of wealthy parents living in one of the most fashionable mansions on Arch street. Her mother had a visit from a Southern friend who entertained her hostess with an account of her misfortune in the loss of a favorite slave who had run away from his kind mistress. She dilated upon the the slaves' virtues, his great value and her great loss, but she was consoled that all in this world is not evil, for she had just heard of his whereabouts in West Chester and expected to capture him in a few days. The exact place in West Chester and with whom he lived was detailed and the time and plan of his recovery were stated by this confiding lady. The heart of the young girl was moved; she knew no one in West Chester, but she knew my wife and me—and that we were abolitionists and Chester county people. She went to her own room as soon as she could leave the parlor, wrote down the names of persons and places, and hastened to our house, her face all aglow with excitement as she told her story. We did not know any of the persons named in West Chester, but we knew Simon Bernard who lived there then, and we knew he was true as tempered steel. A letter went to him by the next mail; all was found as described. The slave-catchers made their appearance the next day, but "the bird had flown;" it was off to freedom on the Underground Railroad and the disappointed Southern lady thought this was but a poor world after all!

One noteworthy peculiarity of these fugitive parties was that the babies never cried. Was it that slave mothers had no time to attend to infantile wants and the children found that it did not "pay" to cry, or did the timid mothers teach their little ones to tremble and be still in horrible fear as do the mother partridges impress their young with dread of the hawk as soon as they are out of the shell?

This is a large subject, and a thousandth part of its miseries and heart-breaks can never be written, but, thanks to the Father of the poor, the horror is dead, the bloodhound is no longer on the track, the Underground Railroad is no more.

EDWIN FUSSELL.

REBECCA L. FUSSELL.

Rebecca Lewis, second daughter of John and Esther Lewis, of West Vincent, Chester county, married in January of 1838 Dr. Edwin Fussell. In May of that year, just before Pennsylvania Hall in Philadelphia was burned, her husband and she moved to Pendleton, Indiana. In that State and in Ohio they met all the friends of the slave at the stirring meetings held from time to time during a residence of more than six years there. They were accustomed to go more than a hundred miles, over roads that would appal the traveler of to-day, to attend these meetings, taking with them a baby, as all others did in the West then.

In May of 1843, Dr. Edwin Fussell came to an anniversary meeting in New York with a large company of Ohio abolitionists in a monster wagon, built by Abram Allen, and called "The Liberator." It was made for carrying fugitive slaves. It is believed that they called at the house of Daniel Gibbons in Lancaster county, and certain that they stayed at the house of Dr. Bartholomew Fussell, who then had a school in York, Pa.

At that anniversary meeting the Parent Society in New York appointed a hundred conventions to be held during the year. The lecturers, as far as remembered, were Frederick Douglass, William A. White, George Bradburn, Sidney Howard Gay, James Munroe and Charles Lennox Remond. The convention at Pendleton had the three first named as speakers. The inhabitants of the town were greatly incensed at the attention paid to a "nigger" (Frederick Douglass) and especially at his being an invited guest at the house of Dr. Fussell. The usual remedy for such insults (!) was resorted to. The meeting was broken up by a mob which threatened the life of the distinguished orator. With the quick inspiration of the mother, who felt that even these men frenzied as they were with anger, could not harm a baby, Rebecca Fussell lifted her infant* and held it between Mr. Douglass and his assailants, thus saving him for a time. Afterwards, when separated from these tender protectors, Mr. Douglass was overtaken and mercilessly cut and bruised by the mob, who thought that they had killed him. He required a lengthened period of nursing as he lay prostrated at the house of a sister of Dr. Fussell, who resided near the scene of ac-

*That infant is now Dr. Linnæus Fussell, of Media, Pa.

tion.   The other guests were sent for safety to the
houses of other relatives, while the citizen of Pendleton to a man watched Dr. Fussell's house all night as
the cry " Five dollars for Dr. Fussell!" had been started when they thought they had killed Frederick
Douglass.   That mob broke up the Fussells' western
home.   In November of that year they came east in
time for Dr. Fussell to attend the first decade of the
formation of the Anti-Slavery Society.

The hatreds of that hour have long passed by, and a
number of those engaged in the mob have become good
citizens.   The person who nursed Frederick Douglass
on that occasion was Elizabeth, wife of Neal Hardy.
Recently, in her widowhood, this kind and motherly
woman received an honored visitor, and the town which
once drove him from her midst, and with him some of
her best citizens, was not slow to recognize in this same
orator, the favored official, Frederick Douglass, then
United States Marshal for the District of Columbia.
A later experience in Philadelphia with the popular
hatred of the times, affected a most lovely and innocent
girl just blooming into womanhood. With her friends she
attended a meeting to listen to the eloquence of George
William Curtis.   Whilst there a shower of vitriol was
thrown into the audience and it fell chiefly on her face
and dress.   She was so terribly burned that for weeks
her face had to be excluded from the air wrapped up in
wet cloths.   This was Emma J., eldest daughter of Dr.
Edwin and Rebecca L. Fussell.   Through the care of
her parents she came out of the ordeal unscarred and
her bonnet, riddled with holes, was the only external
memorial of the fiendish vengeance directed, not against

her personally, but towards the assembly of abolitionists of which she formed a part. This experience, no doubt, hastened the maturing of an earnest, deep, and thoughtful soul, such as looks out from the picture she has left behind her. In early life, this devoted girl offered her services as a teacher in the South.* In pity for her youth and in hope of the richness of her promise, J. Miller McKim very kindly, but firmly refused her. He explained to the writer that he did it because he could not endure to see such a martyr. There is no doubt that he was moved by a fatherly kindness which interfered to prevent a needless sacrifice, but the refusal was most painful to her; and to her friends, as the large tears dropped silently, she excused the author of her disappointment by saying he did not know her, nor how her heart was in it.

Soon after this, wounded men from our battles began to arrive in Philadelphia. At one time four hundred and fifty were sent to a hospital near the residence of Dr. Fussell. At midnight, with wine and cordials, father and daughter made their way to where their help was so imperatively needed. As the daughter of a physician, with the knowledge and skill which many willing nurses lacked, she was everywhere in request, and, forgetful of her own needs, she only remembered to supply as far as in her power, those of the suffering around her. It was not at the South, but amid her own kindred that she labored until nature would bear no more. Then she laid down in death, and the martyr soul rose beyond our vision, leaving an agonized memory of what she was and what she might have been. We do not

* At Beaufort, S. C.

question was it wise or well. We only state that it *was,* and that such were the spirits nurtured by the opposition to slavery. Young persons through an illimitable condemnation of an illimitable wrong, rose to the height of their power for time, or else they passed to eternity, and God knows which was best. We only know that the silent dead sometimes influence us more than the living. Children yet unborn may be lifted to a higher plane by spiritual kinship with Emma J. Fussell, aged 23.

NORRIS MARIS.

CHAPTER XII.

NORRIS MARIS.—LEWIS PEART.—A Dream.—EMMON KIMBER.—Sketch of Experiences of RACHEL HARRIS.—"Cunningham's Rache."— Abbie Kimber.—Gertrude Kimber Burleigh.

NORRIS MARIS.[*]

(Fifth Month 24th, 1808.)

While Norris Maris lived on the farm of Esther Lewis and daughters, he was ever willing and ready to assist the fugitive, whether at night when fatigued from the day's labor, or in cold, dreary or stormy weather when less benevolent hearts would seek their own protection and comfort rather than to endure exposure such as that merely to aid a colored stranger in securing liberty. He never looked upon it as a trouble; scarcely as a duty; but simply as a blessed privilege to secure the freedom and happiness of even a few individuals of an oppressed and down-trodden people.

In 1854 he purchased a farm near Kimberton, and his home at once became another "station," and continued as such until the government no longer recognized the negro as chattel property.

Slaves came to his place from the eastern shore of Maryland, from Virginia and from John Vickers. John being a potter, frequently gave them a slip of paper containing the words: "Thy friend Pot," and gave directions how to find the place. In the fall of the year

---

[*]The editors think proper to put upon record here a statement made by Dr. R. C. Smedley to a friend before his death, viz.: that to the interest aroused in his mind by Norris Maris, who told him of what was done by the Lewis family, was owing his determination to give this work to the world.

he impressed the locality more forcibly upon their memory by telling them that after passing a place where they would smell pomace—which was at Abraham Buckwalter's cider press—they were to stop at the first house by the roadside on the right. After delivering the paper to Norris they were free to converse with him and family. With all others they maintained profound reticence.

Norris either took them to Elijah F. Pennypacker's or Lewis Peart's, or sent them in charge of persons living with him. John A. Groff, then a lad, and now an ex-Justice of the Peace in West Chester, was one of his trustworthy conductors. Frequently he gave directions how to find the next stations; and his son George, who was then a small boy, often drew a map of the road for them as far as E. F. Pennypacker's.

While Norris lived on the farm of Graceanna Lewis and sisters, a party of twenty-one came and were cared for by the two families.

So frequently did fugitives come and go that Norris's children while young looked upon providing for them with the same calm, cheerful, "matter of course" feeling as they did upon preparing the daily meals, or attending to the various departments of housekeeping.

LEWIS PEART.
(Born September 26th, 1808.—Died February 14th, 1882.)

Lewis Peart, of Lampeter township, Lancaster county, was one of those quiet, cautious men whose calm, cool determination, serene, deliberate forecast, and unwavering judgment made him a reliable agent on this line of secret transportation. Slaves were sent to him chiefly from Daniel Gibbons and direct from Columbia.

From his house they were sent to Lindley Coates, Thomas Whitson, Thomas Bonsall and others. Some were secreted in the house, and some in the barn. He generally took them himself, after dusk, to other stations, as it were dangerous for negroes to go when the Gap gang was prowling around. When he sent them he gave verbal directions. · If pursuers were close behind, or there was danger, he sent a swift messenger in advance to the next station agent to apprise him of the necessity of hurrying the fugitives along without delay.

In the spring of 1844 he removed to Chester county, near Valley Forge. Here his work in this line of travel was quadruple that which he was called upon to perform while in the Lancaster section of the route; slaves were sent to him chiefly by the Lewis sisters and by Norris Maris. He always kept plenty of horses and either took the fugitives, or sent them by Henry Richards, to Dr. J. L. Paxson, or the Corsons, in Norristown; also to Charles Adamson, Schuylkill, and to James Wood, both of whom were ever willing to assist all who came to them.

Henry Richards owned, and lived on, a lot near Lewis Peart's. He and his wife had both been slaves in Delaware.

One night Lewis saw John A. Groff, in a dream, coming at a distance along the road, with a lot of fugitives he was bringing from Norris Maris. He watched him until he came to the house, when a loud rap at the door awoke him. He arose, went down stairs, and on opening the door, there stood the very boy with the load of slaves he had been watching in his dream.

He believed that many of the African race possessed

J

peculiar susceptibilities, and he had strong faith that in
their flight from bondage they were frequently guided
to a re-union with their friends by the force and inten-
sity of their affections.   In corroboration of this he related an instance of a party of slaves that were concealed in a covered wagon at his place ready to be conveyed by him to another station.   Before starting, a
colored man from another region came up, and learning
that there were fugitives in the wagon, felt a strong and
peculiar drawing toward it.   Going up, he gave a low
tap on the side, and received from the interior the desired reply, which proved to be from his mother.   After
long wanderings, and wide separation, they were thus
re-united.   Many instances of a similar character came
under his immediate observation.

EMMOR KIMBER.

(Born 1775.—Died Ninth Month 1st, 1850.)

Among those who took on early and active part in
the cause of the slave was Emmor Kimber, of Kimberton, Chester county.   His house was a welcome
refuge to all who sought his aid.   He was a man of superior intelligence, extensive education, firm in his convictions, strict in discipline, and was a "recommended
minister" in the Society of Friends.   In 1818 he established a boarding school for girls, which he conducted
successfully for a period of twenty years.

But one incident is related in detail of the assistance
given by him to a long line of fugitives extending over
many years.   A few are referred to in the accounts of
others who forwarded them to his place.   Among the
most noted who came under his roof, whose character-

istic traits and ability distinguished her from all others
and made an impression upon the memory which a mul-
titude of other events could never efface, was "Cunningham's Rache," who was afterwards long and well
known in West Chester as RACHEL HARRIS.   She was
tall, muscular, slight, with an extremely sensitive nervous organization, a brain of large size, and an expression of remarkable sagacity.   She was owned by a man
in Maryland named "Mort" Cunningham.   She passed
into the hands of Henry Waters, a gentleman of estima-
ble character, in Baltimore.   But whether he bought
her, or hired her of Cunningham for a period of time, is
not known.   He was in delicate health, and wished
Rachel to accompany him and his wife to New Orleans
as their servant.   After remaining a short time he returned.   On the voyage he grew worse, and one night
when about to die, a fearful storm arose.   In relating the
incident to the Kimber family, with her remarkable
dramatic powers, she depicted the scenes and surroundings with such powers of speech and expression and
apposite gesticulation as almost to make them feel they
were witnessing the scenes in reality.   She impersonated
the howling wind, the tumultuous sea, the lurching ship,
the bellowing of a cow, frightened by the storm, and
finally the dying man in his last moments of earth.
She described the landing at their place of destination,
and the appearance of the cow as she stepped upon *terra
firma*, and, taking a snuff of the land-breeze, darted
through the crowd.   The captain beckoned to Rache
and pointed toward the cow.   Rache took in the meaning at once, and taking advantage of that moment when
her mistress was occupied in thought, she, like the cow,

darted through the crowd with the quickness of a flash, and disappeared. Making her way northward, she arrived at the house of Emmor Kimber. The family being in need of a servant employed her as cook, in which capacity she served them for a long time faithfully, and was much esteemed. Her slave-name then was Henrietta Waters.

She had a most thorough abhorrence of her former master, "Mort" Cunningham.

She married Isaac Harris, who had formerly been a a slave of William Taylor, Maryland. His slave-name was Joe Lusley.

After their marriage they resided in West Chester many years; the latter part of the time they occupied a small house on West Miner street, where Dr. Thomas Ingram's house now stands. She was ever cheerful and lively, and her clear, strong, musical voice, as she sat in her doorway in the evenings and sang, was heard in all that part of the town. She was employed by as many familes as she could serve to do their weekly washing and ironing; and in house-cleaning times her services were always in demand.

A large reward had been offered for her, and a man in West Chester learning this, and having a more selfish love of money than a regard for her liberty, informed the advertiser where she was living. He came, engaged a constable to go with him, proceeded to her house, arrested her and took her before Judge Thomas S. Bell, to prove her to be his property. While the examination was going on in the judge's office, then located at the southeast corner of Church and Miner streets, she asked permission to step out into the backyard, which was granted, the officer accompanying her. The moment she entered the yard she ran to the board fence surrounding it, about seven feet high, and, as if assisted by an Unseen Hand, scaled it with the agility of a cat, and fled. The constable had not time to seize her, for she left him in the quickness of a flash, nor could he with his best effort climb that fence to pursue her.

Rachel sped out the alley and down Miner street to High, up High to Samuel Auge's hat store, down an alley and through the hat shop, over a vat of boiling ‘ liquid, frightening the men as though an apparition had suddenly darted among them, out through an alley back of Dr. Worthington's stable, and into the kitchen of John T. Worthington's house, where Caleb E. Chambers' leather store is now situated. Rushing up to Mrs. Worthington she threw her arms around her.

" For God sake, take me in, save me, my master is after me !" cried the poor affrighted woman.

" Oh! I guess not," said Mrs. Worthington, trying to soothe her.

" He is! he is! they had me, but I got away from them. Oh hide me somewhere quickly, do !"

Her emotion and piteous appeals convinced Mrs. Worthington that she was actually pursued, and immediately she took her up to the garret, hid her in a cubbyhole, fastened the door, and returned, Shortly after, her husband came home to dinner; the family took their seats around the table, and no sign was manifest that anything unusual had occurred.

The constable, exasperated at her successful escape and mortified at his discomfiture, went back into the

office and told his tale. Bewildered and amazed at such
an instanteous flight, the slaveholder and his aids knew
not for a moment what to do. Gathering their senses
again they determined upon an immediate and vigorous
pursuit. Rushing to the street they looked both ways,
but the fleet-footed Rachel was nowhere to be seen. Not
an individual was in sight save one old man named
James Hutchinson. Hurrying up to him they inquired
if he had seen a colored woman running past there. He
had seen her, and wondered what she was running after.
Taking in at once the facts of the case that these were
negro hunters he promptly replied, "Yes, I did."

"Which way did she go?"

"Shure an' she shot along there like a rabbit," he
answered, pointing in the opposite direction to that in
which she ran. The men being thus misled searched for
her in that part of town.

Hearing in the afternoon that something like a phan-
tom had passed through "Sammy" Auge's hat-shop that
day, they went thither immediately, examined the alley
and Dr. Worthington's stable, and passed by John T.
Worthington's house without calling. The Beneficent
Hand that guided her to this place still threw the protecting mantle around her, and it did not enter the minds
of her pursuers to make enquiries there, but meeting
John on the street, they asked if he had seen or heard
anything of her. He told them he had not. His wife
had fortunately revealed nothing to him.

Rachel had washed for Mrs. Worthington for many
years, and was beloved by her as a faithful, honest
woman, and now, in her distress, she could return the
measure of faithfulness. The colored woman had fre-

quently said she would rather be cut to pieces than be
returned to slavery.

Her husband at that time was working in the brick-
yard of Philip P. Sharples.   By some means, information reached them of where she was.   Philip immediately set to work to devise some measures for her removal from West Chester.   Active search was made for
her during the entire afternoon and evening, and every
movement of those known to be in sympathy with the
fugitive was as closely watched as the movements of an
army by the scouts of the enemy.   It would not be safe
for an abolitionist in West Chester to attempt to convey
her from town, for the scrutinizing eyes of the hunters
were vigorously on the alert.   Philip knew, that as
Benjamin Price's sons were attending the Friends'
school at the High Street Meeting House, and he drove
in town on that evening of the week to take them to a
lecture, the appearance of his carriage standing there
would excite no suspicion.   He visited Benjamin, a quiet
but faithful Underground Railroad agent who lived two
and a-half miles from the borough, and the proper arrangements were made.

About dusk he drove into the sheds as usual, hitched
his horses and went into the school-room where the
pupils were engaged in their evening studies.   As the
hour approached for the lecture, he and his son Isaiah
took their seats in the carriage while the others went to
the lecture.

During this time Rachel was being dressed in male
attire at Mrs. Worthington's, and at the appointed hour
walked out of the house with her husband, attracting no
more attention than two men would ordinarily do, and

went directly to the carriage at the sheds, arriving there a few minutes after Benjamin and Isaiah had entered.

"Is that you, boys?" was inquired from within.

"Yes."

"Then hop right in; we shall be late at the lecture, and we have to go on an errand first."

The darkness of the night, and a drizzling rain descending favored their eluding the observation of any who might be on the watch. They started northward out High street "to attend to an errand first," then turning to the right at the road below Taylor's brewery they drove along a by-way to the State road, and then proceeded directly on their course through Norristown to the residence of a relative, William H. Johnson, in Bucks county, about forty-five miles from West Chester, arriving there about ten o'clock next day. They were warmly received, and the fugitives were taken into the care of the family. Being so far from West Chester, and so little danger of their being discovered there, they remained for a considerable time, and then removed to Canada.

This statement of how she was conveyed from West Chester, differing from that which is given in the History of Chester county, requires an explanation.

The account of her escape from the officer, and her flight from Judge Bell's to John T. Worthington's house, was given by Samuel M. and Cyrus Painter, and others. Her entrance into Worthington's house, her rushing up to Mrs. Worthington and pleading for protection, and the way in which she was secreted, was related by Mrs. Worthington herself. She could not remember who among the abolitionists of the borough she spoke to about bringing a carriage for her, but thought it was Samuel M. Painter, as he conveyed more from West Chester than any other person. He said he did not remember taking her, that he took so many he could not now separate one incident entirely from another, unless something at the time made a special impression upon his mind; but if he did take her, it was to John Vickers', as it was there he took all. Not being able to ascertain anything different from all enquiries I could make, I accepted that as most likely to be correct.

In my subsequent gleaning of incidents I asked Capt. Isaiah Price for some reminiscences of his father's Underground Railroad work. Among them he related the incident of their taking Rachel Harris away while her pursuers were searching for her. This could be accepted then as correct, and was the first positive information received.

Rachel afterwards wrote to Hannah Jeffries and others in West Chester, saying she was contented and happy.

The slaveholder and his assistants continued their search in the borough for two days, and then abandoned it.

For the part Mrs. Worthington took in the grand success, her friends for a long time humorously called her "the little abolitionist."

Some time during their sojourn at Johnson's Rachel and her huband were met by Dr. Bartholomew Fussell and Graceanna Lewis. As was his wont this kind hearted-man soon entered into conversation with her, and in a few minutes discovered that she had once been a pupil of his during his residence in Maryland many years before. At the moment of recognition she sprang up, overwhelm-

J*

ing him with her manifestations of delight, crying: "You Dr. Fussell? You Dr. Fussell? Don't you remember me? I'm Rache—Cunningham's Rache, down at Bush River Neck." Then receding to view him better, she exclaimed, " Lord bless de child! how he is grown!" The Doctor by this time had become quite corpulent.

She then recounted her wretched experiences in slavery while the property of "Mort" Cunningham, who had come to capture her, and rehearsed the incidents of her escape in her naturally dramatic style, and said that from her hiding place in the garret she heard the men hunting for her in the alley below.

Graceanna Lewis, shortly after this event, in a private company, was impersonating Rachel in her description of her escape from West Chester, without telling who the fugitive was, when Abbie Kimber, recognising the description of the woman, and her perfectly natural manner of dramatizing scenes and incidents, at once exclaimed: "That's our Rache."

ABIGAIL KIMBER.

(Born 1804.—Died Third Month 22d, 1871.)

Abigail Kimber, daughter of Emmor Kimber, was a woman of superior mind and excellent traits of character. At the early age of fourteen she became a teacher in her father's school, and soon exhibited rare capabilities for her vocation. Her quick perceptions enabled her to comprehend without an effort the intellectual needs of her pupils, and she applied herself with diligence and tact to supply the helps which each required. Her high standard of worth, her own example and her enthusiastic love for her pupils inspired them with a proper idea of their duty, and no one, it is said, ever left the school that did not carry with her grateful recollections of the care and kindness of Miss Abbie, as well as a warm admiration of her superior intellect and noble nature. She continued in the profession of teaching for thirty years.

At a very early period of the anti-slavery cause she enrolled herself among its advocates, and from that hour she labored with rare devotion and activity in its behalf. At different periods she filled the offices of President, Vice President, and Recording Secretary of the Philadelphia Female Anti-Slavery Society, and for many years she was a member of the Executive Committee of the Pennsylvania Anti-Slavery Society.

In those days when Government officials gave up anti-slavery meetings to the mercy or the fury of mobs, and abolitionists walked to their assemblies and sat therein, solemnly, as confronting mortal peril, she never faltered, nor shrank from the duty of maintaining freedom of speech, and demanding freedom for the slave.

She was a delegate to the World's Convention which met in London in the summer of 1840.

To what great extent the influence of her example and the noble aims and purposes in life she instilled into the minds of her pupils have spread throughout the world as they left the school-room, and in their turn became teachers and mothers, or to what extent she swayed the sceptre of good over matured minds in those days when it required a vast amount of heroism and moral stamina in woman to come publicly to the front and advocate the rights of humanity, no pen can tell, nor mind can adequately conceive.

" As tiny pebbles cast in sea
    Make circles to the farther shore,
  Brave woman shall thy power be felt
    The wide world o'er."

GERTRUDE KIMBER BURLEIGH,

sister of Abigail Kimber, was also endowed with superior intellectual gifts and moral force of character. She
became the wife of that able apostle of anti-slavery and
temperance, so well known and beloved throughout
Chester county, Charles C. Burleigh. I append a communication sent me by one of her friends and a former
pupil of their school.

Gertrude K. Burleigh, youngest daughter of Emmor
and Susanna Kimber, was born at Kimberton, Chester
county, Pennsylvania, on the 14th of June, 1816.

In a cultured home, she was remarkable for her
sprightliness and power of entertaining others. In this
she had a life-long training.

Her mother, a member of the Chester county Jacksen
family, was characterized by such sweetness of disposition that everybody loved " Friend Susan," and
throughout the wide circle of the pupils educated at the
Kimberton Boarding School, few were greater favorites
than she. The rare qualities of her nature reappeared
in her daughters as an active benevolence which had for
its object the welfare of others under all the circumstances of the life which surrounded them. Gertrude
was a most loyal friend, noble and high-minded to a
superlative degree, exercising a powerful influence on
the pupils of the school. As a matter of course, she
became an enthusiastic anti-slavery woman, and when
in the height of his splendid oratorical powers, C. C.

Burleigh was welcomed to her father's residence, mated natures were found.

In writing concerning her, William Lloyd Garrison says: "Mrs. Burleigh, long before she became a wife and mother, warmly espoused the cause of the enslaved millions at the South, and throughout the long and eventful struggle for the overthrow of slavery, remained faithful to her early convictions and cheerfully accepted whatever of private ostracism or public obloquy attended those not ashamed to be known as abolitionists of an uncompromising stamp. In whatever she did she was sure to be thoroughly persuaded in her own mind, and to act independently of all considerations of selfishness or worldly expediency. She had rare elements of character, which, as opportunity presented, fitted her to be a true heroine; one afraid of no deprivation, disposed to shrink from no cross, and at all times prepared to decide for herself what was right and where the path of duty lay. I shall always cherish her memory and remember with pleasure that she placed me on the list of her closely attached friends."

She died at Florence, Mass., on the 26th of August, 1869, in the fifty-fourth year of her age, mourned and loved by the community in which she had zealously labored. Her true worth was fully understood and most highly appreciated by these co-workers, and at her funeral, Florence Hall was so densely crowded that all could not find seats, some of the discourses being exceedingly appropriate and touching.

CHAPTER XIII.

ELIJAH F. PENNYPACKER.—Incidents.—Parentage.—Member of Legislature.—Marriage.—Enters Ministry.—JOSEPH P. SCARLETT.—Saved Life of Dickerson Gorsuch at Christiana.—Arrested.—Acquitted.—THOMAS LEWIS.—THOMAS READ.—Incidents.—Daniel Ross.—Amusing Incident at Company.—Public Opinion.—DR. JACOB L. PAXSON.—Assists Parker, Pinkney and Johnson.—Interesting Colored Family.

ELIJAH F. PENNYPACKER.

(Born Eleventh Mo. (Nov.) 29th, 1804.)

Of the many hundreds of fugitives whom Elijah F. Pennypacker assisted on their way to freedom, no record was ever kept. And of the hundreds of incidents relative to their passage through his hands, a distinct recollection of the entire circumstances connected with one case apart from others was not so engraven upon the mind as to be related with accuracy after the lapse of many years. The aid given to each one of this poor oppressed portion of the human family, as they individually applied for assistance, was the work of the moment prompted by the spirit of benevolence, of right, of justice, and was only fixed in memory as the consciousness of a good act done leaves its impress upon the mind for time and for eternity.

The cause which they almost always said induced them to seek freedom northward was the natural inborn love of liberty in connection with a sense of the tyranny and injustice of the slave system. Ill treatment was ofttimes an exciting cause. The traffic in slaves be-

E. F. Pennypacker

tween the Northern Slave States and those bordering
on the Gulf, was always a terror to the slaves. They
had a deep and intense horror of being "sold to go to
Georgia," as they expressed it. If they saw a slave-
trader, or overheard some remarks which induced them
to believe there was to be a sale, their only safety was
in escape. This they effected by night, starting on foot,
or taking their master's horses and wagon, and going as
far as they could toward the North Star by morning,
then turning the horses loose, secreting themselves by
day and traveling at night. The many expedients resorted to by them for escape, which they related to
Elijah, he has remarked, would fill a volume.

There was generally an influx of fugitives after the
Christmas holidays. They took advantage of the privileges given them at that season, many having passes
given them by their masters to attend meeting, or to
visit some distant relatives, which they used as passports to freedom.

Men frequently said that if an attempt were to be
made by their masters to reclaim them it would involve
a question of "liberty or death."

One stalwart man who had lived in that vicinity
many years went back to Maryland after the Emancipation Act to visit the old "quarters," the abode of his
early years. While it was to him a matter of special
interest to view the old slave-buildings, the fields where
he and others had toiled under the austere commands
of a driver, where weary backs and limbs had accomplished tasks under the daily crack of the whip, and
where the soil had been watered by the tears of sorrow-
ing hearts whose children, parents, companions or loved

ones had been sold and driven off, they knew not where, he could not say with Woodworth:

> " How dear to this heart are the scenes of my childhood
> When fond recollection presents them to view !"

But now how marked the change! The prayers of the bondman and the prayers of Northern abolitionists had been answered. The quondam slave stood there a free man, and all around were free.

The residence of Elijah F. Pennypacker was the most eastern station in Chester county, and the point where the three most important routes converged. One having its starting point in York, Adams and other counties westward along the line bordering on Maryland and Virginia, passing through Columbia, Lancaster and the northern part of Chester county; and another starting along the line of Delaware and Maryland, passing through the middle of the county and joining the former at John Vickers, whence they passed on as one by way of Kimberton; and the third starting from the same points as the latter and passing through Kennet and Willistown.

From Elijah F. Pennypacker's the fugitives were sent to Philadelphia, Norristown, Quakertown, Reading and to various other stations, as occasion demanded. They crossed the Schuylkill river into Montgomery county at different points. Some crossed the bridge at Phœnixville, some at Pauling's, and some in paddle canoes at Port Providence. It is recalled to mind that in one year forty-three were passed over within a period of two months.

From this the reader may form some idea of the amount of business conducted at this station, bearing in mind however, that all fugitives were not passed along these three lines. Hundreds were sent to the many branch stations along interlacing routes, and hundreds of others were sent from Wilmington, Columbia, and stations westward direct to the New England States and Canada. Many of these passed through the hands of the Vigilance Committee connected with the anti-slavery office in Philadelphia.

Elijah kept a large two-horse dearborn in which he took loads of fugitives by day and by night. If they reached his house in the night, and there was urgency to proceed, they were taken on without delay. In case they were taken in day-time, the women and children were placed in the rear end of the wagon, the children covered up, and the women disguised by wearing veils. The men walked singly so as not to excite suspicion. They were sensible that their security from arrest depended upon their getting away from the Slave States as fast as possible.

One man arrived at Elijah Pennypacker's, leaving his wife behind in slavery. He remained and worked until he had acquired sufficient means to obtain her escape. Their reunion took place at Elijah's. They then went to Canada. They wrote back some time afterward stating that they were doing well, and acquiring property.

A remarkably kind, obliging and noble man, who had escaped from Maryland, arrived here and remained two years. He went to school two winters and made progress in learning. When the Fugitive Slave Law was passed he went to Massachusetts. The climate not agreeing with him, he became consumptive and died.

Just after the passage of the Fugitive Slave **Law**, twelve fugitives who had been residing temporarily in Elijah F. Pennypacker's vicinity, summarily left. **He** took a two-horse dearborn load of women and children **to** Philadelphia and the men walked. From there **they** scattered in different directions, some to New **York**, some to Massachusetts and some to Canada.

One time when Elijah's mother was staying with her daughter, Catharine Rinewalt, two fugitives came there and got refreshments and went on. They felt they owned themselves and walked off from their reputed master. Soon after they left two men came and inquired for them. His mother said they were not there, knowing at the same time they were not far away. After a little parley she invited the pursuers to stop long enough to have some coffee and refreshments. They objected and wished to hurry on. She insisted with such friendliness and hospitality that they eventually said: "Well, madam, we are hungry and will be glad of some coffee." Gifted with the power of being entertaining she used it to good advantage on that occasion in detaining the two men while John Rinewalt, Catharine's husband, who carried on merchant milling at Moore Hall mill, took the fugitives across the river to a place of security.

Elijah F. Pennypacker owns and resides on part of a large farm formerly owned by his father in Schuylkill township, Chester county. He was born at the mansion place of that farm Eleventh mo. (November) 29th, 1804. His parents were both of German descent, and in early married life were connected with the Society of Mennonites. Later in life they connected themselves with

the Baptist denomination, and were earnest and devoted members of that sect of Christians. They were
both very exemplary and circumspect in their life; felt
an interest in the temperance and anti-slavery movements, and in the success of the workings of the Underground Railroad.

His mother was remarkable for wisdom and an in-
tuition or insight into questions or movements which
relate to the present and their bearing upon the future.
This innate quality of mind was transmitted in a large
degree to her son.

He was a member of the State Legislature four sessions—that of 1831–2, 1832–3, 1834–5 and 1835–6, was
elected secretary of the Canal Board, Second mo. (February) 1836, and continued in that position till Second
mo. 1838, when he was appointed by Governor Ritner,
a member of the Canal Board.

In Second mo. 1839, he retired from political life,
and soon thereafter engaged heartily in the anti-slavery
cause, and also in the Temperance movement. His
mind was so constituted as always to be directed toward
reform. His fine organization was such as to sympa-
thize with the suffering and the oppressed wherever
found, or from whatever cause. His great and sincere
object in life was to strive by precept and example to
make men purer, wiser, better.

"For mankind are one in spirit, and an instinct bears along
Round the earth's electric circle the swift flash of right or wrong:
Whether conscious or unconscious, yet Humanity's vast frame,
Through its ocean sundered fibres feels the gush of joy or shame,
In the gain or loss of one race all the rest have equal claim."

During his connexion with the affairs of the State
he was much interested in its improvements by railroads

and canals, in a general system of education by common schools, the currency question and the protective system. And now, when the period of seventy-eight cycles marks the point he has attained in the pathway of time, it is a satisfaction, while looking back through the vista of years to feel and know that all the public positions he held were voluntary offerings—the gift of a people who acknowledged and appreciated his intelligence, sincerity and marked probity. It was said of him by one who was intimate with his private and public life, "that mentally and morally, as well as in physical stature, he stood head and shoulders above the majority of others."

He has been twice married. His present wife, Hannah, is a daughter of Charles and Mary Corson Adamson. His first wife, Sarah W. Coates, to whom he was married in the Tenth mo. 1831, descended from Moses Coates, one of the earliest settlers in that vicinity, and who purchased a tract of one hundred and fifty acres in 1731. Both his wives were in full sympathy and accord with him in assisting fugitives, and both were members of the Society of Friends. He united himself with that religious organization about a year after his retirement from political life.

About two years after his admission to membership he obeyed the Master's call to the ministry. Being a radical and progressive thinker his communications received the approbation of those who united with him in the sincere and earnest support of every reform calculated to advance the welfare of humanity, while they were as heartily disapproved by those who were content with

"Treading the paths their sires before them trod."

and who looked upon reforms as heterodox innovations and fanatical errors.

During the course of a sermon one First-day (Sunday) morning, in Philadelphia, in 1848, he said: "My mind has been occupied with *the misdirection of the human mind*, by which man's veneration and devotion are excited toward organizations and conventional laws, rather than the truth of God in his own soul; and men are led to tolerate and patronize legalized and popular crimes, while they denounce individual sins." He then expatiated upon the evils of war, slavery and intemperance. This was too much for some of the staid and conservative Friends, who would rather let God remove these curses to humanity "in His own good way and time" than to bring the subject into the church and make themselves active agents in His hands for the removal of those specified crimes. An uneasiness was manifest among some of the Friends when one arose and requested him to take his seat. Another, speaking commendably of his remarks, and of his being a member of that Quarterly Meeting, hoped he would be allowed to proceed without interruption. Another Friend "relieved his mind" by requesting the speaker to sit down, and then in religious accent counselled patience among the members, which advice, remarked the reporter, seemed very much needed on the "high seats." At this several members requested him to go on. A woman then fainted, and amidst the confusion the meeting was broken up by some of the elders.

A correspondent of one of the papers in commenting upon this transaction said: "Thus, a man universally beloved and revered by those who know him, for his gentleness of spirit, his integrity of character, benevolence of heart, and soundness of mind; an irreproachable member of that society, whose pure life is an ornament to his professson—was silenced in his own society. Had Elijah F. Pennypacker spoken thus in any political, social, or religious meeting in Phœnixville, (near which he resides), we believe he would have been heard with respect, for however men may differ with him in opinion, they there know and esteem him too well to lay a finger upon those lips which always breathe blessings and speak words of love."

He does not believe in mystifying religion, but in making it so plain and applicable to our every-day transactions in life that "he that runs" may comprehend its meaning, its laws and its requirements. He recognizes as a fundamental principle, that the whole universe of mind and matter is governed by fixed and immutable law; that God is as immanent in a grain of sand or the lower orders of nature, as in the highest which is the mind of man:

> "Breathes in our soul, informs our mortal part,
> As full, as perfect, in a hair as heart."

He does not inculcate the belief that the divinity of Jesus was super-natural, but that his divinity was *natural*—the gift of the Creator (differing in measure) to every rational being—"the true Light which lighteth every man that cometh into the world:" or as George Fox succinctly termed it, "*the Light within.*"

He has lived to see the national sin, slavery, which disturbed the fraternal relationship of the country, abolished; he maintains with wonted vigor his testi-

mony against the legislative sanction of liquors as a
beverage; he is desirous of promoting that policy between governments of settling differences by arbitration
instead of the sword, that the finer sensibilities of man
may not be blunted, nor his fiery passions inflamed by
scenes of war and bloodshed; that the love of the
Father may unite His children upon earth into the one
great brotherhood of man, and that Peace may yet
weave her olive branch around every nation's sceptre.

JOSEPH P. SCARLETT.

(Born Third Month 15th, 1821.—Died Seventh Month 14th, 1882.)

Joseph P. Scarlett, Philadelphia, resided during the
earlier period of his life on the farm of his mother,
Elizabeth Scarlett, in Robinson township, Berks county,
six miles from Morgantown on the Chester county line.

As far back as 1838 slaves were sent to their place,
chiefly by James Williams—" Abolition Jim"—of Sadsbury, Chester county. Williams gave them a paper
containing the names Waynesburg, Morgantown,
Joanna Furnace, and Scarlett's. Arriving at the latter
place they were cared for, and assisted on their way toward Canada. No especial plan was taken to secrete
them. Being so far from the Border Slaves States, their
section was rarely visited by slavehunters.

Fugitives frequently hired with farmers in the neighborhood. One named Washington lived with Elizabeth
Scarlett a number of years. Yearning to see his wife
and children again, and if possible have them with him,
he went back to his former home in Virginia, hoping to
be able by some means to succeed in bringing them
North. He saw them, but before he could consummate

any plans for their escape he was captured and sold to
go South, and never saw his family again. He was kept
at hard work and closely watched, but finally succeeded
in getting away, and made a safe journey to Daniel
Gibbons. After resting awhile he proceeded on the balance of his way to Elizabeth Scarlett's, having been absent about six years. He was now becoming an old
man, but was industrious and honest, and was given
constant employment by the neighboring farmers among
whom he lived the remainder of his days.

After Joseph P. Scarlett moved into Lancaster county
he frequently gave employment and assistance to fugitives, but did not engage in the work as a regular agent.

He was living near Christiana at the time of the riot
in that place. His interest in the colored people and
the excitement occasioned by the firing led him to the
spot during the contest to see what was happening. Arriving at the place where Dickerson Gorsuch lay
wounded, and seeing some of the colored men who were
frenzied by the fight pressing forward with vengeful
spirit to kill him, he placed himself between them and
Gorsuch, and advised them against taking his life.
Having great respect for Scarlett and a warm attach-
ment to him as their friend, they yielded to his moni-
tions and left their enemy in his protection. Yet, notwithstanding he thus calmed the fury of the negroes in
the intensest heat of their excitement, and saved the
life of one of their antagonists whom they sought to destroy, the very fact of his being on the ground at the
time of the conflict and of his being a well known
abolitionist who would not under any circumstances assist in arresting a fugitive and remanding him to

slavery, were sufficient grounds for rewarding his kindness by arrest and imprisonment upon charge of aiding and abetting armed resistance to the enforcement of the Fugitive Slave Act, constituting as they alleged, High Treason against the United States.

Accordingly, a few days after the riot, a constabulary force of twelve men came to his place at Cooperville, arrested him, and with Castner Hanway, Elijah Lewis, and thirty-five negroes arrested under same charge, he was cast into Moyamensing prison in Philadelphia, and confined there ninety-seven days. After the acquittal of Castner Hanway, he and the others were released without a trial, but were immediately taken to the jail at Lancaster to answer at the next term of court to the charge of riot and murder. He was released on bail. At the opening of next court the jury, as stated in the chapter on the Christiana tragedy, ignored the bills, and all were set at liberty.

THOMAS LEWIS.

The home of Thomas Lewis, Robinson township, Berks county, was one of the stopping places of the fugitive on his way to Canada, after leaving the border of Chester county. Many were either brought or sent by Joseph Haines, near Christiana, while many came by way of other stations. Some remained a few days to work and earn money. One, while sawing wood in the cellar, observed his master ride by. As soon as he was out of sight the colored man left.

Slaves came, showed papers, or gave some signs of recognition, were fed, cared for in whatever way was necessary and passed on. All was done in such a quiet, smooth way that persons about the house seldom ob-

K

served any difference between them and other colored people.

A party was brought there one very wet day by two colored men from Joseph Haines. At dinner some curiosity was manifest as to their character and purpose. Seeing this they said they were moving and that the other part went by way of another road.

They certainly were *moving*.

THOMAS READ.

(Born Second Month, 1798.—Died Ninth Month 23d, 1856.)

In 1841, Thomas Read lived in a retired place along the Schuylkill, four miles west of Norristown. The fugitives he received were chiefly men, who following directions given them, came in the night. Some were brought. He sent many to J. Miller McKim, at the anti-slavery office in Philadelphia, William Still being generally the receiving agent. Others were sent in various directions. Some remained and worked for him when required.

At one time four came, three of whom were large, intelligent young men, the other was an old man who was making his second effort at escape. His first attempt was successful, and he had enjoyed his freedom for some years, when he was betrayed by a *colored* man and reclaimed by his master. These four men were, therefore, very suspicious of persons of their own color in the North. They remained for some time and worked for Thomas Read; but one day a colored man appeared who said he was a fugitive, and showed numerous scars, but from his actions was suspected of being a spy. The four men threatened him with instant death if they discovered his story was not true. He left the next night, but so frightened were the real fugitives that they were anxious to leave the place. They were at once forwarded further North.

A mulatto came and remained during the winter. Toward spring he became frightened at rumors that slavehunters were on his track, and he was anxious to make his way to Canada. He was taken by Thomas Read to Philadelphia. The day was very cold, and he wore his coachman's overcoat of a peculiar light color. When nearing the city he grew apprehensive that the color of his coat might identify him too easily, and he insisted upon removing it and riding in his shirt sleeves, which he did, bearing the cold without a murmur; believing that his ruse made the chances of detection less. He reached Philadelphia safely, and was forwarded to more Northern agents.

In 1848 Thomas Read moved to Norristown, and the fugitives received there were mostly women and children. For years they were forwarded to Quakertown, but this system was too laborious, the distance being twenty-two miles, and the driving to be done at night. To change this a few abolitionists organized to unite their efforts in securing money to forward fugitives by night trains to the anti-slavery office in Philadelphia. The prime movers in this were Rev. Samuel Aaron, Dr. Wm. Corson, Isaac Roberts, John Roberts and others, whose names are not now recalled. The fugitives were housed by an old colored man named Daniel Ross. He started out with his basket and gathered up clothes, money and provisions, provided by this abolition organization. He was questioned at times by Mary R. Roberts, daughter of Thomas Read, whether or not all were fugitives; were there not some imposters among so many? "Oh, no, ma'am," he replied, "I'd know dem ole Maryland clo'es anywhars."

After the passage of the Fugitive Slave Law the determined members of the organization still persevered in their efforts to aid the fugitives to escape. Others faltered and knew not what to do.

At an evening company where several of these faltering ones were in attendance, two young school girls were present and listened to the conversation. The thought occurred to them to test by actual experience the standing of those present. Leaving the room upon some pretext they shortly after knocked at the kitchen door, and closely disguised and muffled, said they were fugitives, and asked for help. This brought the question home to the men present, "Would they give aid?" A long parley ensued, the girls being left in the kitchen. It was finally decided to take them to a neighboring house and, as soon as a wagon could be procured, two of the men volunteered to drive them to Quakertown. By this time the girls were so full of laughter at the success of their plan, that when passing close to a light their emotions were discovered to be other than those of grief and fright, and the disguise was detected. But the joke was so serious to some of the men that they could not laugh at it. The girls were severely reprimanded ; yet all concerned were glad at heart that they had discovered how those present stood in regard to the Fugitive Slave Law.

At a convention held in the old Court-house in Norristown shortly after the enactment of that law, a committee of prominent anti-slavery advocates was appoint-

ed to circulate petitions for signatures asking for a re-
peal of the law. Thomas Read's daughter Mary was
appointed one of the committee. Being young at the
time, she thought she had but to present the petitions,
and names would willingly be put thereto. But she was
astonished at the almost universal reception she met
with. Doors were shut in her face as soon as she
made known her desire. People insulted her, snubbed
her, and would not talk with her on the subject. One
minister, however, thought it *his duty* to talk with her,
and pointed out the wrong she was doing; "nay! she
was committing a crime, for laws were made to be up-
help, and not to be opposed." His morality took the
law without question, and he wanted her to do the
same. Needless to say she did not.

While this describes the general public opinion, there
were many benevolent individuals who had not courage
to express their secret convictions, yet were willing to
aid the abolitionists by pecuniary contributions. John
Augusta, an old colored resident of that place, and
an important attache of the Underground Railroad said
that many citizens came to him and remarked: "John,
I know you must be needing considerable money to forward passengers on your road. When you need contributions come to me, but do not let my name be mentioned as one contributing."

Norristown first became a station of the Underground
Railroad about 1839, the year of the first meeting of the
Anti-Slavery Society at that place. The number of fugitives who passed through there, assisted by their friends,
increased from year to year—as many as fifteen or twenty
being occasionally concealed within the town at one time.

A very strong and bitter animosity existed there against the abolitionist, especially in the early days of the anti-slavery agitation; and for individuals to make any active efforts in behalf of fugitives was to incur general denunciation and social ostracism. Malignant threats were made, but never carried into effect. The furthest extent of a mob demonstration was the stoning of the Baptist Meeting House and the breaking up of an anti-slavery meeting which was being held there. This was the only building in which these meetings were held in the early part of the work in that town.

In later times when public sentiment was growing strong in favor of emancipation, very many, even among public officials, were hearty sympathizers and silent helpers. The positions which they held, depending upon public suffrage or popular favor, made it politic for them to enjoin secrecy when bestowing aid, and to make their sentiments known to but few, even of the well known and trusted abolitionists.

DR. JACOB L. PAXSON.
(Born June 17th, 1812.)

As public sentiment in Norristown was inimical to the anti-slavery cause until the exigencies of the times and the acknowledged justness of universal liberty throughout the country made it popular, the harboring of fugitives in that place was particularly hazardous. Yet among those who dared to do it, who was openly known to do it, and who built a secret apartment in his house for that especial purpose which it was almost impossible to discover, was Dr. Jacob L. Paxson. Independent and fearless, he did his own thinking, kept

DR. JACOB L. PAXSON.

his own counsel, took his own course, and concealed, fed, and forwarded hundreds that even the anti-slavery people knew nothing of. He kept a horse and wagon, and took them himself to William Jackson, Quakertown, Jonathan McGill, Solebury, and William H. Johnson, Buckingham, all in Bucks county. He entertained abolition speakers after the passage of the penal slave law, when they were refused admittance to the hotels.

One evening when Garrison, Burleigh and several others were at his place, Samuel Jamison who owned a large manufacturing establishment adjoining, came in and informed him of a conversation he had just over-heard in a small assemblage of men, concerning a plot which was being laid to burn his house if he did not dismiss his guests.

"Tell them to burn it," said Paxson, "and scatter the ashes to the four winds: I'm a free man."

A few days after the Christiana riot, Parker, Pinkney and Johnson, an account of whom is given in the description of the tragedy, and the narrative of Isaac and Dinah Mendenhall, came on foot in the night to Norris-town, accompanied by another person whose name is not known. Dr. William Corson announced their arrival to John Augusta. The four men were concealed in a lot of shavings under a carpenter shop which stood three feet above ground on Church street, near Airy. There they remained four days, and were fed with food passed to them upon an oven-peal across a four-foot alley from a frame house in which Samuel Lewis, a colored man, lived. During this time the United States Marshal's detectives were watching every part of the town. On the fourth day a meeting was held by a few trusted friends in the office of Lawrence E. Corson, Esq., to devise means for their escape. Dr. Paxson proposed engaging five wagons for that evening, four to be sent in different directions as decoys to lead off the vigilant detectives. The plan was adopted, and the wagons and teams were engaged of Jacob Bodey, whose sympathies were known to be in favor of fugitives. But he would accept no pay, saying he would do so much as his share. The first was sent up the turnpike road and shortly after, the second was sent down that road; another was sent across the bridge toward West Chester, and the fourth out the State road toward Downingtown. The attention of the alert officers being now attracted in these directions, the men after having shaved, and otherwise changed their personal appearance, walked from the carpenter shop to Chestnut street and down Chestnut to the house of William Lewis, colored, where the fifth wagon which was to go directly through the town and up the Mill creek road was waiting for them.

Dr. Paxson was there also, and saw the men with William Lewis, colored, as their driver start safely for Quakertown. Lewis was a little tremulous with fear at the perilous undertaking, which, with the haste, somewhat confused him at the start. On the road he became bewildered, and went several miles out of the way, which gave Parker the impression that he was partly intoxicated—a condition in which Lewis never was known to be. From Quakertown they journeyed to Canada, traveling part of the way on foot and part by public conveyance.

On the following day the United States Marshal was

informed that they had left Norristown and were out of his reach. Officers were at once despatched to Quakertown, but the Underground Railroad there disappeared from their view, and its passengers could be tracked no further.

At the close of the war, Judge Smyser, of Norristown, was returning on a train from Philadelphia, and seeing Dr. Paxson in the same car called out to him, "Paxson, is that you? I was at an entertainment last night, and some of the party said I was as great a radical as you are. I replied, 'I thank God that I am!' But," he continued, "there was a time when, had you been convicted under the Fugitive Slave Law, I would have given you the extent of the penalty; for I looked upon you as one of the most dangerous men in the community, on account of your utter disregard for that law."

On Dr. Paxson's return home one afternoon in 1846 he saw on his back porch a very black, gray-haired woman, about sixty years of age; also a mulatto woman about thirty, and a small, very fair child, with flaxen hair, of about six or seven summers. The old woman was conversing with Parker Pilsbury. Her cultivated thought and remarkable gift of language excited their interest and attention. On questioning her they found that she, her daughter and granddaughter, were all slaves. Paxson interrogated her relative to their escape. She stated that they had traveled through Maryland on foot by night, and during the day they crawled under cornshocks or hid under leaves in the woods; their principal food being roots and corn for many days. He said to her, "Did you not know that you were running a great risk of being caught and taken back, tortured with the

K*

lash and sold upon the auction block, and separated from your child and grandchild?"

She answered "Yes," and the tears rolled down her cheeks; "but I believed that God would help those who tried to help themselves; and with confidence in that power I started out, and it has brought me here. And may God be praised!"

"Now tell me," said Paxson, "what induced you to make this effort."

Rising to her feet, and turning deliberately toward her child, with utterance choked by emotion, she said, "See you not, marked upon her features, my own pollution that the white man has stamped there! See you not upon this grandchild, with its flaxen hair and florid face the pollution of a fiendish nature over her! It was to save that grandchild from the terrible pollution which slavery sways over all whom it dare call a slave; it was to save that fair and beautiful creature from a life of shame that I dared, and have accomplished what I did; and there shall ever go forth from my innermost nature a feeling of gratitude that I have her thus spared."

Dr. Paxson is now residing in Philadelphia. With an active temperament, a good constitution and good health, he possesses mentally and physically the vigor and elasticity of his early manhood, when he displayed earnestness of purpose and determination of will to dare and do for the right.

CHAPTER XIV.

JOSEPH SMITH.—Incident in Canada.—Marriage and Death.—OLIVER FRIENDS.—JOHN N. RUSSELL.—THOMAS GARRETT.—Inspiration.- Marriage.—Arrested and Fined.—Prospered Afterward.- Reward Offered.—Plan of Management.—Woman Escaped in Wife's Cloth- ing.—Death.—JACOB LINDLEY.—Earliest Worker.—Death.—LEVI B. WARD.—Kidnapping.—JAMES N. TAYLOR.—Assisted Parker, Pinkney and Johnson.

JOSEPH SMITH.

(Born Fourth Month 15th, 1801.—Died Seventh Month 19th, 1878.)

Among the first fugitives that came to Joseph Smith's, Drumore township, Lancaster county, was one from Maryland, in June, 1844. It was early in the morn- ing. The man was without hat or shoes. His appear- ance suggested that something was wrong. Joseph's anti- slavery principles were known; and as the men whom he had working for him were then at breakfast, and were opposed to interfering with slavery, although they were members of the Society of Friends, he ordered the man to be kept out of sight until he could have the op- portunity to question him.

The fugitive stated where he was from, and, using his expression, said, "his master was h—l." He was fed and concealed during the day, and at night was sent in care of one of Joseph's colored men to Thomas Whit- son, who sent him on the following night to Lindley Coates; from there he was safely sent from friend to friend until he reached Canada.

After this, many came and were forwarded to other agents, and his house became widely known as one of

the important stations on this long line of nightly travel
with its many branches like arms of beneficence extended to the hunted slave to aid him on his way from
a land of bondage, to seek freedom within the American
domain of England's Queen.

The largest number that came at one time was thirteen—all from Virginia. On being asked where they
first heard of Joseph Smith, they replied, "Down where
we come from. They don't like you down there. They
call you an abolitionist."

"And was that the reason you tried to get here?"

" Yes, sir, it was. We know'd you'd help us on to
Canada where we'd be free."

They were asked how long they were planning their
escape, and said "several weeks, and we've been just
three weeks getting here. We were afraid of being
caught and taken back, and every little noise scared us.
But we were determined to be free.   We traveled only
at night, and in day time we lay in swamps where the
thickets were almost as dark as night itself. There were
plenty of them in Virginia, but we didn't find any in
Maryland. Sometimes we were two or three days without anything to eat."   One of this number was a lad of
fourteen.

Many of the farmers in Drumore township went to
Baltimore market with loads of produce, taking with
them their colored drivers. The slaves sought opportunity
to talk with these teamsters and to ask them many
questions, as to where they came from, whom they
lived with, and what kind of work they did, how they
were treated, etc., etc. These colored teamsters gave
them all the information they could, which was liber-

ally conveyed to others, and especially to the slaves who accompanied their masters from the planting states to Baltimore on business. These would tell it to other slaves on their return South, and say "if they could only get to Joseph Smith's in Pennsylvania he would help them on to a land of freedom." This stimulated their inborn love of liberty to devising plans by which to reach Smith's, and from there be assisted to where no task-master should exact from their weary limbs the daily requirements of uncompensated toil. And so successful was the management of this station that all who reached it were passed on safely toward the goal of their desires.

An old colored man living near Baltimore who was acquainted with Joseph Smith, gave passengers a start at that end of the road by piloting them to another colored man near the Susquehanna. This man would go in the night, see them across the river, and direct them to the house of Isaac Waters, living near Peach Bottom Ferry, York county, and then return before morning. Waters would then take them to Smith's. Here they were concealed in the back part of a dark apartment in the barn entirely underground, and victuals carried to them while they remained.

While Joseph had many pro-slavery opponents, yet none, he believed, informed on him—at least they gave him no trouble. One of them, while at the ferry, on his return from York county, observed some men waiting, whom he ascertained were slaveholders coming into Lancaster county in search of slaves. Thinking if there were any fugitives in that neighborhood they would most likely be at Smith's, he sent him word that these

men were " hunting their niggers, and might give him
trouble." The act of warning him was certainly kind,
even if the language was uncouth. The notice, however,
did not alarm him, as no slaves were then about his
premises. His only fears were that some might come at
that time. The following morning four men were seen
coming up the road toward the house; they looked
steadfastly at it, but passed by. During four days they
were observed to pass frequently along the road. On
that fourth night the family kept watch and saw them
several times lying in wait around the house, evidently
determined not only to foil any effort clandestinely to
aid fugitives in escaping, but to prosecute those who
attempted it. It was subsequently ascertained that these
were the four men whom Smith was apprised of, and
that the slaves they were in search of had not left the
plantation when they started in pursuit of them. Learning the course their masters took, they left in another
direction, crossed the river at a lower ferry, and made
an easy and safe transit to their prospective homes of
freedom.

Smith's house was never searched, except once. At
that time some hunters drove up under pretence of
looking for stray horses. After a short conversation
they arrogantly demanded of him to "bring out his
niggers." He replied that he had none. Unwilling to
accept his word as truth, they proceeded, without permission or ceremony, to search the house. This was
peremptorily refused them, unless it be done legally.
Whereupon some of the men went to a Justice of the
Peace to procure a warrant, while others were stationed
to guard the house. After the warrant arrived a search

was instituted, Joseph's daughter, Rachel, accompanying them. But no "niggers" were found. Two weeks
after, the family learned from a friend of theirs that he
had taken that party of negroes to Lindley Coates, and
by that time they were out of the reach of slavery. The
hunters had missed the trail.

The last slaves who came to Joseph Smith's were a
woman and her two children. Her master had once been
in affluent circumstances, but was now very much reduced
in his possessions. His next move to raise funds was to
sell this woman and her children. His son, a young
man of tender feelings for others, felt it an act of cruelty
to sell her and her children who were entwined within
her affections, and thus to thrust them out upon the
uncertainty of having a good or a bad master told her
of the decision of his father and advised her to go away.
He and his wife were acquainted with Joseph Smith
and family, and had visited them and others in the
neighborhood. He directed them there, saying that he
would be chosen to go on the hunt of them, and he
would be sure *not* to go to that place.

They were taken to Smith's in the night. During the
day she said in a pathetic tone that "she did pity her
young Missus, for she didn't know how to do any work,
and she did wonder how they would get along without
any one to help them."

In October, 1859, Joseph's daughter Rachel visited
Niagara Falls, and registered at the Cataract House.
The head waiter, John Morrison, seeing her name and.
residence upon the book, approached her one day and
politely made apology for intruding himself; but said
he would like to ask if she knew a man named Joseph

Smith in Pennsylvania. She replied that he was her
father. He continued, " I would like to tell you about
the poor fugitives I ferry across the river. Many of them
tell me the that first place they came to in Pennsylvania was Joseph Smith's. I frequently see them when
I visit my parents at Lundy's Lane. Many of them
have nice little homes and are doing well." He ferried
some across the river during two of the nights she was
there.

Joseph Smith was a member of the Society of
Friends. He was born near London Grove Meeting
House, Chester county, Fourth mo. (April) 15th, 1801 ;
removed to Drumore, Lancaster county, Third mo.
(March), 1818 ; was married to Tacy Shoemaker, Ninth
mo. (September) 17th, 1823 ; and died Seventh mo.
(July) 19th, 1878.

OLIVER FURNISS.

(Born near Chadd's Ford, Chester county, Pa., First mo. 11th, 1794.—
   Died in Little Britain Township, Lancaster county, Eleventh mo.
   19th, 1858.)

Oliver Furniss, of Little Britain, assisted in a quiet
way all fugitives who came to him. It was a custom
with himself and family to ask them but few questions
about where they came from. They were always received warmly and kindly by him as human beings
whose misfortunes, to be born and owned as slaves
claimed his sympathy. He was known as the "fugitives' friend," and they often expressed themselves as
" feeling safe in his hands." The neighbors were not
generally disposed to interfere much with the colored
people, or to throw obstructions in the way of assisting
fugitives to freedom. If any who appeared to be

strangers in the neighborhood inquired for work, or for persons friendly to colored people, they were directed to his place. From there they were sent on different routes through Lancaster and Chester counties.

As the family were always reticent upon the subject of the aid which they contributed, no reminiscences of individual cases, or the amount of work done, aside from the general labor which all performed, has been gleaned. Theirs were good works quietly accomplished.

JOHN N. RUSSELL.

(1804—1876.)

John Neal Russell, of Drumore, Lancaster county, received fugitives from different points, and forwarded the greater number to Henry Bushong, about nine miles distant. His place was well known throughout Lancaster and the adjacent counties as one of the regular and prominent stations on the slaves' route toward the *North Star*. Many interesting incidents could be related, and some of them full of romance.

During the height of the Torrey campaign, when Charles T. Torrey was making his adventurous and precipitate excursions into the very heart of the slave States, gathering up large numbers of slaves who wished to be free, and conducting them northward, a company of twenty-two was brought to John N. Russell about twelve o'clock one night by Samuel Bond, a thick-set, heavy, stout mulatto, who frequently piloted the ebon-hued travelers in their nightly peregrinations toward an abiding place of freedom. He threw a pebble against the window of the sleeping room occupied by John and his wife. The signal was understood, the window raised, and "Sam" spoke with his peculiar guttural sound of voice, "Please come down quick; I got a whole field full of 'em." They were taken into the sitting-room and a large table of substantial food was soon set for them in the kitchen. They sat down to it, and one of their number, a very black but intelligent man asked a blessing with uplifted hands. He seemed to be the leading spirit among them, and said that he was a body-servant of Dr. Garrett, of Washington; that the Doctor was a kind master, and had often promised him he should be free; but somehow he always forgot it. It went hard with him, he said, to leave "massa" and "missus," but when his friends who were not so well treated, were going away, he could not stay behind. While he was a fine specimen of a well-bred negro, the others presented quite a different appearance—coarse, dejected and ignorant, and were evidently field-hands. Supper over, they tumbled themselves into a four-horse covered farm wagon, and were driven to Henry Bushong's house.

The editors of this work have received from Slater B. Russell, Esq., of West Chester, Pa., the following interesting reminiscences: "My father, the late John Neal Russell, was born of Quaker parents in Brandywine Hundred, Delaware, on the third day of July, 1804, and died in Drumore township, Lancaster county, Pennsylvania, December 23d, 1876. He was quite a small child when the family moved to Lancaster county. They bought and settled on a large farm in the valley of the Conowingo in Drumore township, at a point about eight miles from the Delaware line.

The proximity to the slave border afforded my father,

while yet a small boy, a good insight into the workings
of slavery. When he was about ten years of age, a
light colored woman, the mother of two small children,
was taken quite near his father's house in broad daylight, tied, gagged, thrown into a wagon and, amid the
cries of the little ones, hurried off across the border.
She was sold into Georgia, and the children grew up in
my grandfather's family.

This incident, in particular, seems to have stirred the
boy's nature to its depths. He became the champion
and friend of the fleeing slave from that hour and remained so till slavery was abolished. He was fearless
and resolute, not to say rash. I often look back in
wonder at the spirit of defiance he manifested toward
his pro-slavery antagonists on both sides of the border.
It must have been that his very boldness was his safe-
guard. * * *

My father's house sheltered most of the prominent
abolitionists of the land. Garrison, the Burleighs,
Thomas Earle, Lucretia Mott, Daniel Gibbons, J. Miller
McKim, Thomas Whitson, Lucy Stone, Robert Collyer
and many others. I was just at an age to enjoy their
rare company, and what a coterie of noble spirits
they were! How can we reverence them enough?
* * * I have a particularly distinct recollection of Thomas Earle; I remember he was a man to take
notice of a boy of twelve or fifteen. What most impressed me in him was his exceeding mildness—as gentle
as a woman was he. He dressed well, too, I remember,
and was tall and elegant looking. * * *

There is another character I will describe to you, who
lived in Southern Lancaster county, Joseph C. Taylor.

* * * He was a young farmer. One June morning some one rattled and shook his door furiously, at the same time setting up an unearthly yell that caused him to put his head out of the window in short order. The cause of the noise was that a colored girl had been kidnapped near by, and that the kidnappers were making off with her in a covered wagon at break-neck speed toward the Maryland line, about three miles distant. In less time than it can be told, Taylor was mounted on the bare back of a plow-horse that had only a "blind" bridle, and, hatless and bootless, away he went. He had time to think, going along, and he thought how foolish would be his journey without arms. Just then he came to Jacob Kirk's store. The clerk was taking down the shutters. "For God's sake, give me a gun," said Taylor. There happened to be one in the store which he took and away. His steed was too fleet for the Marylanders. He overtook them, within, I think, about one hundred yards of the line. Riding around the wagon, he wheeled in the road, aimed his old fowling piece at the driver's head in a way that seemed to "mean business," and brought the horses to their haunches as he exclaimed: "Stir another foot and I'll blow your brains out!" A part of the sequel is that he marched the party back to a magistrate's office, had the girl discharged and the kidnappers put in jail. That is not the best part of the sequel, however; that remains to be told. The old gun hadn't the ghost of a load in it! Taylor didn't know this, neither did the kidnappers, of course, but the old gun not loaded served its purpose just as well as though it had been. * * *

THOMAS GARRET.

THOMAS GARRETT.
(1789—1871.)

Thomas Garrett, the uncompromising advocate of the emancipation and education of the colored race, was born in Upper Darby, Delaware county, Pennsylvania, on Eighth mo. 21st, 1789; he was a son of Thomas and Sarah Garrett.

A member of the Society of Friends, he held to that faith which is one of their cardinal principles, that God moves and inspires men to fulfill the work which He requires at their hands; from this conviction he never swerved, no matter what labor it cost, nor what vicissitudes and trials might beset him. His motto was "Always do right at the time irrespective of consequences."

He was married twice. His first wife was Mary Sharpless, of Birmingham, Chester county, Pennsylvania, who died at Wilmington, Delaware, Seventh mo. 13th, 1827; his second, Rachel Mendenhall, who died Fourth mo. 20th, 1868. He survived them both. Whilst yet living at his father's house, on his return from a brief absence from home, he found the women in great distress, two men having kidnapped a colored woman in the employ of the family, and removed her in a wagon; mounting a horse, he followed them rapidly by means of a mark left by a broken tire. They went to the Navy Yard, Philadelphia, and thence to Kensington, where he saw the wagon. The men were in the bar-room—the woman was in the kitchen and was taken home with him.

It was during this ride, while meditating upon the wrongs and oppressions of the colored race in bonds, that he felt the call to aid them in throwing off the yoke of slavery, as his special mission in life. He devoted himself there after fearlessly and faithfully to this work.

He removed to Wilmington, Del., in 1822.

It is a remarkable fact that, while living in a slave state, and in the largest city in that State, with a population hostile to abolitionists, and his house frequently under the rigid surveillance of police, that of the nearly twenty-nine hundred fugitives who passed through his hands, *not one was ever recaptured*, with the exception of a man who had lived some years in Canada and returned to Wilmington to preach. Remaining there some time, he was seized and returned to bondage.

He would never directly nor indirectly entice a slave to leave his master, but when one applied to him for aid in escaping from bondage, he never refused assistance, let the consequences be what they might.

Open assistance given at one time involved him in a law suit, an account of which we extract from William Still's "Underground Railroad."

"He met at New Castle a man, woman and six children, from down on the Eastern Shore of Maryland. The man was free, the woman had been a slave, and whilst in slavery had had, by her husband, two children; she was then set free and afterwards had four children. The whole party ran away. They traveled several days and finally reached Middletown, Del., late at night, where they were taken in and cared for by John Hunn, a wealthy Quaker. They were watched by some persons in that section, who followed them to New Castle, arrested them and sent them to jail. The sheriff and his daughter were anti-slavery people and wrote to Mr. Garrett, who went over and had an interview; after finding that four of the party were undoubtedly free, he returned to Wilmington and, on the following day, he and United States Senator Wales went to New Castle and had the party taken before Judge Booth, on a writ of *habeas corpus*. Judge Booth decided that there was no evidence on which to hold them and that, in the absence of evidence, *the presumption was always in favor of freedom*, and discharged them.

Mr. Garrett then said, " Here is this woman with a babe at her breast, and the child suffering from white swelling on its leg; is there any impropriety in my getting a carriage and helping them over to Wilmington ? " Judge Booth responded, " certainly not." Mr. Garrett then hired the carriage, but gave the driver distinctly to understand that he only paid for the woman and the young children; the rest might walk; they all got in, however, and finally escaped; of course the two children born in slavery among the rest.

Six weeks afterwards the slaveholders followed them, and incited, it is said, by the Cochrans and James A. Bayard, commenced a suit against Mr. Garrett, claiming all the fugitives as slaves. ` Mr. Garrett's friends claim that the jury was packed to secure an adverse verdict. The trial came before Chief Justice Taney and Judge Hall in the May term, (1848) of the United States Court sitting at New Castle, Bayard representing the prosecution, Wales the defendant. There were four trials in all, lasting three days; we have not room here for the details of the trial, but the juries awarded even heavier damages than the plaintiffs claimed and the judgments swept away every dollar of his property."

The amount taken was about $8,000—all he was worth, but his spirits were not in the least affected; and after sentence, he arose in open court and said, "Now, Judge, I do not think that I have always done my duty, being fearful of losing what little I possessed; but now that you have relieved me, I will go home and put another story on my house, so that I can accommodate more of God's poor." Then turning to the large crowd in the court-room he addressed them. He was listened to throughout with the closest attention. Sometimes profound silence prevailed. Sometimes his bold assertions were applauded, while some who felt the keenness of his remarks tried to relieve their feelings by hissing.

But those who prosecuted him, were so impressed with his candor and honesty that one of them came forward and shook him by the hand, asked his forgiveness and desired his friendship, which was fully promised on condition of the person's " ceasing to be an advocate of the iniquitous system of slavery."

His household goods, along with his other property, were sold, but were purchased by his friends and were used by him until he was able to pay for them.

He was at that time keeping an iron store and coal yard. His friends volunteered all the means needed to continue the business, and even more than he required ; they saw his faith, honesty and boldness put through a severe test in the crucible of a Southern court, and that these came out pure as gold.

He was then sixty years of age, but he applied himself assiduously to business, which vastly increased ; he put the additional story on his house, as he promised the Judge; fugitives came to him in greater numbers, for his name became more known in the Southern States than ever before; he aided all who came, at the same time contributing to the relief of other suffering poor, regardless of color, and with all these acts of charity, he was enabled to repay all who had loaned him money, and amassed a competence within a few years.

Charitable friends in England had long assisted him with funds for the relief of the slave, and of later time they furnished more than he could advantageously use in the cause. This excess he returned to them.

In an obituary it is said of him that he seemed scarcely to know what fear was, and although irate slave-holders often called on him to know the whereabouts of their slaves, he met them placidly, and never denied having helped the fugitives on their way, but positively declined to give any information, and when they flourished pistols or bowie knives to force their demand, he calmly pushed the weapons aside and told them that none but cowards resorted to such means to carry out their ends, and that Quakers were not afraid of such things.

On one occasion $10,000 were offered for him in Maryland; he wrote to the parties, that this was not enough; send $20,000 and he would go himself. They did not send it, nor did they make any further efforts to be confronted by a man of such boldness.

For a long time when it was expected that he would be murdered for his avowed interest in the poor slave, many of the blacks would get into his yard by turns and stay there all night to protect him, against his posi-tive orders, for he feared nothing except neglect of his duty to the cause which he had espoused.

He was fertile in plans for directing or conveying fu-

L

gitives out of Wilmington to safer places. As the physician prescribes for each individual case according to conditions and symptoms, so did he promptly advise means to meet the necessities of each individual case that applied to him. Frequently he would give a man a scythe, hoe, rake or some other implement to carry on the shoulder through the town as if going to work, with directions that when a certain bridge was reached to hide the tool under it, then strictly follow directions to the next station.

These tools would find their way back and again be ready for similar duty.

He gave those he sent on foot such directions as enabled them readily to find the places of safety, and gave the fugitives papers by which the persons to whom they were sent would know from whom they came, and that they were neither impostors nor spies.

He wrote many letters to the managers of the anti-slavery office in Philadelphia, informing them of slaves *en route* for their place, sometimes of single individuals, sometimes of parties of from two to thirty or more; if hunters were in close pursuit and large rewards offered, he apprised them of all danger and gave them such directions as were necessary to secure protection and safety. These letters gave evidence of his ever-watchful mind, the secrecy, wisdom, discreetness and success of his plannings, his indefatigable labors and his liberality in paying money where needed for the assistance of " God's poor," as he was pleased to call them, out of slavery.

If he knew of a party coming who were in danger, he sent his agents to intercept them before entering the city, and have them ferried across the Christiana river, where a carriage would meet them, if they were women and children; if men, they were guided to some safe place on foot, and then directions were given them how to proceed.

Joseph G. Walker, now living, Tenth mo. 1881, at the age of seventy-six years, was one of Thomas Garrett's principal assistants in the removal of fugitives out of Wilmington to safe routes northward. Though now quite crippled and nearly blind, he warms up with the animation of earlier days when he recounts the many exploits and the long journeys he frequently made to

> " Point the bondman's way,
> And turn the spoiler from his prey."

During one fall he took away one hundred and thirty slaves; on one occasion he went with seven. From three o'clock in the afternoon until six o'clock next morning he walked over sixty miles; he did complain a little of this, however, and said he would not do it again in the same time. His father was a West Indian and his mother was English or Scotch; hence his inherited powers of locomotion and endurance.

Fugitives were frequently taken from Thomas Garrett's in carriages or on foot, while the reputed owners or their agents were watching his movements in other parts of the city where he was apparently engaged in his business pursuits.

Officers were sometimes stationed around the house to capture slaves who had been traced to Wilmington. At times it was necessary to wade the Brandywine in winter with fugitives; after which careful directions were given and the agents would return by the bridge, on seeing whom, the constables in waiting, on one occasion, said quietly, " it is all over, we may as well go home."

His house being a Southern station of the underground line was the scene of many startling and even amusing experiences.   One summer evening when there was a collection of old plain Friends at the house, he. was called to the kitchen where he found a greatly terrified poor woman who had run away, and from her statement it was evident that pursuers would be there in a few minutes to watch the house.   He took her up stairs, dressed her in his wife's clothes, with plain handkerchief, bonnet and veil, and made her take his arm. They walked out of the front door where she recognized her master as she passed.   He was eagerly watching the house at the time.

(There were several underground stations below Wilmington, nearly all Friends.   Those who resided down the State could be depended upon for the service. John Hunn, spoken of in the extract from " William Still's Underground Railroad," was particularly active and was at one time fined very heavily, perhaps to the extent of his property).

Thomas Garrett, after the opening of the Rebellion, wrote several very strong letters to President Lincoln, urging the " Emancipation Proclamation."   He lived to see his most earnest wish accomplished—that to which he had devoted the energies of a lifetime—viz.: the Emancipation of the Slaves of the United States of America.   On the arrival of the glorious news he was waited upon by a delegation of his colored friends requesting him to surrender himself to them for the day.

He yielded to their wishes implicitly and the event was duly celebrated, without noise but with thankfulness and joy.

He expressed himself as entirely satisfied with his work and died calmly and peacefully on First mo. 25th, 1871, in the eighty-second year of his age.

He was interred in Friends' Grounds at Wilmington, Del.; a vigorous oak (now of good size) was planted between the head and foot stones of his grave.

JACOB LINDLEY.
(1744—1814.)

Jacob Lindley, who lived in New Garden, Chester county, near where the village of Avondale is now situated, and owned six hundred acres of land in that vicinity, was the first to give assistance to fugitives in Chester county, of whom we have been able to glean any account. He aided many on their way to freedom long before the Underground Railroad was established.

About the year 1801, a line was formed by a few friends from Elisha Tyson's, Baltimore, to his place, thence to Pughtown and Valley Forge as described in the account of Abraham Bonsall.

Jacob Lindley was sympathizing and affable in disposition, sensitive in feeling and energetic in action. He was a prominent and powerful minister in the Society of Friends, a man of extraordinary intelligence and ability, a pungent writer when he assailed either open vice or the sinister means used to deceive and wrong others for pecuniary gain.

He possessed a large and strong physique, and a voice of great volume. When addressing an assemblage, and powerfully moved by the earnestness of his feelings in rebuking sin in any phase or beneath any guise, or in pleading the rights of humanity, especially of the down-trodden, enslaved and oppressed African, he expressed himself in words and tone and manner so emphatic as to reach the most common understanding, or to touch the most adamantine heart. While he sent the poniard of conviction directly home to the hearts of the guilty, he was tender toward the feelings of the unintentionally erring, or those who strove to do right against adverse influences of a potential character difficult at times wholly to overcome.

His genuine kindness, and love for all the children of God, was a marked trait of his character. A respectable mechanic who had been the recipient of his hospitality remarked that "the house of Jacob Lindley and his wife was in one respect like the kingdom of Heaven, no profession or complexion being excluded."

Toward the close of his life he wrote: "Oh! surely I may say, I shudder and my tears involuntarily steal from my eyes, for my poor, oppressed, afflicted, tor-mented black brethren—hunted—frightened to see a white man—turned from every source of comfort that is worth living for in this stage of being. The tears, the groans, the sighs of these, have surely ascended to the ears of the Lord of Sabaoth, and as a thick cloud are awfully suspended over this land. I tenderly and tremblingly feel for the poor masters involved in this difficulty. I am awfully awakened into fear for our poor country." He was twice married; both wives being ministers of the gospel.

On the twelfth of Sixth mo. (June) 1814, he attended New Garden meeting, and spoke with his usual earnestness and power. During the course of his sermon he intimated " his conviction that there were those present who would not see the light of another day," and added, " perhaps it may be myself." That afternoon he was thrown out of a carriage upon his head, dislocating his neck. He was aged about seventy.

LEVI B. WARD.

In 1848, two men drove up to the house of Levi B. Ward, East Marlborough, Chester county, while he was absent from home, seized upon a colored boy seventeen years of age, and claimed him as their property. Mrs. Ward remonstrated against their taking him, but they replied that they had papers to prove that he belonged to them. They did not show the papers, but hurried away with the boy and the family never heard from him after-ward.

It was supposed that the men were kidnappers who had been waiting an opportunity to take him when no one but women was about to interfere.

JAMES N. TAYLOR.
(Born Third month 4th, 1813.)

James N. Taylor, from early boyhood, felt an interest in the anti-slavery movement, and a sympathy for the fugitive. In 1841 he removed from East Fallowfield, Chester county, to West Marlborough. Prior to that date he assisted all slaves who came to his place, but was not then connected with the Underground Railroad management. After removing to Marlborough, his willingness to aid fugitives being known, his residence was made a branch station, and he received passengers from William Rakestraw and Day Wood, in Lancaster county, and from James Fulton and Amos Preston, Chester county.

One fugitive was so closely pursued that James took him to Lancaster, put him on the cars and sent him to Lafayette, Indiana. He was so nearly white that but few would have suspected that in his veins flowed a trace of African blood.

In 1844, eighteen men, women and children came to his place on their way "toward the North Star." They were sheltered in the depths of some straw, and next night taken to Isaac Mendenhall's.

After the Christiana riot, Parker, Pinkney and Johnson and one other came to his place, and were taken to Isaac Mendenhall's. He was not aware at the time who they were.

The last who came were brought in a dearborn in day-time by Ann Preston and Elizabeth Coates. They were well covered so as to attract no attention.

James N. Taylor assisted in organizing the first Anti-Slavery Society in Chester county.

ISAAC MENDENHALL.

CHAPTER XV.

ISAAC AND DINAH MENDENHALL.—Interesting Incidents.—HARRIET TUBMAN.—Assists Parker, Pinkney and Johnson.—'Squire Jacob Lamborn.—Sarah Pearson Opens Free Produce Store in Hamorton.—Isaac Mendenhall Disowned.—Assist in Organizing Society of Progressive Friends.—Reunited to Original Society.—Golden Anniversary of Wedding.—Original Estate.

ISAAC AND DINAH MENDENHALL.

(Isaac Mendenhall, Born Ninth Mo. 26th, 1806, Died Twelfth Mo. 23d, 1882. Dinah Hannum Mendenhall, Born Tenth Mo. 15th, 1807.)

The home of Isaac and Dinah Mendenhall, in Kennett township, near Longwood, ten miles from Wilmington, was always open to receive the liberty-seeking slave. Their station being nearest the Delaware line was eagerly sought by fugitives as soon as they entered the Free State. They were generally sent by Thomas Garrett, of Wilmington, who, starting them on the road, directed them to " go on and on until they came to a stone-gate post, and then turn in." Sometimes he sent a note by them saying, " I send you three," (or four or five, as the case might be) "bales of black wool," which was to assure them that these colored persons were not impostors.

No record was kept of the number they aided, but during a period of thirty-four years it amounted to several hundred. Many were well dressed and intelligent.

At one time fourteen came on a Seventh-day (Saturday) night and remained over next day. The women and children were secreted in a room in the spring-house,

L*

and the men in the barn. As they usually entertained a great many visitors on First-days (Sundays), and some of these were pro-slavery Friends, the fugitives had to be kept very quiet. On Third-day (Tuesday) night Isaac and Josiah Wilson, who lived near by, took them to John Jackson's, Darby. Josiah and his wife, Mary, were ever ready to give their personal aid and counsel.

One woman whom Thomas Garrett brought there was a somewhat curious, but interesting character, and endowed with a spiritualistic faith. The first night after leaving her master she began to regret and to wonder whether or not she was doing right ; whether she should return or continue her course and risk being captured and taken back. She went into a woods, and sat down and cried. While in that deep, prayerful spirit, as to what was best for her to do, a voice seemed to say to her, " Cheer up, Mary ; go on, I will protect thee." With this fresh cheer in her heart, she went on, arrived at Thomas Garrett's, who, as above related, took her to Isaac Mendenhall's, where she remained three months, and was a most faithful servant. She said they were told in the South that " abolitionists were wicked people," but that " she never knowed there was such kind people in the world as they."

A colored woman named Harriet Tubman, living near the line, was active in helping hundreds to escape. In point of bravery and success she might well be called a second Joan of Arc. She would go fearlessly into the Slave States, talk with the slaves, tell them how to escape, direct them on the road, and thus during one visit among them, would start numbers on their way northward to freedom. Large sums of money were

DINAH MENDENHALL.

offered for her capture, but all in vain. She could elude
patrols and pursuers with as much ease and unconcern
as an eagle would soar through the heavens. She "had
faith in God;" always asked Him what to do, and to di_
rect her, "which," she said, "He always did." She
would talk about "consulting with God," or "asking
of Him," just as one would consult a friend upon matters of business; and she said "He never deceived her."

After escaping from bondage herself, she set about
devising means by which she could assist others in leaving. In her first effort she brought away her brother,
with his wife and several children. Next she helped
her aged parents from Virginia to a comfortable home
in Auburn, N. Y. And thus encouraged, she continued
making these trips, at intervals, for several years.
Many who escaped through her directions to Thomas
Garrett were sent by him to Isaac Mendenhall.

When the war broke out, she felt, as she said, that
"the good Lord had come down to deliver her people,
and she must go and help Him." She went into Georgia
and Florida, attached herself to the army, performed
an incredible amount of labor as cook, laundress, and
nurse, and still more as the leader of soldiers in scouting parties and raids. She seemed to know no fear, and
scarcely ever fatigue. They called her their *Moses*. On
account of the valuable services she rendered, several
of the officers testified that she was entitled to a pen-
sion from the Government.

After the Christiana riot, James N. Taylor brought
Parker, Pinkney, and Johnson and one other whose
name was not known, to Isaac Mendenhall's. When
James returned, the hunters had been at his place in

search of any colored people who might have fled to him from the vicinity of Christiana.

The four men slept in the barn at Isaac Mendenhall's at nights, but during the day they husked corn in the field, with all the appearance of regular farm hands. If pursuers came, the family were to give a certain sound when the men were to flee to the woods. One day a messenger came and said there was a party on the track of these men, and it would not be safe to keep them longer. During the remainder of the day they concealed themselves in the woods. Isaac decided to take them that night to John Vickers; but Dr. Bartholomew Fussell, then living near by, at Hamorton, hearing that the men were there, went to consult with him about them. Learning his decision, he said, "Isaac, I am better acquainted with the route than thee is; and beside, I have no property to sacrifice if I am detected and thee has. Thee start with them on the road and I will meet thee and go on with them and thee can return." After some deliberation, Isaac accepted the proposition, and at an appointed hour in the evening, started.

Dinah Mendenhall, in relating this case, said : "These men were not only fugitives but participants in the tragedy, and harboring them subjected us to heavy fine and imprisonment. But we had always said we would never submit to carry out that accursed Fugitive Slave Law, come what might. But that night when they started, the poor quivering flesh was weak and I had scarce strength to get into the house. But I held to my faith in an Overruling Providence, and we came through it in safety." "These," she remarked, "were the times which tried men's souls, and women's too."

Doctor Fussell, instead of taking them to John Vickers, took them to his niece, Graceanna Lewis, arriving there before midnight. Leaving them in the conveyance, he went to the house, awoke the family, told them whom he had with him and what the danger would be in harboring them. They admitted them, however, and put them in a third-story room, the door of which locked on the inside. They were told not to unlock it unless a certain signal was given. As the girl then living with the family was not to be trusted, they borrowed food for the men from a neighbor, so as not to excite her suspicion. The following day arrangements were made with J. Pierce West, living near by, to take them to the house of a friend in Montgomery county, about a mile or more from Phœnixville. A little after dark he and his brother, Thomas, started with them in a market dearborn, throwing some old carpet over them, just as they would cover a butter-tub. Passing through Phœnixville about midnight, they arrived at the friend's house, whose name is not now remembered, and there left them.

(A further description is given of them in the reminiscences of Dr. J. L. Paxson, of Norristown.)

Fugitives were taken from Isaac Mendenhall's to John Vickers, William and Simon Barnard, John Jackson, in Darby, and to Philadelphia. James Pugh, of Pennsbury, would frequently go to Philadelphia and make arrangements with Miller McKim and William Still, to meet Isaac outside the city and take the fugitives into their care.

Many families along these routes who were inherently opposed to slavery, refused, through fear, to give any

assistance whatever in facilitating the fugitives' escape.
James Russell Lowell truly says :

> "They are slaves who dare not be
> In the right with two or three."

There were many persons in Kennett township who
were not strenuously opposed to the anti-slavery movement ; were inclined to be sympathizers in the cause, but
thought abolitionists were running great risks.

Squire Jacob Lamborn was honestly opposed to the
fanaticism of abolitionists, as their warring against the
institution of slavery was engendering a spirit of animosity in the minds of the Southern people toward those
of the North.   But after hearing a cogent and exhaus-
tive argument by Abbie Kelley, he was convinced of the
true principles upon which they stood and united with
them always afterwards.

Anti-slavery lectures in that township did much to
enlighten the people upon universal liberty and to
soften the asperity of antagonism toward abolitionists,
although many meetings, in the early part of the time,
were but slimly attended.

Many persons in Kennett and vicinity grew to be ·
conscientiously opposed to using the products of slave
labor, as by so doing they were patronizing an evil that
they were endeavoring to uproot.   To meet the demand
of these persons, Sarah Pearson opened a free produce
store in Hamorton, about the year 1844, and continued
it fourteen years.   She was well patronized.   At first
she kept only free produce ; but later kept mixed goods.

Kennett Monthly Meeting of Friends disowned several of its members who had, in a measure, separated
themselves from it, on account of the meeting's not

taking as active a part in anti-slavery, temperance, and other needed reforms of the day, as they held it to be the moral duty of a religious body to do. Isaac Mendenhall was one who came under this decree of disownment, but his wife, as earnest in the progressive movement of reform as he, was never disowned. It is a principle of Friends to act in harmony. In the consideration of her case there was a " division of sentiment."

They united with a number of others in organizing the Society of Progressive Friends at Longwood. In conformity with a " *Call for a General Religious Conference, with a view to the establishment of a Yearly Meeting in Pennsylvania*," a large number of persons assembled in Old Kennett (Friends) Meeting House, on the twenty-second of Fifth month (May), 1853. The house was filled and many could not gain entrance. They invited to membership, " not only members of the Society of Friends, but all those who felt the need of social and religious co-operation, who looked to God as a Universal Father, and who regarded as one Brotherhood the whole family of man." They invited all such persons to take part in the deliberations upon such a plan of organization as might commend itself to their judgment, and to take action upon such other subjects pertaining to human duty and welfare as might appear to demand the attention of the assembly. The call to this Conference was signed by fifty-eight persons, chiefly Friends. Its sessions continued four days and were marked by free and cordial interchange of views, development of thought, and an earnestness and unity of action for the enlightenment, improvement and general welfare of the whole human family. That aged and religious emancipated slave, Sojourner Truth, was there, and spoke on several occasions. She touched the sympathies of all, and reached the deep fount of parental tenderness, when, after a few impressive remarks, she sang

> I pity the slave-mother, careworn and weary,
>   Who sighs as she presses her babe to her breast;
> I lament her sad fate, all so helpless and dreary,
>   I lament for her woes, and her wrongs unredressed.
> O! who can imagine her heart's deep emotion,
>   As she thinks of her children about to be sold ;
> You may picture the bounds of the rock-girdled ocean,
>   *But the grief of that mother can never be told.*

A permanent organization was effected, and weekly and yearly meeting established. Joseph A. Dugdale was appointed their first treasurer. He served for several years. Isaac Mendenhall was next appointed and served until his son, Aaron, took his place.

Isaac was Treasurer of the Chester County Anti-Slavery Society from its organization at Coatesville, in May, 1838, until its labors closed at the termination of the war.

After the downfall of slavery and the establishment of universal liberty by the Government, the great object which had brought them together, had cemented their hearts in the one grand design and impelled them with enthusiasm and unfaltering devotion toward the one great end, was accomplished ; and with one accord they could offer up thanksgiving and praise to the Father of all, that four millions of human beings held as chattel slaves under our laws were now, henceforth, and forever FREE.

After the close of the war, when the slavery question ceased to be a disturbing element, the Friends of Kennett Monthly Meeting invited those back into the Society, whom they had disowned, without requiring of them the usual acknowledgment.

Outside of their daily avocations and domestic duties, Isaac and Dinah Mendenhall were active and zealous workers whenever the cause of humanity needed earnest supporters. They were a firm and solid rock upon which the friends of progress and reform could ever rely. The earnest appeal for temperance, for the advancement of women, for the free expression of thought upon religion, found them strenuously, yet unostentatiously, working in the van.

On the twelfth of Fifth month (May), 1881, their life of united honest toil and faithful devotion to each other, reached the rounded period of *fifty years*. This *Golden Anniversary* of their nuptials was celebrated at their home by the assembling of two hundred and twenty-five guests of all ages, from the little frolicking child to the friends whose advanced age and feebleness rendered it necessary for them to be lifted from their carriages. Yet to these, the happy commingling of old-time friends, enlivened by the sprightliness and vigor of joyous youth, was like the balmy breezes and the fragrant blossoms of the return of spring.

Fifteen of the seventy-two persons who signed their marriage certificate were present at this anniversary, and among them were the two first waiters on that occasion.

Their eldest son Aaron, living on the old family estate, now known as Oakdale, was there with his wife and three children, one of whom bears the name of Isaac. This property was originally purchased of William

Penn, by Robert Pennell and Benjamin Mendenhall, and the deed was signed by his deputies, Edward Shippen, Griffith Owen and James Logan, (Penn being then in England). The deed was dated Fifteenth day of June A. D. 1703, and was for six hundred acres of land, which according to present survey makes one thousand, and for which they were to " yield and pay therefor, yearly from the said date of survey, to me, my heirs and successors at Chester, at or upon the first day of March in every year forever thereafter, six bushels of good and merchantable wheat, to such persons as shall be appointed to receive the same."

The estate afterwards passed into the hands of Benjamin Mendenhall's son Joseph, then to an Isaac. Since then it has passed alternately from an Isaac to an Aaron, and from an Aaron to an Isaac through four generations. It has descended from the possession of one occupant to the other by will—but one deed was ever given, which bears the date of 1703.

Many testimonials of esteem and love were sent by persons who could not be present. Among these was one from John G. Whittier, who said, " I knew you in the brave old anti-slavery days, and have never forgotten you. Whenever and wherever the cause of freedom needed aid and countenance you were sure to be found with the noble band of Chester county men and women to whose mental culture, moral stamina and generous self-sacrifice I can bear emphatic testimony."

Mary A. Livermore, in a letter addressed to their daughter Sallie, on that occasion says, " With what noble people have they been associated! How rich in reminiscences their memories must be! They have wit-

nessed the unparalled growth of the country, the downfall of slavery, the nation convulsed with civil war,
which ended in the death of a colossal national sin and
the freeing of four million slaves."

Isaac and Dinah H. Mendenhall are living at the present writing. They have reached that summit in the
upward progress of human existence, from which, in retirement, they can look down upon a beautifully diver-
sified landscape, richly adorned with the fruits of their
own labors. The sunset sky, toward which they are
tending, is ruddy in its glow, while the sun of glory
sends forth its effulgent beams from an unclouded sky,
significant of the celestial brightness awaiting them
around the Throne of eternal peace.

[Since the above sketch was written, Isaac Mendenhall has passed away, dying at his home at Hamorton,
" full of years and honors," in peace, after so many con-
flicts; in honor, after so much obloquy.]

CHAPTER XVI.

DR. BARTHOLOMEW FUSSELL.—Parentage.—Teaches Colored School
in Maryland.—Studies Medicine.—Lydia Morris Fussell.—Influence
of Charles C. Burleigh.—Incidents.—About Two Thousand Fugitives Passed.—Women's Medical College.—Death and Burial.—
Incidents Related by His Son.—JOHN AND HANNAH COX.—Incidents.—Take Active Part in Anti-slavery Societies.—Golden Wedding Anniversary.—Greeting.—Death.

DR. BARTHOLOMEW FUSSELL.

(1794—1871.)

Dr. Bartholomew Fussell, son of Bartholomew and
Rebecca B. Fussell, was born in Chester county, Pennsylvania, in the year 1794, and was by birthright, as
well as by conviction, a member of the Society of
Friends. His father, Bartholomew Fussell, Sr., was an
approved minister in that denomination, but of remarkably liberal tendencies, his peculiar mission being frequently to hold meetings among persons of different
beliefs and often in remote country districts where
religious meetings of any kind were rare. To gather
the lambs and the lost sheep into the fold, seemed to be,
largely, the work to which he felt himself assigned. He
was a man of genial and cheerful disposition, often
saying that "he served a good Master, and he did not
see why he should be sad." His conversation was remarkably entertaining and instructive, and he had the
power of winning young people to an unusual degree.
His mother, Rebecca Bond Fussell, was of a shy and
self-distrustful nature, lacking in confidence, but self-
forgetful and devoted to the welfare of others and,

DR. BARTHOLOMEW FUSSELL.

perhaps, one of the kindest of her sex. Their son,
Dr. Bartholomew Fussell, differed from either parent,
and was apparently a new combination, unlike any
one but himself, differing as strongly from his brothers
and sisters as he did from his parents.   In the period
to which his youth belonged, the country schools
in northern Chester county, where he resided, were
not equal to the needs of a few families of Friends.
In consequence his father, Bartholomew Fussell, Sr.,
although unaccustomed to the work, built with his
own hands a school-house, the walls of which are
still in a perfect condition. Here his eldest sister,
Esther, began her career as a successful teacher, beginning when only sixteen years of age, with her brothers
and sisters and the children of a few friends. To this
sister, more than to any one else, Dr. Fussell always referred as the person who had stimulated, aided and
encouraged him in his efforts to obtain a broad and
useful education.

Removing with his father to Maryland, he decided
upon the study of medicine, teaching school by day,
and reading for his profession at night.   But even this
heavy strain upon his energies was not sufficient. Being
deeply impressed with the ignorance, misery and degradation around him, he sought to alleviate the condition
of the slaves, by opening a Sabbath School and inviting
their attendance.   Here he taught the rudiments of
knowledge, not for a few hours only, but for the whole
day, frequently having as many as ninety pupils in attendance, their advancement being the sole reward he
desired or obtained. When they had progressed sufficiently to be able to read the Bible for themselves, it

was a manifest source of satisfaction and delight to them and it was too early for the slaveholders to see in his efforts any occasion of danger to themselves. We do not learn that he met with any opposition from the masters, while he did win the life-long gratitude of some of his pupils. It was an evidence of the splendid physical constitution of the young student, that his health did not break down under these exhausting efforts. He continued on every occasion to manifest his opposition to slavery, becoming the friend and co-laborer of Elisha Tyson, one of the most courageous and devoted philanthropists that the institution of slavery ever called into existence. At the time of his graduation, and in the face of the most influential slaveholders belonging to the medical profession in Baltimore, Dr. Fussell uttered his solemn protest against slavery, as a fruitful source of disease and demoralization and as a stigma on the race of those who enslaved their kind.

Returning to Pennsylvania to practice his chosen profession, he became eminently successful, both on account of his knowledge and judgment, and his intense sympathy with suffering, which seemed to inspire him with the faculty of entering into the feelings of others, of tracing the hidden sources of disease, and of keeping his mind ever on the alert, to select and administer the proper remedies. These principles actuated him just as much in the hovel of the poor as in the elaborately furnished mansions of the rich. When life was hanging tremblingly in the balance, when the closest watching and the strictest care were needed, when the timely administration of a remedy, or judicious nursing might save life, or the neglect of these imperil all chances of recovery, he would spend whole nights by the bedside of the indigent where he expected little or no reward, with just as assiduous devotion to the suffering family as if he were attending the only daughter of a millionaire whose recovery would compensate him with a worldly fortune. His heart was in the welfare and happiness of the human family, and not in his purse.

He was fortunate in selecting for the companion of his life one who entered fully into sympathy with him, and who aided him in all his endeavors with wifely devotion. Lydia Morris ˙Fussell was greatly beloved, not only in his own family, but in the neighborhood, where she was a spirit of kindness, doing good wherever opportunity afforded. She was an admirable hostess, and her doors were ever open to the most generous hospitality; her cheerful spirit and free social nature making her home a delightful place of sojourn. Many were the guests there entertained, only to speak her praises. None knew her that were not attracted to her. During the greater part of her married life she and her husband owned the dwelling afterwards occupied by Chandler Darlington and his wife, near Kennett Square, Chester county, Pennsylvania, and as this house was always open to fugitives and their friends, it has already become historic. Nearly all of the distinguished persons who visited Kennett Square, in the exercise of anti-slavery duties, were at one time or another entertained there as guests.

This house soon became the goal of the slaves and thither they made their way long before the general public was awakened to the iniquity of the system of slavery. Dr. Fussell had become a strong and determined oppo-

nent of this evil by seeing its ruinour effect and its inhuman cruelties in Maryland, and his own convictions
had been intensified by his association with Elisha
Tyson, so that he was fully prepared to attend the Anti-
slavery Convention in 1833 and to append his signature
to its immortal " Declaration of Sentiments." He was
a subscriber to the *Liberator* from the time the first
number was issued until, the battle being ended, the
last number was announced.

The real earnestness and activity of Chester county
abolitionism had its date with the advent of Charles C.
Burleigh, who, about the year 1835, appeared as a
lecturer in the neighborhood of Kennett Square.

There being at that time no railroad or stage facilities by which he could be accommodated, and being a
remarkable walker, this gifted orator left Philadelphia
for Dr. Fussell's, one mile east of the village of Kennett Square, traveling on foot over bad roads, the whole
distance. Arriving at his destination in the evening, he
learned that the doctor and his wife had already departed to attend a discussion on the subject of Phreno-
logy, in the village. Tired as he was and supperless,
our friend immediately followed, and soon overtook and
passed the doctor and his wife in their carriage. Being
excessively muddy with travel, this young athlete did
not present an extraordinarily attractive exterior. The
first impulse of the kind doctor had been to invite the
stranger he saw passing to a seat in his carriage, but a
glance at his boots, and a thought of the wife by his
side checked the impulse, and the wayfarer was allowed
to pass on. When they reached the place of meeting,
he was already there, and during the debate which fol-

lowed he modestly asked permission to speak, exhibiting such an amount of knowledge, extent of research, profundity of thought, and such oratorical and logical powers as to astonish and captivate his hearers. Dr. Fussell used often to tell the story of how he was cheated of doing a kindness to Charles C. Burleigh, by allowing himself to be governed by a pair of muddy boots.

At this meeting, all were so delighted that Charles C. Burleigh had only to express the wish to have appointed and announced a meeting on the subject of slavery. This meeting was largely attended, for the fame of the speaker had gone abroad. Here he pictured slavery and liberty in such clear contrast, and depicted the Christian duty of man to his fellow men in such glowing colors, embellished by the sublime rhetoric of which he was master, that the latent sense of justice and anti-slavery emotions were stirred up in the hearts of the good people of Kennett, and organization and agitation were at once instituted. From that time onward until emancipation was effected, Kennett Square was noted among those who were slow to accept the movement, as the " hot-bed of abolitionism " while the earnest sympathizers with the negro in bondage, in this and in other States, found here kind-hearted, able, and intelligent men and women to aid in the cause, ever ready to assist with their money and their labor, and in whose homes they always had a hearty welcome. It was the cynosure alike of the fugitive and his friends.

Discussions were now held in West Chester, Lionville and various other places throughout the country, between the abolitionists and colonizationists, each side

M

being supported by able speakers. These discussions aided greatly in arousing public sentiment, which grew in favor of freedom for the negro under our own Government.

Dr. Fussell was an intimate friend of Thomas Garrett, of Wilmington, and laboring in connection with him and many others at available points, about two thousand fugitives passed through his hands on their way to freedom. Among these he frequently had the pleasure of welcoming some of his old Maryland Sabbath School pupils, who made the knowledge he had afforded them of service in their escape from slavery long years afterward. The delighted recognition of him by these poor beings in a strange land, was the occasion of the most heart-touching scenes.

In his practice as a physician, while at Kennett Square, Dr. Fussell occasionally met with colored persons whose constant dread of being recaptured so affected their health as to render his medical services necessary. In one instance, the shocking details of which are omitted, he was called upon to save the life of one who had preferred death by his own hand to such a fate. In many cases he gave far more sympathy than medicine, benefitting each by administering what their needs required, whether it be clothing or food, encouragement, mirth or reprimand, which latter was sometimes needed, but was kindly and wisely given.

During their residence at Kennett Square, both he and his wife were untiring in their efforts to aid all persons of color, whether bond or free. Towards the close of the first decade of the anti-slavery agitation, they removed to West Vincent, Chester county, purchasing a farm adjoining that of their sister Esther Fussell Lewis, herself a well-known abolitionist, and there they continued their work of receiving fugitives. About the year 1838, Lydia M. Fussell died, mourned by all who knew her and leaving a young and helpless family to the care of her husband.

After his second marriage with Rebecca C. Hewes, he removed to York, Pennsylvania, and opened a school there, doing anti-slavery work as formerly. Later he came to Hamorton, not far distant from his former residence, at Kennett Square. Here he gave a practical illustration of his principles by admitting colored youth to his school.

At all times he took an active interest in all educational and moral reforms, but was addicted to the use of tobacco, which habit he had acquired while young. When he was about seventy years of age, a very aged relative earnestly remonstrated with him against the continuance of this habit, as being inconsistent with a life devoted as his had been to the advocacy of many different reforms. On his replying that a sudden cessation from a practice so long indulged in might result in his death, her answer was, " Well, die then, and go to heaven decently." He delighted in after years to recur to this conversation, feeling that the faithfulness of his mentor, had stimulated him to the resolution of abandoning a habit so much at variance with his otherwise exemplary life.

From early youth, owing to the aid rendered him by his eldest sister, he had been led to consider the fitness of women for the study and practice of medicine. On his own graduation, he mentally resolved that if ever he had the opportunity, he would do what he could to aid them in acquiring a knowledge of the principles and practice of medicine. This purpose he frequently conversed about, and in it he had the cordial sympathy of his wife before she died. Even as early as 1840 he had given regular instruction to a class of women. In 1846 he communicated to a few liberal-minded men of his own profession, a plan for the establishment of a college of the highest grade for the medical education of women, holding a meeting for the purpose in his own house. Those comprising the meeting were Dr. Ezra Mitchener, Edwin Fussell, M. D., Franklin Taylor, M. D., Ellwood Harvey, M. D., and Sylvester Birdsall, M. D., including himself, six physicians. In inviting a beloved niece to be present, he reminded her that it was for her mother's sake—she who had more than any one else, moulded his character, and inspired him with the purpose. This niece still lives to testify that it was from the germ of his thought, hallowed by brotherly affection, that the Woman's Medical College of Philadelphia, grew into existence, one of its early graduates being Ann Preston, so long a part of the life of the college. Although never at any time officially connected with this institution, he yet regarded it as the result of one of his best efforts, and he continued through life to consider its welfare with the deepest interest.

Like other early abolitionists, he had his share of persecution to endure, and was occasionally mobbed while making anti-slavery speeches. This occurred once in West Chester, but he was supported and protected by the best citizens, more particularly by Hon. William Everhart, who lost no opportunity of allying himself with the oppressed and their defenders, at that period so unpopular.

At another time, while speaking at Centreville, Delaware, he was attacked by a party of Irish from Dupont's Powder Mills, who were incited to violence by a person who told them that Dr. Fussell had said that "the colored persons made better citizens than did the Irish." During the most vigorous period of the anti-slavery agitation his life was an almost continual warfare with the opponents of that cause, he being prompted by no hope of reward, present or prospective, but like other abolitionists, solely by benevolent purposes, and by a sense of justice and of right; and no aspersion, however infamous, no contumely, however vile, no ostracism, however cold, could turn these from the fulfillment of what they conscientiously held as a Christian duty. A part of his days towards the close of his career, were spent with his son, Joshua, at Pendleton, Indiana, and as age and infirmity increased, he was most faithfully and tenderly cared for by his children, in the home of his son, Dr. Morris Fussell, near Chester Springs, Chester county, where he died on the fourteenth of Second mo., 1871. His mortal part was interred near those of his ancestors and by the side of his wife, Lydia M. Fussell, in Friend's grave yard at Pikeland, where formerly stood a meeting house, now gone to decay.

His son, Joshua L. Fussell, contributes a few incidents which he can remember connected with the escape of fugitive slaves. There was an old man named "Davy," who gained a livelihood by selling peaches, fresh fish, and other commodities, purchased in Delaware, and sold in the neighborhood of Kennett Square. This person became a very important agent between Thomas Garrett and Dr. Fussell. His business being known it excited no suspicion to see his frequent journeys to Wilmington and back, nor was there anything remarkable in his being accompanied by friends of his own color, either by day or night. There can be no doubt that many loads other than fish or peaches, came in the dark from Thomas Garrett's to the house of Dr. Fussell, and were forwarded by him in safety.

One fugitive from the far South, was guided alone by the " dipper." He knew there was a land of liberty somewhere at the North, and that if he directed his course to the right or to the left, as that constellation turned around the polar centre, he would reach the land he sought. This much he seemed to have learned even in the darkness of slavery. Where freedom depended on observation, these bondmen became intense watchers of the stars at night.

All who were interrogated as to why they left their homes, gave nearly related answers. In the majority of cases it was the fear of being sold to go further South. Being " sold to Georgia " was the terror of plantation life, although the testimony usually was that very few slaveholders would do this unless compelled by needy circumstances. Hence the slaves learned to look with dismay on extravagances which sooner or later would bring the anguish of parting upon themselves. Some escaped rather than submit to promised punishments. Two good looking women, dignified and upright in department and conversation, left for the most womanly of all reasons. They prized their native purity as highly as do the most chaste and refined of their sex, and only by escaping to a land of freedom, could they preserve it.

One man leaving the South in mid-winter, had his fingers frozen so that the flesh was sloughing off, the ends of the bones protruding half an inch, yet the idea of liberty was so dear to this man that his suffering seemed trivial in comparison with the bondage he had endured.

After Dr. Fussell had left Kennett Square, and resided in West Vincent, as formerly mentioned, a girl named Eliza came to them. She had been a field hand, was only 18 years of age, and was quite masculine in appearance. She had charge of the horses belonging to her master, and being a good rider, she one evening selected a suitable steed, and as soon as it was safe, started northward. Pressed by the fear of capture, she rode *bare-backed*, about forty miles that night, and towards morning, dismounting, she turned the horse homeward, hiding the bridle to thwart the suspicion that she had ridden the horse away. Tired as she must have been with her long ride, she knew no rest, but continued her journey on foot, walking thirty miles by evening, making in all seventy miles of travel in twenty-four hours. She lived for a considerable time in the family, and proved an excellent girl, but was at first extremely awkward in learning anything pertaining to housewifery. She was never better pleased than when permitted to work on the farm, and, as a harvest hand, was hard to excel, even by the stoutest men. Here she became acquainted with James Washington, another fugitive, and after a time the pair were married at the house of Dr. Fussell, by Friend's ceremony—a marriage

certificate being provided for them, signed by the
requisite number of witnesses. On the same evening
another pair was also united in a similar manner, before
the same witnesses. In these times, in the year 1838,
aboltionists felt it needful to be extremely chary about
trusting magistrates with secrets of this or any other
character pertaining to fugitives, but these marriages
were made strictly legal by providing a sufficient number of trusted friends as witnesses.

Earlier than this, another fugitive seems vividly to
have impressed the boyish memory of Joshua L. Fussell. This was George Harris, who was remarkable for
his extraordinary qualities of mind, and for his indomitable perseverance in obtaining liberty. He was reared
in Maryland or Virginia, and had been sold and taken
to Georgia, near the boundary line with Florida. He
was quite a young man, but must have been gifted with
extraordinary geographical powers. Undeterred by the
long distance to be traveled on foot, or the privations to
be endured and risks incurred before he could reach
" Mason and Dixon's line," he started on his journey,
determined not only to attempt the undertaking, but to
succeed in it. For his guides, he relied wholly upon
the course of railroads running northward and upon
his knowledge of the country, gained in his compulsory
journey southward. It is probable that he then had
escape in view, and that all his faculties were bent in
one direction, for so accurate was his memory that he
could enumerate in successive order every county
through which he passed, as evinced by tracing his
course upon the map of the country. The narrative of
his journey abounded in incidents of peril, humor, and

JOHN COX.

even romance so interesting that the friends who listened
to it intended to preserve it. This was, however, never
done, and after leaving Dr. Fussell's, George Harris
hired with Pusey Cland, near Marlborough Meeting
House, and soon afterward died.

Among active abolitionists it too often happened that
one story succeeded another with great rapidity, while
the main thought centered upon the safety of the narra-
tors. Daily life and its duties interfered to prevent a
written record of these narratives, and it is now too late
to restore them with any degree of vividness. Frequently the speed of transit did not admit of sufficient
delay to listen to life histories; and sometimes there was
little to tell except the unconscious heroism of escape
from a system of barbarity, which lifted above the common level of slavery natures which had been depraved
by generations of ignorance, submission, and all the
other vices inherent in the system to which they had
been subjected.

JOHN AND HANNAH P. COX.

(John Cox, Born Third Mo. 12th, 1786, Died Second Mo. 22d, 1880.
Hannah Pearce Cox, Born Eleventh Mo. 12th, 1797, Died Fourth
Mo. 24th, 1876.)

Longwood, Chester county, being one of the first
stations after leaving Wilmington, John and Hannah
Cox, with their children, were frequently called upon,
and generally in the night, to aid fugitives on their way
to freedom. This aid was ever cheerfully, gladly given.
They fed all, clothed those who needed clothing, and
either conveyed or directed them to stations further
northward. As it was unsafe to keep them so near the
M*

State line, no delay was risked in moving them northward beyond the precincts of danger.

The women and children who were brought to their place from Wilmington, were generally conveyed in a dearborn by a colored man named Jackson. If men were along, and the party small, they rode. If there were several, the men followed on foot. When arriving, Jackson gave three distinct raps upon the pale-fence. This awakened the family who responded: "Who's there?" "Friends," was the reply. Jackson then immediately turned his vehicle and left. The fugitives were admitted, a good supper given them, and a speedy conveyance furnished to other friends. Thus hundreds were aided, and instances of peril and anxiety were not rare. Many came directly from their owners in Delaware, Maryland, Virginia and North Carolina. Few questions were asked beyond what were necessary to satisfy themselves that the parties were really fugitives from slavery.

A man and woman with their child, tired and hungry, called at their place one night. They had come from near Elkton, had ridden one of their master's horses as far as they dare, then traveled the rest of the way on foot. They were attired in some of "Massa's clo'es." The woman wore a pair of his fine boots. Their reason for leaving was a "fear of being sold to go South." They were fed, properly clothed, and assisted further on their journey.

It was a custom in the South to give slaves once a year a week of holiday in which to enjoy themselves without being required to work, and to visit relatives and friends on other plantations. Many of them were not

HANNAH COX.

required to return or to give an account of themselves during that time. As this week was their own, and some of them liked to earn a little spending money, they remained and worked; the masters paying them for the labor. But many felt that as one week of liberty in a year was a glorious respite from the long weeks of unrequited tasks, a lifetime of such liberty would be better, and they took advantage of that time to leave for the North. So, after the holidays, a greater number of fugitives were passed along. In after years the slaveholders discontinued this custom.

It was after one of these seasons that two fine looking colored men and a woman came from Maryland and were passed to other stations. Several years after, one of the men met Hannah Cox at an anti-slavery meeting, and reminded her of the time she " helped him to freedom."

One woman came there from Wilmington, who was the slave of a Presbyterian minister. She had been kindly treated, but heard a whisper in the family that she was to be sold next day. She was very nervous through fear that her " kind massa" would be after her. While she was secreted in the garret, a carriage drove by which they knew was from Wilmington.

As soon as it was dark she was taken to another station and rapidly sent on to Canada. Next day they heard that some persons were in Kennett Square hunting a fugitive slave, but could not find her.

Eight men came at one time, just after the passage of the " Fugitive Slave Law." They were in haste to reach Philadelphia to meet another party. There being no railroad in the lower part of the county then, J. William

Cox, who was but a lad, took them to West Chester in the night, in time to take the first train in the morning. As the horses were busy he took but one, which he rode; the men followed. Before reaching West Chester he halted and gave them directions to walk by twos at some distance apart, so as not to excite suspicion along the streets and when he arrived opposite the depot he would raise his hat; the first two were then to cross the street and enter the door, the others were to follow. On reaching the place he gave the signal and rode on to Simon Barnard's to ask if he would go to the depot and see that the men were started rightly. He met Simon at the gate, and while talking he was astonished to see six of the men coming up behind him. They had not observed the first two enter the depot, and had followed him. He gave them at once into Simon's charge and left.

. In the summer of 1843, eight men came in the night. It was hay-harvest, and John Cox was needing help. He kept them in the barn to assist. As soon as one cart was loaded it was driven in, and the man returned with the empty one to the field—John and the boy remaining in the barn. The men wondered how they unloaded so quickly. But they were men not to be trusted with the secret, and it was carefully kept from them.

One midnight, in 1857, they were startled by the signal that " Conductor Jackson's" train was at Longwood, with a party that needed immediate assistance. They comprised eighteen in all, seven men, the rest women and children. They had been attacked near Centreville, Del., by a party of Irishmen, whom they took to be kidnappers. They fought desperately; one of the negroes showed a knife with which he had stabbed an Irishman. The whole party were intensely excited and the family very much alarmed, not knowing but that the pursuers were close upon them. A hot supper was at once prepared for them, and as quickly as possible they were taken further North. They had not been gone more than fifteen minutes, when loud talking was heard from two carriages coming from toward Wilmington, and one person was heard saying, "We'll overtake them yet." The anxious family awaited tremblingly the return of those who took the slaves, knowing well the consequences should they be overtaken and captured.

They learned afterwards that the persons who drove by were returning from a party; and that the Irishmen were not kidnappers, but lived in the neighborhood, and had gone out to have a little sport on Hallow Eve. The unfortunate one who received the injury, died shortly after in Centreville.

A slave and a free colored man in their employ were foddering the stock one morning at daybreak, when two men in a carriage stopped near the fodder-stock. One exclaimed, "that is he." At this moment one of the men ran to the stack and caught the negro who was descending the ladder, but who happened to be the free man. A sharp fight ensued, in which the white man received some severe injuries. The colored man declared in emphatic language, not wholly in conformity with one of the Commandments, that he would shoot him. The one in the carriage called out "That is not Sam." Sam knew his master's voice and hid. The free

man ran to the house, got the gun, and started in hot
pursuit of the men; but they drove so fast as to keep
beyond the reach of his ammunition. That night the
slave left for a safer home farther North.

John and Hannah Cox were members of the Society
of Friends, and were endued with a great love of
justice and right, and a desire to fulfill in their lives
the Divine law. It was this inherent principle in
the days of slavery that made abolitionists of men and
women who " considered those in chains as bound with
them."

They became interested in anti-slavery meetings, and
from reading the *Liberator* and hearing Charles C.
Burleigh in one of his lectures repeat Whittier's poem,
" Our Fellow Countrymen in Chains," they advocated
immediate emancipation. They thought with William
Lloyd Garrison that while the slave was made to work
under the lash, that while a husband was sold by a
Virginia gentleman to be taken to Louisiana, children
sold to slave-traders to go under different masters, and
the wife and mother kept at home to pine in a hovel
made desolate, to talk of the *gradual* extermination of
these evils was as unwise in principle as " to tell a man
to moderately rescue his wife from the hands of the
ravisher, or tell the mother to gradually extricate her
babe from the fire." The burning of Pennsylvania
Hall, in Philadelphia, on May 17th, 1838, and what
they saw and heard there, aroused them to increased
interest and activity in the cause. It was there they
became personally acquainted with Garrison and the
warm friendship which began then continued during
life. He was a frequent visitor at their place, especially

during the meetings of Progressive Friends at Longwood, as were also Isaac T. Hopper, John G. Whittier, Lucretia Mott, Sarah Pugh, Abby Kelley, Lucy Stone, Mary Grew, James Russell Lowell, Samuel J. May, Theodore Parker, Robert Collyer, James Freeman Clarke, and a host of others who were interested in the progress and elevation of the human family.

John Cox was President of the Kennett Anti-slavery Society, and both he and his wife were frequently sent as delegates to Anti-slavery State and National Conventions.

On the eleventh of Ninth mo. (September), 1873, the fiftieth anniversary of their wedding was celebrated at their home at Longwood, and eighty-two guests signed the certificate. Many of them were old anti-slavery friends and co-laborers in the various reforms in which husband and wife were so warmly interested.

Their friend and neighbor, Chandler Darlington, in recounting the works of their life in a poem prepared for the occasion, said:

> We saw you early on the watch-tower stand,
> When Slavery's curse polluted all the land:
> You've lived to see that blighting curse removed,
> And Freedom triumph in the land you loved:
> For Woman's right to equal be with Man
> You've borne the taunt and labored in the van:
> Nor were you circumscribed to those alone;
> The Temperance cause you fully made your own.
> In works of Charity, at open door
> Your liberal hands have freely served the poor:
> Where'er was sorrow, suffering or despair,
> Your kindly sympathy was ever there.

Bayard Taylor, whose boyhood's home was near them, sent a greeting from Germany, where he was then residing, in which he said:

> There, as a boy, my heart and mind
>   Oft fed on gentler manna,
> For John was ever firm and kind,
>   And motherly was Hannah;
> And when with hopes of higher law
>   The air of home grew warmer,
> How many a preacher there I saw!
>   How many a famed reformer!
>
> •   •   •   •   •
>
> Nor these alone, though all the land
>   Gives praise where it upbraided;
> There was a sad and silent band
>   Your Christian courage aided:
> They came in fear, and straightway found
>   Food, rest, emancipation:
> THEIR "Cox's House" was underground—
>   A *blessed* railway station!

Their poet friend, John G. Whittier, who was unable to be present, sent them a congratulation, in which, referring to the happy visits he had made to their home, and to the congenial spirits with whom he had there met and conversed, he said:

> How gladly would I tread again the old remembered places,
> Sit down beside your hearth once more, and look in the dear old faces;
> And thank you for the lessons your fifty years are teaching,
> For honest lives that louder speak than half our noisy preaching;
> For works of love and duty that knew no selfish ends,
> For hearts and doors set open for the bondman and his friends;
> For your steady faith and courage in that dark and evil time
> When the Golden Rule was treason, and to feed the hungry, crime;
> For the poor slave's house of refuge when the hounds were on his
>   track,
> And saint and sinner, church and state, joined hands to send him
>   back.
> Blessings upon you! What you did for each sad suffering one,
> So homeless and faint and naked, unto our Lord was done!

Since then John and Hannah Cox have ceased their labors upon earth. The fruits of their good works remain behind them; the record of their earnest, faithful lives preceded them into eternity. After a long life of rare goodness and usefulness, we can but feel assured that the Master's call was theirs, " Come ye blessed of my Father, inherit the kingdom prepared for you from the foundation of the world," and that a blissful immortality is now their glorious reward.

CHAPTER XVII.

SIMON BARNARD.—Differences at Kennett Square.—Incidents.—Arrest of Charles C. Burleigh.—EUSEBIUS BARNARD.—Incidents.—Eusebius R. Barnard's tedious journey.—Eusebius Barnard's Ministry. —William Barnard with Eusebius and Others Assists in Founding Society of Progressive Friends.—Kidnapping at house of Zebulon Thomas.

SIMON BARNARD.

(Born Eighth Mo. (August) 7th, 1802.)

Simon Barnard, of Newlin, was one of the ablest advocates of the anti-slavery cause within that southern section of Chester county. Possessing more than ordinary mental ability, sound in logic, clear and convincing in speech, and undaunted in purpose, he was looked up to as the leader and pillar of the anti-slavery movement in that vicinity.

The opponents of anti-slavery there had well-grounded reasons, as they thought, for adhering to the claims of slavery. The Constitution of the United States guaranteed it; it was an institution of the South, and we had no right to meddle with it; slavery was not so bad as it was represented to be; slaves did not want to be free, except a few who were made dissatisfied by abolition preaching and disturbances; if they were set free they would all come North; they were property by inheritance, and belonged to their masters as much as our land belonged to us, and the doctrine of States Rights had been so well digested and proclaimed in the South, and disseminated in the North, that the majority of the people felt themselves absolved from all responsibility pertaining to it. This was the firmly maintained public opinion which the rising spirit of abolitionism in and around Kennett Square had to contend against, and it required a man of Simon Barnard's nerve, intelligence and ability as a speaker, to take a position in the van, to breast this tide of opposition and subdue its force.

Meetings were frequently held in that neighborhood, addressed by the ablest speakers. In the earlier days of the anti-slavery uprising these were but poorly attended. Those who were opposed to the movement, and who should have attended the meetings to know whether or not the arguments advanced were valid, remained at home, and many of these discouraged others from going. Simon Barnard on some occasions traveled many miles, day and night, to give information of meetings, took speakers to and from them and was rewarded for his labor by an audience of less than a dozen—nearly all abolitionists—and that, too, at one time, when the speaker was the eloquent Charles C. Burleigh.

Behold the difficulty of instructing and convincing individuals upon any reform or upon any subject in which they feel no interest, and upon which they do not wish to be convinced.

At that time the church, of all denominations, condemned the movement as fanatical and incendiary. And the church sways a power like Archimedes' lever. But no great reform, however salutary, no great first step in the advancement of science calculated to benefit the human family in its entirety, has ever been adopted without earnest opposition. Even the broad doctrine of Christianity, of salvation through Jesus Christ, was bitterly opposed, and Jesus was put to death. Men and

women have been tortured upon the rack, buffeted in
the streets, and have had their tongues pierced with red
hot irons for preaching religious doctrines different
from the belief of others.   Michael Servetus and John
Rogers were both burned to death for this offense.
Galileo was imprisoned and threatened with death for
teaching the theory of the earth's motion.   Harvey lost
a great portion of his practice for a time after he published a Treatise upon his Discovery of the Circulation
of the Blood.   He was defamed by eminent professors
and by the older members of the profession generally.
Jenner was stigmatized for introducing vaccination,
doctors refused to try it, and it was denounced from the
pulpit as "diabolical."   Franklin had evil things said
of him for interfering with heaven's lightning, in attracting it from its course and making it to lie down
harmless at his feet.   We are not to wonder then that
abolitionists were reviled throughout the whole country,
mobbed in the North, and tarred and feathered in the
South for advocating freedom to the negro.   The spirit
of denunciation is not confined to any age of the world,
nor to any race or sect of people.   But Progress is a
law of Nature, stamped upon our being by the hand of
Deity, and cannot be inhibited or repressed.   Radical
thinkers are necessary for the enlightenment and advancement of every age, and the slow and deliberative
reasoning of conservatives is oft-times essential to the
modifying and maturing of original thought.   Hence
all fill important niches in the onward progress of the
world's events.

As it is not to be expected that all will see and believe
alike at the same time, a respectful consideration for the

honest views of others is ever due from man to man. And as religious beliefs and tenets are always dear to those who espouse them, it was as painful a course of action for the reformatory Friends in Kennett Square and the vicinity who sought, by extraordinary and ultra means, to ameliorate the condition of humanity, to absolve themselves from allegiance to their former religious ties, as it was for those who remained within the pale of the church to disown from membership their former co-laborers.

Times since then have changed. A new era has dawned upon our nation. Differences have been settled. Over all the past the veil of charity should now be tenderly drawn, and the warm hand of love and friendship be cordially and tenderly extended.

The house of Simon Barnard being on the direct line of "underground" travel, was an asylum for the hunted slave on his perilous nocturnal journeyings toward the North Star and freedom. Hundreds received the usual attention, were harbored, fed, clothed and forwarded to other friends. But scarcely any reminiscences can be given in detail. *Secrecy* in the work was the one great feature, and not to know or remember too much was one of the essentials. The younger members of the family were exhorted to silence. They would hear whisperings, sometimes see colored people; the very atmosphere seemed laden with an impressive hush; then soon, all was again as usual.

The effort was to pass all fugitives along as quickly as possible. Simon Barnard kept a large, two-horse, close-covered wagon, which was called "Black Maria," and by hanging a quilt close to the front seat where he sat, he could carry ten or a dozen men, women and children, with several babies, well concealed. His fear always was that the babies would cry. But the women seemed to have an astonishing power in stopping their cries. The moment one would begin, it was silenced as if by magic. This was a fortunate circumstance, for had the little ones cried when passing through a village at midnight, or by a hotel where, perchance, a slave-hunter was sleeping, as was sometimes the case, the success of the undertaking would have been seriously endangered. Marshallton, Downingtown and West Chester were in his direct routes to other stations.

A party of thirteen came to Simon Barnard's house one night and were taken to Nathan Evans. The men were well armed. There was cause for apprehension as they passed through West Chester at midnight, but all were delivered safely.

A party in a wagon of peculiar construction which was easily tracked, arrived at one time at his place in Newlin. He piloted them to John Vickers by way of Isaac Meredith's, taking Isaac with him through Marshallton. This ride was in the very face of most imminent risk, for slave-catchers were in close pursuit— somewhere in the neighborhood, they knew not where. It was discovered afterward that they had stopped for the night at a tavern in Marshallton, and were quietly sleeping there when the party passed by the house. [A further description of them is given in the account of John Vickers.]

So close was the chase sometimes that Simon thought it best to encumber his property that it might be unavailable for damages to slave *property*.

On one occasion, Charles C. Burleigh was arrested in Oxford and sent to jail in West Chester. He was in custody of a constable passing through Unionville, when word was sent to Simon Barnard, who immediately started, although the roads were deep with mud. He arrived there just as the door of the jail was about to close upon Burleigh, and took him out of custody on bail.

Burleigh deeming his mission at Oxford unfinished, repeated his offence by preaching abolition and selling his tracts there on the next Sunday. He was re-arrested, and on the evening of a bitter cold day, he and the Oxford constable drove up to Simon Barnard's comfortable house, nearly perished—both nearly frozen. The ludicrous part of the scene was keenly relished by Simon, who used to say that instead of the constable taking Burleigh to jail, Burleigh was conducting the frozen officer to the house of his friend, where they were both kindly treated to a warm supper, lodging and breakfast; not only they but their horses. Next morning they departed, and Simon humorously remarked afterward that he was left in doubt as to whether the constable took Burleigh, or Burleigh took the constable.

His home was the frequent visiting place of the eminent abolitionists of those times, then unpopular, but now renowned, such as Isaac T. Hopper, Edmund Quincy, William Lloyd Garrison, Wendell Phillips, Theodore Parker, John G. Whittier, Frederick Douglass, Charles C., William and Cyrus Burleigh, James Russell Lowell, Lucretia Mott, Joshua R. Giddings, and others.

In his humanitarian labors he was warmly seconded by his wife, a woman of superior intelligence and character. She died in March, 1881.

Simon Barnard, a son of Joseph Barnard, and his wife, Mary Meredith, was born in Newlin, Chester county, Eighth mo. (August) 7th, 1802, on ancestral lands acquired in 1726 by Richard Barnard, the second, who was a son of the emigrant ancestor who arrived here in 1685.

In Tenth mo., 1827, he married Sarah, daughter of Emanuel and Martha Darlington, of East Bradford. In 1852 they removed to West Chester, and in 1863 to Philadelphia, where he still resides in the enjoyment of good health.

He was engaged in farming until about his fiftieth year. In West Chester he engaged in the lumber business and the building of houses; and in Philadelphia in the manufacturiug of bricks by steam and in real estate investments. He is now enjoying in retirement the fruits of an active life.

The Barnards were all abolitionists. Richard M. Barnard, a brother of Simon, and occupying an adjoining farm, rendered some effective service to fugitive slaves, but he was more of a politician in those days, and more conservative. He was a representative in the Legislature at Harrisburg in 1837–38. He was a prominent and influential man of the neighborhood, and was much relied upon as an umpire in disputed questions, being a clear-headed accountant, mathematician, surveyor, conveyancer and man of affairs.

EUSEBIUS BARNARD.
(Born Seventh Month (July) 1802.—Died 1865.)

When the number of slaves that were forwarded by Daniel Gibbons to friends in Lancaster county and the northern part of Chester county, and by Thomas Gar-

EUSEBIUS BARNARD.

rett to Philadelphia and other places, became so great as to necessitate another route through Chester county, Eusebius and Sarah P. Barnard, of Pocopsin, were among the first to make their residence an established station on this new line of travel. Slaves came to their place chiefly from Thomas Garrett, Isaac and Dinah Mendenhall, Dr. Bartholomew Fussell and others. If they arrived in the early part of the night, they were fed, and about two o'clock in the morning were taken to other stations, generally by Eusebius himself, until his sons were old enough to be sent on these hazardous missions. During his absence on one occasion, his wife sent their oldest daughter Elizabeth. If fugitives arrived in busy seasons, or at other times when their labor would be of service, and there was no immediate danger, they remained a few days, worked, and were paid the customary wages. If women and children came, they were taken in a dearborn to other places. If there were no children along, and the fugitives were able to walk, they were taken part way to some other station, generally to William Sugar, six miles distant, and given a slip of paper containing his name, and directions how to find his place.

Seventeen men came on foot one evening, when no one was at home but the daughters and the youngest son, Enos. He knew where his uncle William Barnard lived, and being just old enough to ride a horse, he mounted one and rode in front of the men to the place, and delivered his charge safely.

A party of six or eight came one First-day (Sunday) morning, just as the family were starting for meeting. Eusebius and his brother William were on a religious

N

visit to Ohio, and were expecting some of the family to meet them on their return to Downingtown the next day. Upon the oldest son, Eusebius R., now devolved the task of conducting these passengers. It was somewhat hazardous to venture out with them at that time of day, but he loaded some in a dearborn so as to give them the appearance of going to a colored Quarterly Meeting, then in session near by. The balance of the party were to walk far enough behind to keep in sight of the dearborn, while he rode on horse-back some distance in advance. He took them to Dr. Eshleman's, left the horse there which he rode, and returned with the dearborn. They met a great number of persons, but no one suspected that the load of dusky humanity which passed, were passengers on the "Underground Railroad," traveling in open daylight, with their conductor in front, piloting them with as much calmness as though he were riding on an ordinary errand. On the following day the dearborn was driven to Downingtown, Eusebius and William returned in it, and the horse was ridden home from Dr. Eshleman's house.

On the 27th of October, 1855, while a number of friends were assembled at Longwood to level the ground and make arrangements for building sheds, a party of eleven came there from Wilmington; they were kept until evening, when Eusebius took them home with him, gave them supper and lodging, and at two o'clock next morning sent Eusebius R. with them to Downingtown. To avoid suspicion which so many in one gang at that place would excite, he was directed to divide the party before reaching there, to take those in the dearborn to

SARAH P. BARNARD.

Zebulon Thomas, and send the others on foot to Dr. Eshleman. Arriving at a wood near the town, he separated them as directed. When he arrived at Zebulon Thomas's house and Zebulon saw the number he had, he advised him not to stop a moment, but to keep on toward John Vickers. Eusebius remarked that he thought he had gone far enough, but Zebulon, knowing the risk of delay just then, replied, "We cannot talk now, this is a very dangerous pro-slavery place; keep on and I will gear up and overtake thee soon." As he was starting he saw the remainder of the party still following him. Whether they had failed to comprehend his directions, or were afraid to go without a guide, or were unwilling to be separated from the others, he could not devise, and he began to tell about them. Zebulon quickly interrupted him and told him to go on and he would attend to them. He drove on some distance to a suitable place, where he waited until Zebulon with his colored men came up with the others, and took them on toward John Vickers' place. Returning to Thomas's, he ate his breakfast, had his horses fed, and then started homeward, rejoiced that he had passed them so far in safety.

This party left their master's plantation in Maryland about eight o'clock the night before, taking with them a couple of two-horse carriages, and arrived in Wilmington early next morning. They went immediately to Thomas Garrett's. He told them to leave the horses hitched on the street, while he conducted them quickly out of town, and directed them up the Kennett "pike," to friends at Longwood. Their meeting with a number of them together at that place was casual.

About eleven o'clock Thomas Garrett passed along the street and called attention to the horses; said they looked in bad condition, and wondered whose they were. No one knew, but some observed that they had seen them there since early in the morning. He suggested their being taken to a stable and cared for. Perhaps some people had stolen them in the night and driven them to Wilmington for a ride, or for some other purpose. If the owners should call they could be told where to find them, and the matter be explained. The crowd which had then collected thought this the best thing to do, as the horses looked badly in need of provender. The news soon spread over town. In the afternoon the slave-hunters came, and were told where the horses were. They supposed then that the slaves were hidden somewhere in the town, and would be crawling out of their coverts at night. So every suspected place was well watched—Thomas Garrett's in particular. The hunters remained in town a day or two and continued an assiduous and determined search, but hearing no tidings whatever of their slaves, they abandoned their efforts and returned home.

The fugitives reached the home of Graceanna Lewis and sisters, where they were separated and forwarded on different roads toward Canada.

About the middle of March 1861, two women, both somewhat crippled, with four children, were brought to Eusebius Barnard's place late in the evening. The reasons given for leaving their master, were that one or more of the children were about to be sold, and that in their own crippled condition they could not perform the tasks given them each day without great fatigue and suffering. They were given food and comfortable beds. At two o'clock in the morning Eusebius R. was called. He had retired early in the evening, before the party arrived, as he had to prepare a lecture next day to deliver at the close of the session of Fairville Seminary which he was attending, five miles from home.

It was the custom to select one or two members of each class to give a lecture on Commencement Day upon such subject as the professors might select. One hour was allotted to each class for this purpose. The subject given to Eusebius R. Barnard was Electricity. Being called at two o'clock, the hour invariably fixed for starting with fugitives, he knew well what it meant. He was always willing to rise at night and do whatever was asked of him, but having only three days left of the session, and that being the last day of the week, on which they had but few lessons to recite, he wished to devote the whole day, aside from the time required for those lessons, in preparing himself to meet the large audience which always assembled on those occasions, to give an instructive lecture in a clear manner, and to make it still more interesting by illustrating different parts of it with appropriate apparatus. He therefore asked to be excused from going that morning. But excuses were vain. The demand was absolute. The women and children had to be hurried along as fast as possible, and no one could then go in his stead. For once he arose with reluctance, and mused pensively over the gloomy prospect of preparing his lecture that day.

He took them to the nearest station, one to which he seldom went, thinking if they could be received there it would enable him to return soon. But peculiar circumstances just then made it impossible for the family to give any assistance at that time. He went to another place, which formerly was a good station, but the member of the family who had given it his personal supervision for years, having recently died, the others did not feel easy to undertake the continuance of the work. This second refusal came to him like a stunning blow. He knew not what to do next. He was off his usual route. It was then breakfast time, and he had been travelling since two o'clock through deep, muddy roads. He was asked to get out and take breakfast, but he declined. The women were invited; they accepted. But he was not in a mood to wait for them. He said they were cripples and bundled up, and it would take too long for them to get out and eat. The family then brought victuals out to them, and a plate for him. But he again declined, saying "he could not eat anything; it would choke him." The disappointment that morning had spoiled his appetite. He was in a complete dilemma as to what to do. He inquired for a place he had frequently heard his mother speak of. The family advised him not to go there, but directed him to a person in Coatesville. He persisted in going to the nearest place. Again they advised him not to go, but gave no reasons. But he wanted to unload quickly and get home, and was therefore willing to risk more than usual. He went there. He was not acquainted with any of the family. He asked first for the man; was told he was not at home. Then he asked for the wife, to whom he told his errand. She would not accept the fugitives. He begged her to accomodate him that time. But she still refused, as they were not in that business and didn't wish to begin it. On his way out the lane he met a man whom he supposed to be the one he wished to see; but he was afraid to importune any further, and passed silently by. In a few days Eusebius Barnard received a note from this man requesting him not to send any more fugitives to his place as he did not wish to identify himself with the work.

Thus disappointed at every step, Eusebius R. Barnard started next for the place of their old, tried and true friend, Dr. Eshleman. It was nearly night when he arrived there; neither he nor his horses having eaten anything all day. While dragging along at a slow, labored gait, through the deep, heavy mud, he met a stranger who looked scrutinizingly at him, and then peering into the wagon, asked what he had there. Fear for a moment tingled through every nerve. He imagined the man must be a slave-hunter, for he could not suppose that any other stranger would have the audacity to act in that manner. He gave a short answer, and drove on with apparent unconcern. The inquisitive stranger stood there for awhile gazing at him, and then started off, much to the relief of Eusebius' mind.

It was nearly night when he reached Dr. Eshleman's. He related his day's tribulations to the good doctor, who told him to unload and he would take care of the party. These were the most joyous words that fell upon his ears that day.

> " Joy never feasts so high,
> As when the first course is of misery."

After the women and children were taken into the house, he was asked to stay, have supper, and let his horses be fed. He accepted the invitation for the horses, but declined for himself. The fatigue and disappointments of the day had destroyed all appetite.

He had now but two days left in which to prepare his lecture, in connection with other school lessons. But

> " Like a ball that bounds
> According to the force with which 'twas thrown ;
> So in affliction's violence, he that's wise,
> The more he's cast down will the higher rise."

He applied himself with redoubled energy, and when the day arrived he and another student, who was at the same time a teacher of some branches, were to occupy the hour allotted to that class. Eusebius was called first, although he wished the teacher to lead off in the programme. Tremblingly, but trustfully, he stepped upon the rostrum and faced his audience.

He expounded the principles and properties of electricity, illustrating the lecture with the apparatus at his command ; nor was he conscious of how time was passing until nearly the whole hour was consumed. The second speaker had scarcely finished his exordium when the bell tapped, announcing the expiration of the time—much to the disappointment of the latter as he had prepared with great care a very elaborate speech for the occasion.

This terminated the labors of Eusebius Barnard in the Underground Railroad work. These were the last fugitives that called on him for assistance. The war broke out soon after and he lived to see the glorious work accomplished—the abolition of slavery—for which he had given his time, labor and money for a number of years.

Like all others on regular routes he had passed hundreds on their way to freedom.

The old house is still standing, and the kitchen floor upon which so many fugitives lay and slept upon comfortable beds waiting for the "two o'clock A. M. train" to leave, frequently calls up reminiscences of by-gone times.

Eusebius Barnard was a "recommended minister" in the Society of Friends, and a member of Kennett Monthly Meeting. He spoke at anti-slavery and temperance meetings, and preached against the evils of slavery and intemperance in the meetings for worship in the Society. He was disowned from membership along with William Barnard, Isaac and Dinah Mendenhall, Isaac Meredith and other reformers. He then united himself with the Progressive Friends. At the close of the war when slavery was no longer an exciting topic, and Friends were no longer exercised upon the subject, he was about asking to be again taken into membership when he died.

His first wife, Sarah Painter, was an excellent woman and united with him in all his religious and reformatory labors. His second wife, Sarah Marsh, was also in sympathy with him in all the good works that characterized his life. Thus two congenial companions were faithful helpers to him in the performance of his life's mission.

WILLIAM BARNARD.

(Born Fourth Month 16th, 1800.—Died First Month 22nd, 1864.)

William Barnard, of Pocopsin, Chester county, began assisting slaves about the year 1840. They came to him chiefly through the hands of Thomas Garrett and Dr. Fussell, and were from Delaware, Maryland, Virginia, and as far South as Georgia. When they were on foot, and were asked how they found his place,

N*

they said "they followed *the star* by day and slept in the woods or in the houses of colored people by night, and were directed from place to place until they reached there." They were very guarded in conversation until assured, when talking with William, that he was "Massa Barnard," when they would tell him "We'se some cul'lud folks goin' North." If it was in the early part of the night, they were given a good supper and beds, and started again on their journey before daylight. If very weary from traveling a long distance, they were kept until next night. Women and children were always brought and taken in covered wagons. If there were reports of close pursuit they were sent onward without delay.

After the enactment of the Fugitive Slave Law, three rough looking men drove up in front of the house, whose demeanor aroused suspicion that they were looking for negroes. There were six concealed in the house at that time. These were hurried out the back-door into a wheat-field, while William engaged the men in conversation.

Immediately after the Christiana riot, when the whole country was aroused, the vicinity of the tragedy in a state of excitement, and the negroes around there were hunted in every direction, a number of them came to William Barnard's almost crazed with fear, and asked for protection. They had traveled all night. A good breakfast was given them, and as houses afforded but doubtful security then from officers with search warrants, they were put into shocks of corn-fodder in an adjacent field. Next night they were taken further from the scene of disturbance.

William Barnard was a man of warm, social nature, strongly attached to friends, and, having a Christian love for the whole human family, his desire always was to promote their best interest and happiness.

Firm in his adherence to what he believed to be right, conscientious in his business relations, and keenly alive to the wrongs of slavery, he abstained from the use of all articles produced by the unpaid labor of the slave.

Being descended from a long line of Quaker ancestry, his love for that Society was strong; but when they were unwilling to advance as far as he in works of moral reform, his feeling of unity with them began to wane, and by an act of the Society, he, with several others of a reformatory spirit, ceased to be members. He then gave his support in organizing the Society of *Progressive Friends.*

He was a sincere seeker after truth, and always welcomed to his home and heart all who sought to promote the higher culture of humanity, however much their views might differ from his own.

> " No soul can soar too loftily whose aim
> Is God-given Truth and brother love of man."

He was twice married, his second wife being a sister of that earnest pioneer in the anti-slavery cause, Benjamin Lundy.

The name of Zebulon Thomas, (Born 1781—Died 1865), occurs several times in this history. His house in Downingtown was the scene of one of the most infamous cases of kidnapping that ever took place in Pennsylvania. This event occurred early one morning in the Fourth Month (April) of 1848. The colored boy had

just arisen, opened the house and was kindling the fire
when three white men entered. Frightened at their
appearance he ran and hid. Taking the lighted candle,
they went up stairs directly to the chamber where the
poor girl lay sound asleep. They lifted her from the
bed and carried her down stairs. In the entry of the
second floor they met one of the women who, hearing
an unusual sound, had sprung from her bed. Her
screams and those of the girl, aroused Zebulon, who
hurried, undressed, from his chamber on the ground
floor. He endeavored to save the girl, but his efforts
were powerless against the three. . With frightful im-
precations they hurried her to the carriage which was
in waiting, and drove off. Quickly as possible he
started in pursuit. Reaching West Chester he learned
that they had driven through the borough in a two-
horse vehicle at full speed a half an hour before.

This stealing of the girl must have been concocted,
and the carrying out of the plan aided by persons well
acquainted with the premises and the town. And a
knowledge of the scheme was not confined to those who
came to the house, as three or four men of that village
took a position in a barn close by, to " see the fun."

Through the efforts of many friend, this unfortunate
child was rescued from the hands of slave-traders in
Baltimore and, with her mother, was afterward helped
on to the North. When Zebulon Thomas's family last
heard from mother and daughter, they were living in
Canada.

CHAPTER XVIII.

ISAAC AND THAMAZINE P. MEREDITH.—MORDECAI AND ESTHER HAYES. —MAHLON AND AMOS PRESTON.—CHANDLER AND HANNAH M. DARLINGTON.—BENJAMIN AND HANNAH S. KENT.—A Large Party of Fugitives.—ENOCH LEWIS.—Conscientious Labors.—Redeems a Negro at Great Risk.

ISAAC AND THAMAZINE P. MEREDITH.

(Isaac Meredith, Born Eleventh Mo. 18th, 1801.—Died Ninth Mo. 28th, 1874.) (Thamazine P. Meredith, Born First Mo. 11th, 1812.)

The home of Isaac and Thamazine P. Meredith, Newlin, Chester county, was situated in a secluded spot, and therefore possessed rare advantages as a station for the aid of "God's Poor" to freedom. Slaves were brought there from Thomas Garrett, John Cox, Simon and William Barnard, Moses and Samuel Pennock, Dr. Fussell, and frequently from other places; and were generally taken to Dr. Eshleman, Gravener Marsh, Benjamin Price, John Vickers, Nathan Evans and Maris Woodward.

Simon Barnard frequently brought them part way, then gave them a slip of paper with writing to show they were not imposters. Isaac Meredith, or some other trusted person, took them to other stations, or so far on the way as to obviate the necessity of their making any enquiries along such sections of the routes as were known to be hostile to them.

There were more arrivals in winter than in summer. Scarcely a week passed during that season in which one or more " trains " did not arrive with passengers leaving the pleasant breezes of the South for a more rigorous climate North, that the natural rights and blessings of liberty might be enjoyed by themselves and their children.

A slave woman was at one time brought by her mistress to Wilmington. While in the back yard adjoining Thomas Garrett's residence, his hired girl told her that if she wished to be free, she could be. She accepted the offer, and was taken to Dr. Bartholomew Fussell, from there to Isaac Meredith and thence to Joseph Hawley's house, where she hired. She soon became discontented on account of her husband and child, whom she had left behind. She "wanted to go back to massa," for, she said, "we'll all be free some time; we'se all prayin' for it; and we'se sure de Lord will set us free soon. I knows he will; he will hear; 'cause we'se all prayin.'" She went back, but the family never heard from her afterward.

Six large, strong men, were brought to Isaac Meredith's house at one time by William Barnard. They had escaped from Maryland, had been pursued and shot at, and the bullet-holes in their coats attested to the proximity of the death-dealing missiles to their bodies. Isaac Meredith and Lewis Marshall took them to a station further northward.

Many fugitives when arriving were weary and exhausted from anxiety and rapid flight. If immediate danger was not apprehended, they were kept a few days to rest.

John Cox's train, conducted by his son, J. William, frequently came well laden. He announced his arrival by a rap at the door; and when called to from a window above "Who's there?" replied in his familiar, cheerful style, "Will Cox; got a wagon load."

One cold November night about twelve o'clock, he brought fifteen men, women and children, cold, hungry and excited. They had come from Delaware City, and were brought to John Cox's by "Conductor Jackson," who drove fast with the women and children while the men ran. The women at John Cox's prepared a hot substantial supper for them, but they were afraid to take time to eat. They warmed themselves while the horses were being harnessed to a large dearborn. The moment he drove up to Isaac and Thamazine Meredith's house, their son who had been away, returned. The fugitives were affrighted, thinking he was one of their pursuers and had overtaken them. And he, just being able in the darkness to distinguish a dearborn and persons moving hurriedly around it, thought they were robbers. Both parties were for the instant surprised, and not a little disconcerted. By some, almost involuntary, expressions, each at once recognized the other's voice—a mutual relief.

The fugitives were willing to remain there long enough to eat. The women had just finished a baking, of which, after the fifteen had satisfied their hunger, unlike the loaves and fishes told of in the Scriptures, there was nothing left.

Isaac and his son took this party on different roads that night, and met at a designated place above Marshallton; then separated and met near Downingtown, where they made a disposition of them among agents at and near that place.

Isaac Meredith was a member of Kennett Monthly Meeting of Friends, took an active part in the business of the Society, and was clerk for many years, until the anti-slavery trouble in the meeting reached its climax, when he and his wife, who was also a member and an earnest co-worker with him, came under the ban of condemnation and their life-long connection with the Society was severed.   They then united with the *Progressive Friends.*

The war over, slavery abolished, the Dove of Peace settled down once more upon the Society, and the olive branch was tendered to Isaac and his wife, who accepted the offering and the unity of former days was again established.   They, however, maintained their freedom of thought, and their desire to see and aid the advancement of all necessary reforms.

MORDECAI AND ESTHER HAYES.

(Mordecai Hayes, 1794—1837.)   (Esther Hayes, 1788—1869.)

Mordecai and Esther Hayes, Newlin, were among the first agents on that branch of the route through Chester county.   They were earnest in the cause, and no weather, however stormy, deterred them from attending anti-slavery meetings within reasonable distance.

Fugitives were brought to their place from Wilmington, from William Barnard's and other stations on that route, in numbers ranging from two to a wagon load. It was customary for those bringing them to drive under an open wagon-shed, arouse the family, and then unload. They were secreted in the house and at the barn. Mordecai's son, Jacob, took them at night in a dearborn to Gravener Marsh, Dr. Eshleman, Esther Lewis, John Vickers or Nathan Evans.   If there was but one or two, they were given a slip of paper with directions either to Gravener Marsh or Dr. Eshleman.

MAHLON AND AMOS PRESTON.

(Mahlon Preston, 1781—1855.) (Amos Preston, Born Seventh Mo., 15th, 1786. Died Twelfth Mo. 2d, 1856.)

Mahlon and Amos Preston, two brothers, members of the Society of Friends, the latter a minister, lived on adjoining farms, near West Grove, Chester county. Their places were not regular stations, but when fugitives came, they always gave assistance.

About the year 1819 or 1820, a colored man named Jarvis Griffith, with his wife and three or four children, came to Amos Preston's, and was allowed by him to live in an apartment over his spring-house. The man and wife proved to be industrious, faithful, hard-working people, and Amos was so well pleased with them that he built a small house for them on one part of his land. The children were put under the care of farmers in the neighborhood. All went on well for about two years, when one morning, about daylight, a person came running to Mahlon's house with a message that kidnappers were at Jarvis's. . He hastened there and found three or four rough men with pistols. They had obtained entrance into the house by finesse, had pinioned the father, mother and youngest child, and were about starting with them for Maryland, when a number of the neighbors, who had by that time arrived, deterred them. Slave-hunters were not quite so bold and defiant then as in after years, when the Fugitive Slave Law gave them greater authority upon free soil, and these men were compelled to go to West Chester to prove their property before a judge. After hearing the evidence, the judge gave them the requisite authority to carry the family back to Maryland. A few months after, a person, purporting to

come from that part of the State, said that Jarvis and
Mary were both working for their master and professed
to be glad they had got back; that the master was well
pleased with them and had made Jarvis foreman on his
plantation.

A few weeks later, a knocking was heard one morning
before daylight at Mahlon Preston's door. He arose,
went down, and there were Jarvis and Mary, tired and
foot-sore, just arrived from Maryland. The horses
were hitched to a dearborn as quickly as possible, and
with utmost speed they were taken to one of the stations
in the Great Valley, from which they were passed beyond the reach of any slaveholders' claims in the
future.

Their profession of contentment was a mere ruse to
gain the favor of their master; and their industrious
habits and the knowledge they had acquired of the
northern method of farming, which was superior to the
negligent practice which prevailed to a great extent in
the South, made them valuable hands on the plantation.
They had been given a holiday of two days to attend a
meeting; which time they employed in making their
escape on foot.

One morning soon after this, a daughter of theirs,
about twelve or thirteen years of age, living with
Mahlon, was missing, and was never heard from afterward. It was supposed that slavehunters had been
lying in ambush about the premises and when out at
one of the buildings which stood some distance from the
house, she had been seized, gagged, and carried off by
them.

Their oldest son, William, a bright boy, received a

fair education, and several years afterward went to
Wilmington, where he was employed to teach a colored
school. One day his master with an officer entered the
school-room while he was in the midst of his duties,
seized him as a fugitive slave and took him before a
magistrate, who, after hearing the evidence for a few
minutes, gave judgment in the master's favor, and
William in charge of a constable was hurried down the
street to where a carriage was in waiting to take him to
Maryland. On the way he remarked that the watch
he carried belonged to another person, and he would be
obliged to return it. This was refused, the officer saying he would return it to the person named as the
owner. At the instant the officer reached out his hand
to receive it, William took advantage of the slackened
grasp upon his arm, broke loose and dashed down the
street with a speed that defied all efforts to overtake
him. He was noted at school as being a fast runner.
How little did he then, or any of his schoolmates whom
he distanced in the race, suspect that those fleet limbs
would one day in the future bear him from the very jaws
of the monster slavery into which he was being led by a
policeman's grasp, and secure to him the undisturbed
rights of a free man! Yet they were the means at his
command in the hour of necessity, and very effectually
did he use them, for he out-ran all his pursuers, and
eluded every effort made to retake him. He reached
New York safely, where he hired with a gentleman as
coachman. His employer became so much attached to
him, that in order to secure his absolute freedom from
any future molestation, he wrote to the man who
claimed to be his master, offering to pay him fifty dol-

lars for a full deed of manumission; assuring him that nothing more would be paid and he had "Hobson's choice" to take that or nothing. He acceded to the proposition, and William henceforward breathed the air of undisputed freedom.

Thus every member of that family, with the exception of one girl, was rescued by devoted friends from a system which held them as chattel property.

CHANDLER DARLINGTON.

(Chandler Darlington, Born Eleventh Mo. (November) 4th, 1800. Died Third Mo. (March) 29th, 1879.) (Hannah M., Born 10th Mo., 29th, 1808.)

Chandler and Hannah M. Darlington were well known as friends of the slave. Their place was not a regular underground station. Their locality and surroundings were unfavorable to concealment, or escape, in case of search. The slaves who were helped on their way were from the District of Columbia, Virginia, Maryland and Delaware, under the auspices of Thomas Garrett. They were brought from the vicinity of Wilmington by a conductor in a close carriage, arriving about eleven o'clock, P. M. A gentle tap was usually heard at the window, and a suppressed call, " Can you care for these people?" giving the number. They then alighted from the carriage, and the escort left immediately, without being known to any one; the shutters were closed, a light was struck, the slaves were taken into the house, served with coffee and supper, packed into a carryall dearborn, and Chandler drove the team to the house of one of the Barnard family, or, if time and the roads permitted, to a more distant station.

Some mornings there were questions and evasive

answers: "Anything the matter last night? I heard a noise." One dark, dismal night, the transfer was rendered difficult by bad roads ; dawn of day approached before the horses were in their stall. A member of the household hastened from the barn to announce the fact that "somebody had the horses out last night ; they were all over wet and muddy," and one of " Miss Opie's white lies " could scarce appease his consternation.

Occasionally a footman presented himself, offering a small piece of paper with a written request, " please help this traveller to a place of safety," or something of similar import.

BENJAMIN AND HANNAH S. KENT.

(Benjamin Kent, Born Third Mo., 23d, 1805.—Died Eleventh Mo. 29th, 1881.) (Hannah S. Kent, Born Second Mo., 13th, 1806.—Died Seventh Mo., 4th, 1882.)

Benjamin and Hannah S. Kent, Penn township, were zealous laborers in the anti-slavery cause. While taking an active part at public meetings, their greatest work was done in a quiet, private way. They assisted in organizing the Clarkson Anti-slavery Society at West Grove Meeting House, about the year 1831. They gave of their means for anti-slavery purposes, and while their home was not on the main route, it was a branch station where the fugitives who came that way received prompt assistance.

At one time Benjamin Kent, with others, went on a hazardous journey into Maryland to bring away thirty-five men, women and children, who were awaiting means of escape. With prayerful hearts, and trusting in Divine guidance and protection, they made the trip safely and successfully. The fugitives were armed with pistols, axes, knives, corn-cutters and old scythes, evidently intending that if forced by pursuers to turn thei r faces toward the South, it would be in a bloody combat for liberty. The whole party were taken to the house of Mahlon Brosius, reaching there between daylight and sunrise. They were quickly secreted in the barn, and being quite hungry, it required no little amount of food to supply their needs. The next night the women and children were taken in two wagons, (commonly used for hauling earthenware) to James Fulton's and Gideon Pierce's, at Ercildoun, a distance of twelve miles; the men being compelled to walk. Their only guides were Mahlon's two sons, Edwin and Daniel K., then but lads. But their youthful spirits, animated by the importance of the trust, proved equal to the occasion. On approaching a burning lime kiln near their journey's end, they knew that the light from it across the road would expose the whole party to the view of those at work, and thus excite suspicion if they attempted to pass in a body. To avoid this, they drove the wagons by at such distance apart not as to attract attention, while the colored men were ordered to take a circuitous route through an adjoining wood. They met in the darkness beyond, and traveled the remainder of the way without interruption.

From Ercildoun they were sent to John Vickers, thence to Kimberton, and thus by way of the various stations to Canada.

Quite early one morning, Benjamin Kent sent a slave boy who was working for him on an errand to a neighbor's while he fed the stock. The boy had just got out of sight when the owner, with a constable and two or three others, came to the barn in search of him. Benjamin told them there was no slave about his premises. The constable knowing his conscientious regard for truth could take his word on all occasions; but in his official capacity felt that he must go through the routine of search, which he did. Satisfied that the boy was not there, the party left only a few minutes before he returned.

In 1833, Benjamin and Hannah S. Kent bought a woolen factory and store at Andrew's bridge, Lancaster county, to which place they removed. They were instrumental there in organizing the Coleraine Anti-slavery Society, and their house was always open to the reception of all anti-slavery speakers who held meetings in that section of country. There were many opponents of "abolitionism" in that vicinity, and their factory and store, with a hotel close by, made their place too public to be a safe station for fugitives, and but few called.

In 1842, their store, factory and dwelling were burned. They rebuilt, and in 1845 sold and removed to Jackson's Valley, West Grove, Chester county, and continued their anti-slavery labors as before. After the Christiana riot, six colored men who had been engaged in it came to their place in the night, were kept in the house until morning, and at the barn during the day. Next night, their son Henry took them to Dr. Bartholomew Fussell.

Their family of seven children were so imbued with opposition to the unjust principle of slavery, from daily conversation and example, that they would eat nothing, not even confectionery, that was the product of slave labor.

About the year 1837, Elizabeth Kent, sister of Benjamin, began keeping a free-produce store at Andrew's Bridge, for the accommodation of herself and friends who bore a testimony against using the products of the slave's uncompensated toil. Although her pro-slavery neighbors refused to buy at her store, she received a fair share of patronage. Benjamin manufactured free satinetts for her—always at a loss to himself as flax was higher priced than cotton.

After remaining there five or six years she removed to Penn's Grove, Chester county, and opened a store for the sale of free produce exclusively. As this could not complete in cheapness with that of slave-labor, the profits were much less. She furnished clothing and money when needed for the aid of fugitives. Among her free-produce customers were Thomas, Eli, and Charles Hambleton, of Chester county, and Joseph Smith, Thomas Whitson, and William Brosius, of Lancaster county.

Benjamin and Hannah Kent were distinguished as active abolitionists for a period of thirty years—until slavery had no longer an existence.

ENOCH LEWIS.
1776—1856.

Enoch Lewis was an active and energetic friend of the colored race. When quite a young man and a teacher at the Friend's Boarding School at Westtown, he was frequently applied to, on behalf of colored persons claimed as fugitives from labor, and in such cases he exerted himself to the utmost to prevent free persons from being carried off as slaves. For upwards of a quarter of a century free negroes were subject to the danger of being sent into slavery on certificates of Justices of the Peace fabricated by kidnappers for the purpose. When a negro was arrested as a slave, all that could be done was to attend the hearing before the justice, ascertain the character of the evidence exhibited by the claimant, and present such proofs of a contrary tendency as could be had. Enoch Lewis was very well acquainted with the law relating to the rendition of fugitive slaves, and his services on such occasions were valuable in keeping the justices, who usually favored their claimants, to the strict line of their duty. It not unfrequently happened that persons supposed to be free were unexpectedly found to be slaves, and that all efforts to rescue them from the hands of their captors were unavailing. One instance of this kind is recollected. While Enoch Lewis was a teacher at Westtown, he was aroused from his bed before daylight one morning by a negro woman in great alarm, who came to inform him that her husband had been arrested in the night by slave-catchers, and carried off to West Chester.

Her husband was an industrious and well-behaved colored man, who had lived in the neighborhood some eight or ten years, and was supposed to be free. He was taken before the judge of the district at West Chester, and before Enoch Lewis arrived the hearing had begun, and the man had acknowledged that he was the slave of the claimant. Enoch Lewis then proposed to purchase the man, and after some negotiation the master agreed to take $400 for him in cash. Enoch drew up a paper, to which he subscribed his own name as one of the purchasers and in a short time $100 were thus raised. The other $300 Enoch himself paid, taking the

o

negroe's own bond for the money, and manumission papers were therefore executed in due form. As Enoch Lewis's salary as a teacher was then but $500, his loss of the money vested upon the integrity of the poor fugitive would have been somewhat serious. But his confidence was not misplaced. By small installments every dollar of the money was paid, and the quandom slave established the character of a good citizen. After paying his bond given for his freedom, he purchased a house and lot of some ten or twelve acres of land and lived comfortably and respectably to a good old age.

The residence of Enoch Lewis, at New Garden, was long a station on the Underground Railroad, during the time of Isaac Jackson, its former owner, and it continued to be so, many years after. Although Enoch did not approve of encouragement being given to slaves to leave their masters and he thought no general good would be accomplished by it, if a fugitive sought a temporary asylum beneath his roof or a helping hand on the way, when fleeing from slavery, his claim to hospitality and charitable aid in the name of humanity was not to be denied. When a slave-catcher appeared in the neighborhood, Enoch Lewis was usually one of the first that was informed of it, and a horse and carriage to convey the fugitive who was supposed to be in danger of arrest to a safe distance were promptly furnished. Enoch's eldest son, Joseph J. Lewis, of West Chester, informs me that when a boy he was once sent to Nixon's factory on Pickering Creek, with a load of wool in a one-horse covered cart and a colored woman and her child packed in behind the wool, on a report that the former master of the woman had obtained a

warrant for her arrest and was in search of her.   The
route taken to Nixon's factory was by no means the
most direct, but was deemed the most safe.   It led by
Kimberton where the woman and child were left in the
charge of Emmor Kimber, who gave them, the same
night, a free passage to the next station northward.

A fugitive once stopped at Enoch Lewis's and remained several days.   He was a preacher and had fled
from the far South, and, after a series of romantic adventures, effected his complete escape.   The narrative
of his experiences was so interesting that Enoch Lewis
assembled his pupils in his school-room to listen to it.
One incident is still remembered.   A short time after
the fugitive left his master, he took refuge with a colored friend who found him a well-contrived hiding-
place.   Though well secreted he became forcibly impressed one night, though without any apparent reason,
that he was not safe where he was, and that he must
immediately seek some new covert.   Obeying the moni-
tion, he left his place of concealment and, entering a
small stream of water which flowed near by, he followed
it for a short distance, so that the scent of his foot-steps
could not be traced by dogs, till he came to the over-
hanging branches of a tree of thick foliage.   This he
ascended, and found himself well hidden within an
hundred yards of his former hiding-place.   " Jist," said
the narrator, " as I'se got fixed, lyin' strait out along a
big lim', when here dey come, massa and a dozen more
on hoss-back, hollowin' and screetchin', de hosses at full
jump, and de dogs yelpin', right up to de little cave
whar dey spect to find de poor nigger.   But no poor
nigger dar.   Den de dogs run about from cave to de

creek, and from creek back to de cave, smellen' de groun'. De men stamp and thrash about, ride up and down de creek pass my tree. De moon perty bright, but de same good speret what tell me to git away from de cave, wouldn't let 'em see me dar lyin' on dat lim' like a coon." '

This colored preacher brought with him to Enoch Lewis's a little nephew, about five years old, whom Enoch reared and educated. Being inclined to adventure, this boy was given his liberty when about eighteen, became steward on a passenger ship plying between New York and Liverpool, and subsequently on a large steam-boat on the Hudson, and when last heard from was thus employed and prospering.

The outrages formerly inflicted on free colored people by the slave system, are illustrated by an instance which occurred over sixty years ago. A free negro, residing in the western part of Londongrove, or in one of the adjacent townships, had occasion to go to Baltimore on business. Having no pass from any slave-owner, he was liable to arrest on suspicion of being a runaway slave, under a law of Maryland, and advertised, and if, after a certain number of days, no claimants appeared, the suspected runaway was sold for his jail fees at public auction. The man, in this case, being found without a pass, and knowing no white man in Baltimore to vouch for him, was arrested and thrown in prison, and no person appearing to claim him, he was advertised to be sold on a certain day. Information of the facts having been communicated to Enoch Lewis and his friends in the neighborhood, Israel Jackson, who knew the man, hastened to Baltimore, procured a writ of habeas corpus,

proved his freedom, and, after a pretty sharp contro-
versy as to the legal right of the authorities to detain
him, obtained his release and brought him away with
him.

Evan Lewis, the youngest brother of Enoch, resided
in Wilmington, Delaware, and was a zealous and active
abolitionist. His house was for many years a much
frequented station on the Underground Railroad. The
fugitives who came his way were generally forwarded
in the direction of Philadelphia, but some, when circumstances required that they should pursue a different
route, took the road to New Garden and were committed to the care of Enoch Lewis for such friendly aid as
was needed.

By an Act of Congress of February 12, 1793, Judges
and Justices of the Peace of the several States were
authorized to issue warrants for the removal of negroes
and mulattoes claimed as slaves. Under this Act many
and terrible abuses were practiced. On fictitious claims,
free colored persons were arrested without notice and
hurried before justices favoring this species of kidnapping, and sharing with the perpetrators the profits of it.
When thus arrested, the alleged fugitives were summarily dealt with. On hasty examinations, conducted
with little regard to rules of evidence or considerations
of justice, warrants of removal were granted. The
victims of these practices, when once fairly within the
clutches of these manstealers, were not likely ever to
return. They were usually sold to some trader, who
carried them far South, whence there was little chance
of escape. To put a stop to this odious traffic, it was
necessary to obtain a law of our State Legislature, de-

priving justices of the peace of jurisdiction in cases of claims to fugitive slaves. As justices of the peace were State officers, it was competent to the State Legislature to define their jurisdiction. Enoch Lewis was one of those who made earnest efforts to procure the passage of an Act prohibiting justices from issuing warrants of removal. He called public attention to the subject in various newspaper articles and visited Harrisburg in conjunction with certain members of committees of the Meeting for Sufferings and other Society Organizations of Friends, to hold conferences with members of the Legislature. At length in 1820, by an Act passed the twenty-seventh of March of that year, the object of these efforts was attained.*

A good deal of excitement and annoyance in the Southern townships of Chester county were formerly caused by the incursions of slave-hunters from Maryland. These men were generally of loose morals and lawless conduct, profane in language, coarse and brutal in appearance and swaggering in their demeanor. They inspired a feeling of detestation wherever they appeared, none favored their nefarious enterprises except the very lowest and meanest of the population. Among such they were accustomed, not unfrequently, to find spies and informers. A posse of these miscreants once started a negro whom they took to be a slave or wished to make one, from his covert in the neighborhood of Pleasant Garden Forge and chased him to the vicinity of the Forge. The fugitive took refuge in the dwelling

---

*The Act of Congress authorizing "Aldermen or Justices of the Peace to issue warrants of removal of any negro or mulatto, claimed to be a fugitive from labor," was passed on the twelfth day of February, 1793.

of Samuel Irwin, the proprietor of the Forge, and was
directed by some of the family to ascend to the second
story, which on the opposite side was on a level with the
ground, and to make his egress on that side. As the
pursuers approached, Mr. Irwin took his stand at the
door, which was divided in the middle, one-half being
open and the other closed, and standing behind the
lower part which was closed, stopped the rush of the
party and parleyed with the leader who demanded
entrance to search for the fugitive. The men were
hot with the chase and fierce and furious, and the
leader, who represented himself as the owner of the fugitive, insisted on his right to enter and capture his
" nigger," whom he had seen pass into the house.   Mr.
Irwin met the demand with great coolness and perfect
civility, stated that he did not at all believe that the
" nigger " was in his house, demanded to see the warrant
authorizing the arrest, and by a series of questions in a
quiet and gentlemanly tone contrived to detain the
claimant and his crew for several minutes before allowing them to enter.   When they entered he offered them
every facility for a thorough search, conducted them
leisurely through every room in his house, opened every
closet, and showed them every nook which might
serve for a hiding-place.   In the meantime, the poor fugitive was busy in putting as much space between himself and his pursuers as possible, and he made so good a
use of his opportunity as to effect his escape.   Mr.
Irwin used to tell of another slave-catcher who, by a
singular series of coincidences, was baffled in the pursuit
of his pleasant occupation. Passing on horseback by
the hut of a negro family on one of the roads near

Pleasant Garden Forge, he leaned forward to get a view of the interior of the cabin and was seen to scan with an inquisitive air the family group within. The mother of the family was of large size and determined character. Observing the demeanor of the stranger, and rightly judging his purpose, she suddenly snatched a large butcher-knife and rushed at him furiously. He immediately put spurs to his horse, and getting beyond her reach, pushed on his way. He had not gone far before he saw a couple of negroes coming out of a bushy piece of woodland trimming ox wattles which they had just cut, while their teams were standing in the road. The slave-catcher, still nervous from his adventure with the woman, suspected that the wattles were intended for him, and not daring to face his supposed antagonists, he turned his horse and rode back a few hundred yards to a place where the road forked. Taking the other prong of the fork, he followed it for a short distance and then happened to see two men, one white and the other colored, approaching him in such a way as to intercept his progress, with guns in their hands. Alarmed at this additional manifestation of hostility, the poor slave-catcher hurried back to the Forge, and calling upon Mr. Irwin, claimed his protection against the "niggers" of the neighborhood who, he believed had formed a conspiracy to murder him. Mr. Irwin, perceiving from the man's own statement that the cause of his apprehensions was his own consciousness of his detestable purposes, assured him that if he would take the road leading south and pursue that to the State line he would escape all molestation; but that if he ventured to go in a different direction, he, Mr. Irwin, would not insure his life for an hour. This excellent advice was followed thankfully, and the face of this redoubtable slave-catcher was not seen afterwards in those parts. Verily, "the wicked flee when no man pursueth."

Enoch Lewis was born in Radnor, Delaware county, First mo. (January) 29th, 1776. He was mainly self-taught. His opportunities for receiving an education when a boy were quite limited. Yet having an insatiable fondness for learning, he found the time and means to acquire knowledge by unwearied diligence, and at the age of fifteen began his successful career as a teacher. He was the author of several works on mathematics, one on Grammar, several on religious and moral subjects; edited at different times the *African Observer* and the *Friends' Review*, and contributed many essays to leading journals upon various subjects.

On ninth of Fifth mo. (May), 1799, he married Alice Jackson, daughter of Isaac and Hannah Jackson, of New Garden, Chester county, a woman of fine education and of literary taste. She died Twelfth mo. (December), 1813. In Fifth mo. (May), 1815, he married a daughter of Jonn Jackson, of London Grove, a first cousin of his first wife, and woman of excellent mind and more than ordinary culture.

He died Seventh mo. (July), 1856. He was a member of the Society of Friends, as were both his wives, and was scrupulous in his attendance at both the First-day and mid-week meetings.

An interesting biography of him has recently been published by his son, the Hon. Joseph J. Lewis, long the oldest member of the West Chester bar, and who

o*

was employed as one of the counsel in the defense of
Castner Hanway; an account of whose trial is given in
Chapter Eight of this work.

CHAPTER XIX.

BENJAMIN PRICE.—His Father, Philip Price, Assists Runaways.—Incidents.—Golden Weddings.—SAMUEL M. PAINTER.—Abraham D. Shadd, John Brown and Benjamin Freemen.—NATHAN EVANS.

BENJAMIN PRICE.

(Born Twelfth Mo., 1793.—Died First Mo., 8th, 1871.)

Taken by permission from the MSS. Memoir of Benjamin and Jane Price, now in course of Preparation by their son, Isaiah Price, D.D.S., Major 97th Pennsylvania Volunteers. Author and Publisher of a "History of the 97th Pennsylvania Volunteers during the War of the Rebellion," etc., etc.

"About the earliest knowledge we had of the anti-slavery cause was derived from the experiences related to us while very young children, by our parents and others, of incidents in the perilous service of aiding fugitive slaves in their escape from bondage, so courageously engaged in by many of the humane inhabitants of the country early in the present century.

"Our father entered upon this fulfillment of the Divine command in his youth, following the example of his father, and took *his* place upon the road at a very early age.

"When he was about sixteen, a case of threatened re-capture of some slaves then at his father's and on the adjoining farm, demanded the utmost care and skill in extricating the fugitives from the grasp of the slave-catchers who had reached the neighborhood. Being apprised of the danger, our grandfather, Philip Price, hurried the three—two men and a woman, the wife of one of the men, to a hiding-place in the thicket, then abounding near his place. The woman was disguised as

a man. He directed them to emerge at dark and make
their way across the fields to an unfrequented road in
the vicinity, in a direction not likely to be observed by
their pursuers, and to look out for a guide with horses.
At nightfall he directed his son, Benjamin, to mount
one of the horses and to lead another, and take some
bags as though going upon an errand to the adjoining
mill. This was then a frequent mode of bringing home
the grist. Grandfather had also given him the requisite
directions for overtaking the fugitives upon the unfrequented road.

"He thus safely eluded observation and joined the
party on the road ; these then mounted, one behind him
and the other on the other horse, and passed by the by-
road across the Wilmington road and through by Jesse
Mercer's place, and out on the street-road east of Darlington's Corner Inn, which was regarded as too public
for them to pass. They then went on safely to a designated station, not now remembered, somewhere in the
neighborhood of Darby.

"Our father returned alone ; being familiar with the
road he had no difficulty in finding his way going or returning, and was capable of finding safe shelter from
pursuit, had any been made, by taking to the by-lanes
and roads or even to the woods, if none of those were
at hand.

"Having reached Osborn's Hill on his return, about
two A. M. his attention was arrested by the sound of
the distant clatter of horse's feet and the rumble of
wheels upon the stony road-bed, mingled with voices
in boisterous rage, oaths and curses being distinctly
heard. Rightly conjecturing that these sounds might

proceed from the disappointed slave-hunters, either returning for another search at his father's house, or on their way to Wilmington by the road he was on, he retraced his road a few paces and entered the lane leading to John Forsyth's place, which would shield him from observation, the hedges being much overgrown, and thus he could escape if they should enter after him, by passing out toward Forsyth's. But the sound soon indicated that the party had passed toward the Brandy-wine, the last he heard being the clatter of crossing the bridge at Wistar's. He then emerged from his concealment and soon found a welcome needed rest at his home where his anxious parents had become quite uneasy at his prolonged absence. Having also heard the noise of the disappointed hunters, they feared he might encounter them in the road upon his return.

"Our father has told us of the thoughts that occupied his mind, as he rode beneath the canopy of stars, going and returning upon his errand of mercy; how his abhorrence of slavery grew into a glowing purpose to do all in his power to aid those seeking to escape from its grievous injustice. Never was a fugitive turned away from the shelter of his home, or bid to pursue his toiling journey unrelieved by food, raiment, means, or a conveyance to some other shelter on the way beyond.

"There was no record kept of the cases in which our father actively aided in the escape of fugitive slaves. He did what he could for them, in that judicious prudent manner in which it is enjoined to 'let not the left hand know what the right hand doeth,' not through any fear of the reproach of men, but in order the better to serve and to shield those whom he would aid from the dangers which a garrulous tongue might entail upon them.

"He received fugitives from almost every station between his home and the land of bondage. It canont now be ascertained what directions these received, or what were the particular landmarks or other indications by which they found their way to his home. They came from his cousin, Thomas Garrett, of Wilmington, Del.; Eziekel Hunn, of near Camden, Del.; William Jackson, Londongrove; Isaac and Dinah Mendenhall, Simon and Sarah Barnard, at Avondale; from Jacob Lindley's home (to his father's during his boyhood); Amos Preston's at West Grove, and from many others not now recalled.

"He forwarded them to various points beyond: To John Sugar, West Bradford; John Vickers, Uwchlan; Dr. Bartholomew Fussell and Graceanna Lewis, West Vincent; Emmor Kimber, Kimberton; Elijah F. Pennypacker, Benjamin Garrigues, Montgomery county; Jacob L. Paxson, Norristown; to his brother-in-law, William H. Johnson, Buckingham, Bucks county; John Sellers, Darby, Pa.; Eli D. Pierce, Providence, and John Jackson, Darby, Delaware county, Pa.; to his cousins, Philip, Isaac and Samuel Garrett, Delaware county, Pa., and to many others of which there is no record.

"Our earliest recollections are dotted with the memory of strange, dark faces, coming in at nightfall, partaking of supper, and afterward being mysteriously stowed away, with blankets for covering, in the barn or on the garret floor, where, in some instances, they remained concealed for a few days and nights, being fed cautious-

ly at our meal-time ; and on some propitious night they
would disappear and be heard of no more, and the
horses in the stable next morning would bear evidence
of having traversed the roads during the night and the
carriage wheels would still be moist with fresh mud,
when we *knew* they were dry on the on the evening before.   Our father, (an unusual occurrence at other times)
being not yet astir, we were cautioned by our mother
' to make no noise to disturb father's rest, as he had not
gone to bed till late.'   His errand was not concealed
from us, but we were thus taught *practically* to *leave un-
spoken* the words that might give improper *information*
to others less cautious and considerate of the peril of
those fleeing from bondage.   In some instances, when
the fugitives were considered to be in less immediate
danger of pursuit, they were given work on the farm or
in the house, where they remained for some weeks or
months, earning means to enable them to reach Canada,
the only place of absolute safety.   Of these, the earliest
recollected arrived on a stormy day in December, 1829.
We first encountered him in the granary getting chaff
to mix feed for the stock ; we had just returned from
school, and one of us asked ' who is this ? ' and received
the answer, ' Ned Wilson, sir,' and his white teeth dis-
closed the ' open countenance ' of a genial nature, to
which boys naturally take with a sincere appreciation.
From that day, while he remained with us, ' Ned
Wilson, sir' and the boys were fast friends.   At every
opportunity we sought him at his work, or wherever he
might be, and in the evening we became his instructors
in the alphabet, which, with great perseverence, he
mastered ; then in writing and spelling, until the difficul-

ties of these elements were surmounted and he became enabled to read with more facility than is often reached by younger scholars in the same period. His interest and gratitude were unbounded. His safety at length rendered it necessary for him to 'run on,' and he left us with saddened heart at the parting, yet with grateful remembrance of his sojourn in our home.

" The next remembered were John and Araminta Dorsey ; they came at the pork-butchering-time ; the year not recalled. The impression of their advent is that seeing the woman engaged at the table where the sausages was being prepared, her name was asked. ' My name is Arrowminta, but you may call me *Minta*, for short,' and ' Minta ' became established in the kitchen at the head of the culinary department, proving to be an excellent helper to our mother, capable of relieving her of many cares. Her husband, John, had been a minister or exhorter among their people ; he was intelligent and with some qualifications for a preacher if he had had a better opportunity for education ; but he did not take ardently to work, and was fonder of an argument than such employment as required the diligence of his hands. After remaining a short period they were forwarded to our Uncle William H. Johnson, and from there subsequently proceeded to Canada.

" One of the most exciting incidents of capture and escape which occurred in West Chester, was that of Rachel Harris. The successful manner in which she was conveyed out of West Chester, by Benjamin and Isaiah Price, is narrated in her History.

" A later case was that of Henry Clark, alias Andrew Commegys, who was a character of notable interest. He arrived at the farm-gate one sultry summer morning, enquired the way to Mr. Benjamin Price's, and was quite glad to find himself so near his destination. Being piloted to where our father was at work in one of the fields, he told the story of his escape. He was owned by a Mr. Commegys, who lived near Cantwell's Bridge in Delaware. To avoid being sold at the settlement of his late master's estate, or of falling into the hands of the young master, whose disposition was recklessly cruel and extravagant, he resolved upon flight. He was familiar with the roads to Wilmington and the vicinity, where, as the trusted servant of his old master, he was often permitted to drive his carriage and teams, and even to go there alone on some holiday excursion to visit his friends.

"He made his case known to the veteran friend of the slave, Thomas Garrett, who gave him accurate directions for finding our father's place. He had set out before midnight and had reached his destination in safety, and without having made a single enquiry, until he asked his question at the gate. He afterward said that 'his heart jumped right up in his mouth as he asked, from fear of being betrayed and sent back,' and he thought that every eye that looked toward him, as he came along after daylight, might be an enemy who would give information that he had been seen upon the road.

"It now seems incredible that it should have been deemed safe for him to remain in a neighborhood so little removed from the vicinity of his former home. But he became impressed with a feeling of security, resulting from his confidence in our father, which made him reluctant to leave us. He engaged in work on the farm and proved to be an industrious and reliable hand, was a great talker, very jocular, was notionate and peculiar to a degree, somewhat superstitious, and had imbibed a dread of medical students, whom he called 'Studeons,' getting possession of his body after death. He was something of a wit and became a great favorite with us all, in our work together on the farm. He continued with us for some years, during which time he became desirous of having his wife and family join him. They were free and had for some time resided in Wilmington, but it was deemed inadvisable on account of increasing his liability to recapture. The only communication between them was through Thomas Garrett. He now began to entertain the project of purchasing his freedom from his young master, who, it was ascertained, had taken the absconded chattel at a risk at a moderate rate, upon an appraisement in the adjustment of the estate. Negotiations for this purposes were opened through Thomas Garrett, which, after much unsatisfactory parley and delay, evidently prolonged in the hope of discovering the refuge of the slave, were finally successfully accomplished and the money paid by Thomas Garrett, who then received a clear bill of sale.

"Henry had been very saving and had a considerable sum laid by for this purpose. Some contributions were added and he was soon enabled to clear his indebtedness. He now rented a house belonging to the late James Painter which stood by the road-side, between Painter's dwelling and the Street Road; here his family came to live, and remained for several years. Having now obtained his freedom, Henry resumed his former name of Andy (Andrew) with his master's surname, as of old, and by this name he was afterwards known. He continued to work for our father for a considerable period ; but his landlord having need of a large force of help, became desirous of his services if he should continue to occupy his house. After this he only worked for us occasionally, when he could get off from his employer, at the end of harvest, corn-husking, etc. In later years he became afflicted and helpless from the exposure and overwork of his early years under the task-master. His constitution, originally of the most robust character, became broken and he gradually succumbed to the encroachments of disease. He died in the old log house at the corner of the Wilmington Road and the road leading to Jessee Mercer's place, in the year 18—. Our brother, Dr. Jacob Price, of West Chester, long gave him comfort and faithful attention and strove, as far as possible, to smooth the declining path of the faithful servant of many years in our early home. He was always grateful for the kindness and care manifested for his welfare, which he felt had been uninterrupted from the morning he first entered the lane to our parent's dwelling.

"These few cases may serve to give some insight into the unobtrusive fulfillment on the part of our parents of the Christian command, 'As you would that men should do unto you, do ye even so unto them.'

"Benjamin Price, son of Philip and Rachel Price, of East Bradford, Chester county, was born Twelfth Month, (December) 17th, 1793. He died First Month (January) 8th, 1871. Jane Price, daughter of Jacob and Mary Shaw Paxson, was born in Abington township, Montgomery county, Tenth Month (October) 18th, 1791, and died at West Chester, Fifth Month (May) 8th, 1876. They were married at Abington Meeting House, on the 12th of Six Month, 1817, and celebrated their golden wedding 12th of Sixth Month, 1867.

SAMUEL M. PAINTER.

Samuel M. Painter, of West Chester, was an earnest advocate and supporter of human liberty and of justice to all; and, like Abraham Lincoln, " he would that all men, everywhere, were free." He was an outspoken, uncompromising opponent of negro bondage; and as a consequence, had just as outspoken proslavery opponents. He kept a book store and circulated many anti-slavery tracts from the central anti-slavery office of J. Miller McKim, in Philadelphia.

At one time a prominent citizen of West Chester, purchased paper at his store, which his wife chanced to wrap in an anti-slavery tract. Seeing the word *anti-slavery*, he tore off the wrapper, threw it way contemptuously, and walked out saying " I didn't come here to be insulted."

A neighbor remonstrated with the subject of this sketch for being an abolitionist, and proceeded to advise him in the matter. Samuel replied, " My religion is to relieve those who are oppressed, as I would have them do for me under similar circumstances."

" Yes," responded the neighbor, " you would wrong the Southerners and sell your soul for a nigger."

A young, genteel, intelligent looking colored man, once called at the store with a note from Thomas Garrett, Wilmington, written in hieroglyphics, and said he knew his pursuers were close after him. He was well-bred and used extraordinarily good language.

Samuel kept him until night and then took him to John Vickers, whence he was sent to Emmor Kimber, Kimberton, thence to Boston. He had been brought up as a house servant. His suavity and intelligence won for him the esteem of some friends who took him to Europe. Here he met with unexpected success, and wrote back to the friends who assisted him, expressing his deep gratitude for the unselfish, unrecompensed kindness they had bestowed upon him in his hazardous journey from bondage to freedom.

A messenger came in haste to the store one night and told Samuel that he was wanted at the Sheriff's office; "that two negro women had been arrested and taken there by their masters who had proven them before Judge Darlington to be their slaves; but the papers the owners presented were defective in some legal point, and P. Frazer Smith, Esq., who was ever active in defending fugitives, seeing this, was demanding their release. While the slave-catchers were devising some plan by which the women could be secured until other papers were obtained, Samuel told these that he wished to see them alone in another room. The owners objected, but he persisted and obtained the interview. He told them to come with him, that he would provide for them during the night and they should not be returned to slavery. They hesitated, saying that their masters had promised them silk dresses if they would return, that they could be in the parlor and would not have to work out, and that they should not be sold. Samuel told them they knew the slave-holders well

enough not to believe that they would go to the trouble
and expense of coming so far and capturing them, just
to take them back and keep them in that style; that as
soon as they returned with their masters they would be
sold into Georgia. They went with him, the slaveholders following them to the house. Samuel forbade
the masters to enter. In the night he took the women
to John Vickers, who immediately sent them with a
colored man to Esther Lewis. The night being very
dark and stormy, the man missed the road and upset
the dearborn. After considerable effort in the impene-
trable darkness, he got it right side up again; but getting
bewildered he started in the wrong direction and finally
found himself at his starting point, at John Vickers'
house. The next night they were more successful, and
the Lewis family started them on a direct line for Boston,
which they reached in safety.

One day a man came hurriedly into the store and
told Samuel Painter he was wanted at the office of
Judge Thomas S. Bell immediately—that a slave had
been brought there. He locked the store-door at once
and started, Just then a Friend accosted him and asked
"why he was locking up at that time of day." Samuel
told him: "Thee had better attend to thy business
and let the niggers take care of themselves," was the
volunteer advice of the man in plain attire. But it did
not accord with Samuel's view of a Christian's duty, and
he proceeded to the judge's office and found there a
woman whom her master had captured and proved to
be his property. The required certi ficate of rendition
had been made out, and the poor woman had to return
to her former dreaded condition as a slave.

It was the custom of slave owners to employ persons in the North known by the sobriquet of "kidnappers" to assist them in catching "runaways." About 1837, a carriage was driven up to the Washington House, West Chester, where David M. McFarland's bank now stands, with two men in it, who, after having ordered their dinners and their horses to be fed, inquired of the landlord where they could find some one who would catch a slave for them, whom they described very minutely, saying at the same time that "he was now in the employ of Joshua Sharpless, near Downingtown." They were referred to one who would do this shameful thing.

· It so happened that Samuel M. Painter was standing unobserved on his doorsteps, directly adjoining the hotel, where he overheard the conversation, and immediately dispatched a messenger to Joshua with the intelligence, who notified the slave of the circumstance, when the latter at once started in haste toward Lionville. Here he met with John Vickers and begged of him to secrete him somewhere about the premises. John knew he would be suspected and was fearful of the result, but finally concluded to take him to his woodpile, where he had a great many cords of wood ranked away. There they fixed him up a secure hiding-place and had but just left when the party who had struck the trail came driving up and inquired if there was such a person about. Vickers said: "There is no such man in my house." "How is it at the barn?" the party inquired. "I know of none there; if there is any such person in any of my buildings it is unknown to me," replied Vickers. The guide told his employers that if Mr. Vickers passed his word there was no use in searching, so they drove on. The stranger was fed in his coop for some days and then sent off for Canada.

In 1862, during the war, a free colored woman in one of the northern slave States, learned one night that her husband, living with his master ten miles distant, was to be sold next day. Braving the darkness of night she started on foot through fields and forests to visit him, reaching the place long before morning. Arousing some of the colored inmates, she told her errand, found the report to be true, and that her husband was then locked in jail to prevent his trying to escape before auction-day. In the morning she remonstrated with his master and implored him not to sell her husband, reminding him of the promise made his wife before her death that he would not sell Mike, but would give him his freedom. The appeal touched a sympathizing cord in the slave-holder's heart, and he yielded to her earnest supplication, so far as to revoke his decision to sell him at that time.

While there, there appeared to her in a dream a northern town and in it a brick house with ivy clinging to the walls; to that place she felt herself directed to go. Being devoted to prayer, and having full faith in the manifestations and directions of Divine Providence, she resolved to leave her husband, take her child and proceed northward, trusting that the way would be pointed out to her, and that her husband would soon find means to escape and follow her. She was passed from friend to friend until she reached West Chester, Pa. Here her child was taken sick. On her way up High street to the office of Dr. J. B. Wood, she saw the identical house that she had seen in her vision. Entering it she found it to be the residence of Samuel M. Painter. He had a sick soldier in the house, whom his wife was caring for, and they were in pressing need of help. After the woman related her story they engaged her to assist them. She remained with them three months, and proved herself an excellent woman and faithful servant. At the end of this time she learned that two men who had fled from the South were then in Kennett; the description of one of them corresponded with that of her husband. Means were furnished her to go there and see if it were he. To her unbounded joy, her fond anticipations were realized. The heart that has never known the ecstasy and sweet delights of home-love can scarcely conceive the rapture of a meeting such as this. Escaped from the bonds of a hated slavery, reunited by the guidance of a Divine Providence amidst friends in a free State, exulting in the consciousness that no slave owner could now separate them, their thanksgiving and praise went up to Heaven as earnestly and devoutly as ever these ascended from the banks of the Red Sea or the Rock of Plymouth.

They went to Samuel M. Painter's, house and in a few days started for Harrisburg.

ABRAHAM D. SHADD, JOHN BROWN AND BENJAMIN FREEMAN.

These three colored men lived in West Chester, and were considered by Samuel M. Painter among his most reliable assistants.

Abraham Shadd owned property and entertained and forwarded fugitives. He was free-born in Maryland, was intelligent and quite well educated.

John Brown rendered assistance at all times when called upon.

P

Benjamin Freeman had not accommodations for lodging fugitives, but gave them food and conducted them to places in and out of the town.

At one time a man and a woman called. He consented to fix a place in which they could sleep that night. Next day he took them as far as the malt-house north of West Chester and directed them to John Vickers. Arriving there, the family had doubts about their being genuine Underground Railroad passengers. A few well-directed questions were put to them, when it was decided they were impostors. They were turned out to take care of themselves.

NATHAN EVANS.

The anti-slavery cause and the negro fleeing from bondage, had no more staunch friend than Nathan Lvans, of Willistown, Chester county. Living in a conservative neighborhood, surrounded by a conservative element, his labors in that vicinity in behalf of the colored race had but few sympathizers and fewer supporters. His honest opponents disparaged him; the bigoted decried him, but

> " Like a firm rock that in mid-ocean braves
> The war of whirlwinds and the dash of waves,"

he was unmoved by any opposition, and maintained calmly, persistently and uprightly what he believed to be the true principles of righteousness and the duty of man to his fellow-man.

He was a minister in the Society of Friends. His discourses were pure, earnest, solid and instructive, but he would introduce into them the subjects of slavery and temperance. These were objected to; they were not popular in his neighborhood, and his persistence in

NATHAN EVANS.

speaking of them in religious meetings and in private conversation made him also unpopular. The meeting admonished him to cease from bringing these subjects into his sermons, or they would have to deal with him for the offence. But he paid no heed to their counsel, believing the cause he advocated to be just and that people must be spoken to before they would learn. He often repeated the couplet :

" Truths would you teach to save a sinking land
All shun, none aid you, and few understand."

He held it to be a religious duty that devolved upon him to speak against all manner of sin or evil, no matter what fascinations it presented, nor how lucrative it might be to individuals, society or the State. If it received the sanction of Government and was legalized by statutes, the church should exclaim against it, and the people be instructed to oppose it.

The opposition to him, however, in the meeting was so strong that he was disowned from membership. He bore this act with patience and charity, never uttering a word of contumely against his adversaries. He was willing to concede that they acted according to the highest light they had received or comprehended. But he considered that they needed more light to dispel the Egyptian darkness through which they were travelling. He continued to attend meeting as before, and took his accustomed seat and preached as usual. A little amusement was created on one occasion when he alluded in a sermon to a party of men and women who had come to his place a few nights before, poorly clad, tired and hungry, their flesh bearing the marks of the lash ; when he depicted the agonies of the mother, whose child had been torn from her and sold to traders, and spoke of his hearers' apathy in this matter as professing Christians, because they were not personal observers of these wrongs and sufferings, and because their own persons, and those of their friends were exempt from this system of holding chattel property in man; and when, at this point, one of the elderly friends in the "gallery" behind him remarked: " Have a little mercy on us," he paused for a moment, turned his eyes reverently upward, and then, with a grave and gentle air, replied: " I have yet many things to say unto you, but I see ye are not able to bear them now." He alluded no more to the subject, but the remainder of his sermon was a touching one on love and kindness.

. Fugitives were sent to his place from West Chester, and from the western and southern parts of Chester county, and were sent, or taken by him to Elijah F. Pennypacker's, to Philadelphia, and to James Lewis's, in Delaware county.

His son David, now living, has kept a diary since he was a boy, in which he noted anti-slavery and Underground Railroad incidents as they transpired, a few of which we extract to show how the business was conducted at that station.

A memorandum is made of the *first anti-slavery meeting in Willistown*, which was held in the Friends' Meeting School House, Twelfth mo. (December) 17th, 1836; addressed by William Whitehead, of West Chester; Nathan Evans presided and Dr. Joseph Hickman acted as Secretary.

Twelfth mo. 30th.—Charles C. Burleigh lectured at the same school house.

1842—Eighth mo. 19th.—I started at two o'clock, A. M., with four colored persons to the anti-slavery office in Philadelphia. They were sent here last evening by James Fulton, in care of Henry Lee (colored). *These were the first taken to the anti-slavery office.*

Eighth mo. 28th.—Two more came from the land of bondage, on their way to Canada.

Ninth mo. 22nd.—About two A. M., Lukens Pierce drove here with a four-horse wagon containing twenty-five colored persons—men, women and children. I took thirteen that evening to the anti-slavery office in Philadelphia; and on the night of the 24th, Davis Garrett, Jr., and John Wright (colored) took the remainder in two dearborns.

Ninth mo. 27th.—Maris Woodward, of Marshallton, brought two colored women, "on their way toward the North Star;" mother took them to Philadelphia on the 29th.

Tenth mo. 10th.—A man and woman came this evening; John Wright took them to Philadelphia on the 12th.

Tenth mo. 19th.—Henry Lee (colored) brought two women and three children from James Fulton's; cousin Joshua Clendenon took them to Philadelphia that night.

Tenth mo. 20th.—Lukens Pierce came with sixteen; father took them to Philadelphia next night. This party was from Washington City and they seemed remarkably well-bred and intelligent.

——— ——— Davis Garret, Jr., took to Philadelphia a man and a woman.

Tenth mo. 27th.—Cousin Joshua Clendenon and mother took three men to Philadelphia.

Eleventh mo. 2nd.—A colored traveler arrived, and

went to Philadelphia with father on a load of hay.
This man informed us that several more were not far
behind.   Accordingly, about two o'clock on the morning
of the 5th, Simon Barnard came with eleven men and
two women; Davis Garrett and William Hibbard, Jr.,
took them to Philadelphia the following night in two
one-horse dearborns.

Eleventh mo. 13th.—Mordecai Hayes arrived about
3 o'clock in the morning with five men. I took them
to Philadelphia that night except one old man who remained and hired with us.

Eleventh mo. 15th.—Three men came, and we sent
them to James Lewis' on the 17th.

These dates of arrival and departure show the amount
of business done at that station, and how it was conducted. It will be seen that the arrivals were frequent,
and that no little labor was required, in addition to farm
and house work, to provide for and to transmit the
number that called yearly. And thus it continued
through a period of several years. Dr. Bartholomew
Fussell, and Joseph Painter, of West Chester, also sent
fugitives to this place.

Nathan Evans frequently said that a great calamity
would yet befall this Nation if the sin of slavery continued to be upheld by the people, and sanctioned by
the Government. He seemed to have a clear, prophetic
vision of the manner in which God would punish the
people of this country if they did not repent and give
freedom to the children of Africa held here in chains.
His predictions, even to the details of the war and its
consequences, have been literally verified.

While the subject of this sketch was unpopular in his

own section, on account of his persistence in speaking of slavery in religious gatherings, and to his neighbors who opposed him, yet amongst abolitionists he was regarded as a worthy, conscientious man, warm-hearted, and, though advanced in years, his hands and heart and and pocket were all combined to aid in the cause. As a speaker at anti-slavery meetings he was regarded as earnest, sincere and truthful, and his discourses were weighty and argumentative, based upon scriptural grounds. Therefore, while they were solid, they did not especially attract the masses, and he was considered a little more tedious than the speaker who warms up with the enthusiasm of the moment, and carries his audience with him upon the tide of pleasing and thrilling thought.

His adherence to the principles of right, as he saw and believed them, in all his intercourse in life, and his charity for those who held views different from his own, drew to him others who began to think and believe with himself. But it was not until during the war when the general opinion of the country concerning slavery was changed, that the principles he maintained were adopted in his own neighborhood—a period he did not live to see.

CHAPTER XX.

JAMES LEWIS and JAMES T. DANNAKER.—Many Fugitives Taken to the Anti-slavery Office, Philadelphia.—ROBERT PURVIS.—The Dorsey Brothers.

JAMES LEWIS AND JAMES T. DANNAKER.

(James Lewis, Born November 8th, 1802.—Died May 25th, 1876.) (James T. Dannaker, Born March 11th, 1814.)

In the latter part of 1837, James Lewis, currier and tanner, in Marple township, Delaware county, ten miles from Philadelphia, felt constrained to give his support to the anti-slavery movement then being agitated throughout the country. He was united with in this advanced step in their neighborhood by James T. Dannaker, an intelligent, radical thinker, then residing with him, and who was his co-worker in the temperance cause. Such was the opposition to this " new departure " of James Lewis that some of his customers withdrew their patronage. But this neither changed his convictions of right nor caused him to swerve from his strictly onward course in what he felt to be a moral duty. As congenial spirits are attracted towards each other, so James Lewis soon found gathering around him new friends whose intellectual and moral worth he highly appreciated ; and his feeling was reciprocated by them. Among these were the younger members of the Sellers families, in Upper Darby. They held private meetings at each other's houses for counsel and encouragement. Finally they decided to have a public meeting, and secured an able speaker. After considerable effort they obtained the privilege of using Marple school-house, No. 1. This

JAMES LEWIS.

caused much excitement, and when the appointed time came the house was crowded with friends and foes, a large number being unable to gain admittance. A gang of twenty came for the express purpose of breaking up the meeting when anything should be said that they could use as a provocation to carrying out their plot. The speaker, Thomas Earle, arrived, accompanied by S. Sellers, and moved through the crowd to the platform. After a few moments of impressive silence, Thomas Earle arose, and in a quiet, dignified manner, said that he had come there for the purpose of talking upon the subject of American slavery, but having heard on his way that there was some opposition, he did not wish to intrude and proposed that James Lewis take the sense of the meeting whether or not he should speak. The vote was almost unanimous for him to proceed. He spoke nearly two hours, and held the audience throughout in rapt attention, as if spell-bound, by his touching appeals and persuasive oratory. He pictured the life of the unrequited laborer, of families separated at the auction-block and fond affections outraged. He brought this condition of servitude directly home to the firesides and hearts of his audience, " remembering those who were in chains as bound with them," and so effective was this portraiture that at the close of the meeting " many who came to scoff remained to pray." Among the first to take the speaker by the hand and thank him for the light and the instructions given, were some of the leaders of the party who had designed to be obstreperous. This meeting was followed by others, and by debates in different parts of Delaware and Chester counties, which largely changed sentiment in favor of

P*

the abolition of slavery. James Lewis now became known as a firm and earnest abolitionist.

About the year 1839, Nathan Evans, an aged Friend, of Willistown, Chester county, who had for years made frequent trips to Philadelphia with large numbers of fugitives, called on James Lewis to ask if he would make his place an intermediate station. This was agreed to, and James T. Dannaker accepted the position of "conductor" on that part of the route. He accompanied Nathan to the city with eight fugitives, the latter then in charge, and was introduced to families with whom Nathan had been accustomed to leave them and told how to manage the business secretly.

If circumstances rendered it inconvenient or dangerous for any one of these families to accommodate the fugitives at that time, they were taken to another.

This trip was, fortunately, rather an eventful one, and the impressions made by this initiary lesson were the more valuable. Nathan had not been accustomed to taking fugitives to the anti-slavery office. On this occasion he wished to go there. It chanced to be at a time when no one was in, and he would not risk waiting, but proceeded to one of his usual stations. Here, as they were about to unload, they observed an inquisitive looking man walking around as if intent upon watching their actions. They judged that he suspected their business, and deeming it unsafe to leave the passengers there, drove one-and-a-half miles to another place, where they unloaded in safety. They remained in the city over night, and next morning learned that the house at which they first stopped had been searched about daylight, but no fugitives found in it.

JAMES DANNAKER.

James T. Dannaker then felt the importance of having several places to call at in case danger should be lurking around any one of them. In addition to the families he had been introduced to, he subsequently, through his friends, became acquainted with others. He made the arrangement with them that when he arrived with passengers he would announce it by *three* distinct raps at the door. The family understanding the meaning of this, would know what precautions to take before going to the door, especially if strangers were in the house. When he had two or more wagon loads, he preceded them a square or two, carrying a white handkerchief in his hand, by which to direct their movements. If they could not be taken in at one place, he went to another, until he found accommodations for all.

James Lewis's house now became a prominent station, and Dannaker an efficient conductor ; never being detected, although he frequently made two trips a week.

At one time Friend Evans kept twenty-six at his place for two weeks, as he heard the hunters were assiduously watching for them in Philadelphia. When danger was past he took them to James Lewis, there they remained until next night, when Dannaker, with two assistants, took them by different routes to Arch street wharf, Philadelphia, arriving there at midnight. He put them on board Captain Whildon's boat, which plied between Philadelphia, Trenton and Bordentown. The Captain kept a state-room in which he carried fugitives whenever they could be put in there without exciting suspicion.

Four brothers and sisters, who had been separated for years, casually or Providentially met at Columbia, and came on this route to James Lewis. These were, as if through the mysteriously directing hand of a kind Providence, sent to Norristown, and there met their father and mother. The joy of this unexpected meeting was a cause of thanks to God from the hearts both of the fugitives and their friends.

Eight arrived at one time from Norfolk, Va. On taking them to Philadelphia, Dannaker found all the stations full, until he arrived at the thirteenth, the home of Hester Reckless,* an elderly colored woman, who was as full of life and enthusiasm whenever she could render assistance to the fleeing slave, as were many who had not attained half her number of years. Having business to transact in the city, he remained until next day. As so many of the stations were full, his curiosity led him to visit them again to ascertain how many were harbored that night, and he found the number was one hundred and sixty-eight. Yet these, without an exception, were moved steadily and safely along to their goal in Canada, with as little outward demonstration as bodies that are carried silently and unperceived along river-beds to the ocean.

Two arrived one evening on their way from Baltimore. One was a bright, intelligent-looking mulatto, owned by Hon. Reverdy Johnson, of that city. He had

*Mrs. Hester Reckless, a colored woman, born at Salem, N. J., in 1776, died at her residence, No. 1015 Rodman street, on the afternoon of January 28th, 1881, aged nearly 105 years. The mother of the deceased also attained the age of one hundred years. Mrs. Reckless resided in Philadelphia for sixty-five years, and was an earnest worker in the anti-slavery movement. She worked with the late Lucretia Mott in the Female Anti-slavery Society, and cherished with great affection two relics of the organization. One was a photograph of its members, and the other was a flag with inscriptions upon it which expressed the strong feelings of the anti-slavery people on the subject. Her memory was good to the last, and she frequently told, with a good amount of satisfaction, the fact that she had several times seen General Washington. One daughter, seventy years old, is the only near relative who survives the old lady.

charge of his master's law office and library, from which he had acquired much knowledge, after stealthily learning the alphabet from white school-boys on the street. The other was a coachman, belonging to a lady, a relative of Mr. Johnson, living in Mississippi, and had accompanied her on a visit to Baltimore. When starting on this journey with his mistress, the idea of coming so near a free State inspired him with a desire and determination to become free himself. While these two men were planning their escape, five fugitives were captured at Wrightsville and returned to slavery. The following night a party was given in honor of the lady from Mississippi. As she was entering her carriage, the Wrightsville capture was being spoken of, when a person remarked to her that she "had better keep a sharp lookout on Charles, the coachman." " I do not believe," she said, "that he could be coaxed to leave me." Charles seized that opportune moment of asserted confidence and replied, "I know when I am well off and well cared for." After stabling the horses carefully, as was his custom, he and his companion started on foot, and the third evening reached James Lewis's house, and in two weeks arrived safely in Canada. When near Wrightsville, after leaving Baltimore, they were accosted by some rude looking men, who attempted to arrest them. Being well armed they drew their weapons upon their assailants, who, doubtless thinking " discretion the better part of valor," fled and gave them no further trouble.

In 1866, while James Dannaker was standing at the depot in Chester, a colored man alighted from a train, and after looking into his face a moment, approached

him, and asked if his name was not Dannaker. He replied that it was. The colored man then introduce:
himself as the slave of Reverdy Johnson, whom he had
helped to freedom twenty-four years before. After
expressing his gratitude he stated that he was then
residing in Rochester, New York; had acquired a
considerable fortune; was married, and was then accompanied by his wife on his way to visit Baltimore.

Many testified to their being well treated and cared
for, both in health and in sickness; but they left through
the fear of their being sold to go South, or of having
their families sold from them.

Occasionally before starting with a load James Lewis
would receive intelligence that the masters, learning
where the slaves had crossed the Susquehanna, instead
of attempting to pursue them in their *underground* route
through the country, had gone directly to Philadelphia,
to intercept them there. He then sent them to Norristown.

At one time, just as Dannaker arrived at a station in
the city with eight, he received word that the pursuers
were close upon them. He took them immediately to
another place, and then returned to watch the course of
their pursuers. They soon arrived with a constable and
search-warrant. After a fruitless search through the
house, the constable remarked that there were two other
places where they might be, and *he knew* they were the
only houses in the city, besides this, where slaves were
harbored. One of them was where Dannaker had just
taken the fugitives. Before the party arrived at this
latter place with another warrant he had his men safely
removed to a secure retreat which the slave-hunting
constable wot not of.

In 1843 James T. Dannaker married and removed to the suburbs of Philadelphia, where he made his home another station. He soon became known in that vicinity as an abolitionist, and his house was closely watched. Knowing this, he ceased to harbor slaves, but took them to the city as soon as practicable after they were delivered into his care.

At one time James Lewis, assisted by two friends, brought sixteen to his place. He accompanied them to the city in the evening, walking as usual on the streets, in advance of the wagons, and directing the course of the drivers by the motions of a handkerchief. They saw they were suspected by a man who followed them a long distance, until they had nearly reached the last station in the lower part of the city, when a furious thunderstorm burst upon them and drove their unwelcome friend to seek shelter. Being thus relieved of uncongenial company, they hastened to the next stopping-place and unloaded in safety.

Two slaves from Havre-de-Grace came to James Dannaker's house one morning before daylight. He concealed them for that day. After breakfast he called on a man residing four doors from his place, for whom he was transacting business in the city. This man had formerly lived in Maryland, but had grown to disapprove of slavery. Quite a facetious smile played over the face of the wife as she met Dannaker, and invited him into another room. He was there introduced to a man from Maryland, in search of two runaway slaves. This man, after a little conversation, gave him one of the handbills describing the slaves, which description tallied exactly with the appearance of the two at his house. In the evening he took them to one of the Philadelphia stations, and related the circumstance of meeting their master. They were kept in the city about a week, and then forwarded to other places. It was not until they were leaving that they were told how near they had been to their master when at Dannaker's house.

An interesting and gratifying occurrence took place on one of James T. Dannaker's visits with a fugitive to the house of two sisters in Philadelphia, whose home was a valued station. The women fixed unusually scrutinizing glances upon this man for a few minutes, and then left the room. In a short time they returned, bringing with them a colored woman, who, as if bewildered with a sudden flash of astonishment and rapture, recognized the fugitive as her husband. The unexpected meeting was equally overwhelming to him. They had been separated from each other nearly four years; he having been sold to a master farther South. He was sold again, and brought back nearer to the free States. Here he heard of his wife's escape, and resolved to follow her. They had taken different routes, were both on their way to Canada, and were thus blest with a reunion in the house of stranger-friends on their road to freedom.

James T. Dannaker is, at the present writing, living at Chester, Pa., a vigorous old man, with remarkable memory. Among the happiest reminiscences of his life is the recollection of incidents—exciting, pathetic and amusing, when, despite the penal laws made in the interest of a slave-holding power, every active worker on the Underground Railroad freely and cheerfully imperiled his own property and even his own liberty to aid the slave in his journeyings for liberty.

ROBERT PURVIS.

ROBERT PURVIS.

In a letter to the editors, under date of April 23d, 1883, James T. Dannaker writes as follows : "And now, at the age of seventy years, the writer looks back upon that part of his life with great satisfaction, his only regret being that he was not able to do more."

ROBERT PURVIS.
(Born August 4th, 1810.)

After describing the manner in which fugitives were assisted through Chester and adjoining counties, many of whom were sent or taken to Philadelphia, the history would seem incomplete without a knowledge of the management of that place. Accordingly the author addressed a letter to Robert Purvis, one of the few surviving members of the 'Anti-slavery Executive Committee, and an agent of the Underground Railroad, and received the following response to the several inquiries made :

DEAR FRIEND :—In compliance with your request, I send you the following statement, as an answer to your inquiries concerning my personal history and connection with the Underground Railroad.

I was born in Charleston, South Carolina, August 4th, 1810. My father was an Englishman, my mother a free-born woman ; a native of Charleston. My maternal grandmother, whose name was Dido Badaracka, was a Moore, born in Morocco. When twelve years old, she, with an Arab girl, of about the same age, was decoyed by a native to go a mile or two out of the city, to see a deer that had been caught.

They were seized, placed upon the backs of camels, and carried over the country to a Slave Mart on the coast, to be shipped to America. This was about the year 1766, when the slave-trade was tolerated in this Christian country ! She was taken with a cargo of kidnapped Africans to Charleston, South Carolina, where, by reason of her comeliness, she was purchased for a maiden lady, whose name was Deas.

Her mistress became exceedingly attached to her, and at her death, when my grandmother was about nineteen years of age, emancipated her; leaving her also an annuity of sixty dollars.

Her Arab companion was not long held in bondage, as the laws did not permit ownership in persons of pure Arab blood. My grandmother, after being reinstated in her freedom, married a German, who professed the Jewish faith.

In the spring of 1819, my father, William Purvis, having retired from business, sent my mother and their three sons to Philadelphia, with the view of going from there to England to reside permanently. The execution of this plan was prevented by his untimely death.

He was instinctively and practically an abolitionist, even at that early date. My first impressions of the evils of slavery were derived from the books he placed into our hands, viz: "Torrey's Portraiture of Slavery" and "Sandford and Merton."

When he arrived in Philadelphia, finding there were no schools of a higher grade for "colored" children, he established a school on Spruce street, near Eighth street, and paid the teacher's salary for one year.

In the year 1830 I became interested in anti-slavery through my acquaintance with Benjamin Lundy, and William Lloyd Garrison—the latter, who called to see me, had just been released from a Baltimore prison, where he was placed for a libel on Francis Todd, of Newburyport, Mass. He unfolded to me his plans for publishing *The Liberator*, the first number of which came out on January first, 1831.

In 1833 the American Anti-Slavery Society was formed in Philadelphia. I was a member of the convention, and Vice President of the society for many years—I was also President for several years of the Pennsylvania Anti-Slavery Society, and a member of the Executive Committee.

I think it was about the year 1838, that the first organized society of the Underground Railroad came into existence—of this, I was made President, and Jacob C. White, Secretary. With the exception of myself, I believe Edwin H. Coates is the only remaining one of the original members.

The funds for carrying on this enterprise were raised from our anti-slavery friends, as the cases came up, and their needs demanded it, for many of the fugitives required no other help than advice and direction how to proceed. To the late Daniel Neall, the society was greatly indebted for his generous gifts, as well as for his encouraging words and fearless independence, for he was a believer in the "Higher Law," and practised it.

The most efficient helpers, or agents we had, were two market women, who lived in Baltimore, one of whom was white, the other "colored."

By some means, they obtained a number of genuine certificates of freedom or passports, which they gave to slaves who wished to escape. These passports were afterwards returned to them, and used again by other fugitives. The generally received opinion, that "all negroes look alike," prevented too close a scrutiny by the officials.

Another most effective worker, was a son of a slaveholder, who lived at Newberne, N. C. Through his agency, the slaves were forwarded, by placing them on vessels engaged in the lumber trade, which plied between Newberne and Philadelphia, and the captains of which had hearts. Having the address of the active members of the Committee, they were enabled to find us, when not accompanied by our agents. Many were sent, by our well known friend, Thomas Garrett, and Samuel D. Burvis, a native of Delaware and a man of marked courage and daring. The fugitives were distributed among the members of the society, but most of them were received at my house in Philadelphia, where by the ingenuity of a carpenter, I caused a place to be constructed underneath a room, which could only be entered by a trap door in the floor. This we deemed perfectly secure, should any search be made by the authorized officials.

THE DORSEY BROTHERS.

Among the hundreds of cases which came under my notice, none excited my interest more deeply than that of four brothers, who came from Frederick county, Md.. and arrived in Philadelphia in the summer of 1836. They were finely developed and handsome young men, reputed to be the children of their master, and after his death, finding themselves slaves, when they had been promised their freedom, they took "French leave," and arrived safely in Philadelphia, under the assumed Christian names of Basil, Thomas, Charles and William; all retaining the surname of Dorsey. I took three of the brothers to my farm in Bucks county—Thomas preferring to live in the city. I succeeded in securing places with some of the neighboring farmers for Charles and William, Basil remaining in my employ. The latter was a married man, having a wife and two children whom he left in Maryland. She was a free woman, and by a previous arrangement with her brother-in-law, likewise free, they were brought to Philadelphia, where I met them and took them to my house.

This man proved afterwards to be a false and treacherous villain. He opened a correspondence with the son of their old master, who bought these men at the settlement of his father's estate and had become their owner. By a well arranged plan, with the assistance of a notorious slave-catcher, they were enabled to surprise and capture Thomas, who was hurried before one of the Judges of the Court and sent back to slavery. He was carried to Baltimore and imprisoned with the view of shipping him thence to the New Orleans market. By the timely efforts of his friends in Philadelphia, money was raised, and the sum of one thousand dollars paid for his freedom. He afterwards became the popular caterer of Philadelphia, and died a few years ago, leaving a handsome competence to his family. Immediately following the the capture of Thomas, by the direction of the brother-in-law, they went to Bristol and secured the services of a constable by the name of Brown, who repaired with the claimant and his friends to Doylestown, and obtained warrants from Judge Fox for the arrest of the three brothers. Basil, while ploughing at some distance from the house, was overpowered after a severe struggle by the slave-holder and his friends, placed in a carriage and taken to Bristol, three miles distant, where he was thrown into a cell used for criminals. I had just returned from the city, and was in the act of eating my supper, when a neighbor's son came in great excitement to tell me that Basil had been carried off. I sprang from the table, and hastening in the direction where I knew the man had been working, learned from the farmers I found assembled there the particulars of this outrage, with the added information that he had been taken to Bristol. Burning with indignation, hatless as I was, I hurried thither, where I found the captors and the captive.

An excited crowd of people was gathered about the market house, whom I addressed and succeeded in enlisting their sympathies in behalf of the poor victim.

After a parley with the slave-holder, it was agreed that we should meet there at seven o'clock in the morning, and start thence for the purpose of appearing before Judge Fox, at Doylestown. Availing myself of the kind offer of a friend, I was driven rapidly home for the purpose of securing the safety of Basil's brothers. I was rejoiced to find them already there. They had heard of Basil's capture and were pursued by a part of those men, led by Brown, who had taken him. These men had halted in a field near my residence, evidently deliberating how to proceed. By my advice, Charles, in whose hands I placed a double barrelled gun heavily charged, walked out in front of the house and defied them. The slave-catchers, thinking doubtless " discretion the better part of valor," instantly departed.   Under the cover of the darkness, I was enabled to convey the two men to my brother Joseph's farm, about two miles distant, and that night, he drove forty miles, and left them in New Jersey at the house of a friend.   There they remained safely, until an opportunity offered to send them to Canada.   The next morning about six o'clock I was on my way to Bristol.   Before reaching there, I met a woman, who informed me that at five o'clock a wagon passed her house, and she heard Basil cry out: " Go tell Mr. Purvis, they are taking me off."   The object of this movement was to deceive me in regard to time and enable them to appear before Judge Fox, and by *ex-parte* testimony have the case closed, and the victim delivered into their custody.   Upon receiving this information I hastened home, and quickly harnessing a fleet trotting horse pursued them.   I left instructions that Basil's wife and children should follow in another carriage.   By good fortune I came upon the *fugitive* kidnappers about four miles from Doylestown, where they had· stopped for breakfast.

I immediately drove to the residence of William H. Johnson, the noted abolitionist, who instantly took hold of the matter, and went out to spread the news far and wide among the anti-slavery people.   I arrived in Doyles-town fully an hour before Basil was brought by his captors, who were of course amazingly surprised to see me.   I at once secured the services of the ablest lawyer in the town, Mr. Ross, the father of the late Judge Ross, who urged the postponement of the case upon Basil's oath of having free papers left in the hands of a friend living in Columbia, Pennsylvania.

Doubtless the judge was deeply impressed by the appearance in the court-room of the delicate and beautiful wife and the young children clinging to the husband and father, who, looking the picture of despair, sat with the evidences in his torn and soiled garments of the terrible conflict through which he had passed.

The claimant obtained legal services in the person of

a Mr. Griffith, a young lawyer. Notwithstanding the urgency of their counsel to have the case immediately decided, the judge postponed it for two weeks.

This was all I expected to obtain. My duty lay clearly before me, and I resolved that no effort should be spared to secure Basil's freedom. With this view I strove to arouse the colored people to rescue him in the event of his being remanded to his captors.

The plan adopted was to assemble in squads about the three leading roads of the town, and use means adequate for the purpose of liberating him. Most fortunately, however, by an unexpected turn of events, a resort to these desperate measures was rendered unnecessary. Desiring to make use of every available means to secure the liberty of this worthy man, I called upon that eminent lawyer and philanthropist, David Paul Brown, and asked him if he would not appear in behalf of the defense. He promptly responded to my request, saying: "I am always ready to defend the liberty of any human being." I then tendered him a fee of fifty dollars, which he at once refused. "I shall not now," he said, "nor have I ever accepted fee or reward, other than the approval of my own conscience, and I respectfully decline receiving your money; I shall be there," and turning to his barber he asked: "Will you get me up so that I can go in the stage coach which leaves at four o'clock in the morning?"

The day of trial came, and the slave-holder was there, bringing with him additional proof in the persons of his neighbors, to swear as to the identity of the man. Armed with the bill of sale, the victory seemed an easy one. The claimant at one time was willing to take five hundred dollars for his slave which we agreed to give, yielding to the earnest entreaty of Basil, although it was in violation of our principles, as we have always denied the right of property in man.

He advanced his price to eight hundred at Doylestown, and when that was agreed to declined taking less than one thousand dollars. Basil then said, "no more offers, if the decision goes against me, I will cut my throat in the Court House, I will not go back to slavery." I applauded his resolution ; horrible as it might be, it seemed better than his return to a living death. Then for the first time I unfolded our plans for his liberation. The case was called promptly at the hour agreed upon, and Mr. Griffith spreading out his bill of sale, and pointing to his witnesses, the friends of the claimant, who had come for the purpose of identifying this man as his property opened his case with an air of the utmost confidence in the result. Mr Brown in his turn quickly arose, and the magnetism of his presence was felt by the crowded court room, nine tenths of whom were doubtless in sympathy with the poor slave. He commenced by saying; "I desire to test this case by raising every objection, and may it please your honor, these gentleman, who hail from *Liberty*, Frederic county, Maryland, are here according to law to secure their 'pound of flesh,' and it is my duty to see that they shall not 'get one drop of blood.' As a preliminary question I demand authority to show that Maryland *is* a slave State."

Mr. Griffith, with a self-satisfied air, remarked : "Why, Mr. Brown, everybody knows Maryland is a slave State."

"Sir, everybody is nobody," was the quick retort of his opponent.

The judge entertained the objection, and Mr. Griffith went out and soon returned with a book containing a compilation of the Laws of Maryland.

The book was not considered authority, and poor Mr. Griffith, confused and disconcerted, requested Mr. Brown to have the lease postponed until afternoon.

"Do you make that request," inquired his adversary, "on the ground of ignorance of the law ?"

Mr. Griffith in an appealing tone said : "Mr. Brown, I am a young man, and this is my first case ; I pray you do not press your objections ; give me some time, for, should I fail in this case, it would be ruinous to my future prospects."

Laying his hand on the young lawyer's shoulder, Mr. Brown replied : " Then, my dear sir, you will have the consolation of having done a good deed, though you did not intend it."

The judge was prompt in dismissing the case, saying that he would not furnish another warrant, but they might secure his re-arrest by obtaining one from a magistrate. Profiting by this suggestion, Griffith and his clients hastily left the court-room. I was equally prompt ; having previously ordered my horse and buggy to be brought in front of the Court House, I took hold of Basil, and hurried him towards the door. In the excitement which prevailed, a colored man, who was outside, seeing me hustling Basil before me, and thinking he had been remanded to slavery, and I was his master, raised a heavy stick, and was about to strike me, when a friendly hand interposed, and saved me from the blow.

We were no sooner seated in the vehicle than the slave-catchers, armed with a magistrate's warrant, came rushing upon us. As they were about to seize the horse, a stroke of the whip on the young and excited animal, caused him to rear and dash ahead. A round of hearty applause from the sympathizing crowd served as an additional impetus to urge us onward. After running the horse about two miles, I came upon a party of colored men who were to assist in rescuing the slave. Resting a short time, I pursued my journey to Philadelphia, a distance of twenty-six miles, and drove directly to my mother's house, where Basil was safely lodged. I afterwards accompanied him to New York, and placed him in the hands of Joshua Leavett, the editor of *The Emancipator*, who sent him to Connecticut to find employment on his father's farm. He remained there some time, and then removed with his family to Northampton, where he worked for Mr. Benson, a brother-in-law of William Lloyd Garrison. Mr. Dorsey died a few years ago, a highly-esteemed and respectable citizen, leaving a widow and a number of children.

Q

Robert Purvis is well known throughout the country as an earnest speaker in the Anti-slavery cause, whose fervid eloquence, when he was warmed up with indignation at the wrongs suffered by the colored race in this country, was like the lightning stroke from heaven. He hated slavery as intensely as he loved liberty.

APPENDIX.

The following letters received by William Still at the *Anti-slavery office* in Philadelphia, illustrate the correspondence between agents.

KIMBERTON, October 28th, 1855.

ESTEEMED FRIEND:—This evening a company of eleven friends reached here, having left their homes on the night of the 26th inst. They came into Wilmington on the morning of the 27th, and left there in the town their two carriages drawn by two horses. They went to Thomas Garrett's by open day-light, and thence were sent hastily onward for fear of pursuit. After remaining all night with one of the Kennett friends, they were brought to Downingtown early in the morning, and thence by daylight to within a short distance of this place.

They came from New Chestertown, within five miles of the place from which the nine lately forwarded came, and left behind them a colored woman who knew of their intended flight and of their intention of passing through Wilmington.

I have been thus particular in my statement, because the case seems to us one of unusual danger. We have separated the company for the present, sending a mother and five children, two of them quite small, in one direction and a husband and wife and three children in another, until I could write to you and get advice; if you have any to give, as to the best method of forwarding them, and assistance pecuniarily, in getting them to Canada. The mother and children we have sent off the usual route and to a place where I do not think they can remain many days.

We shall await hearing from you; H. Kimber will be in the city on Third-day, the 30th, and anything left at 408 Green street, directed to his care, will meet with prompt attention.

Please give me again the direction of Hiram Wilson, and the friend in Elmira, Mr. Jones, I think. If you have heard from any of the nine since their safe arrival, please let us know when you write.

Very respectfullly,

G. A. LEWIS.

Second-day morning, 29th.—The person who took the husband and wife and three lads to E. F. Pennypacker and Lewis Peart, has returned and reports that L. Peart sent three on to Norristown. The women and children detained in this neighborhood, are a very helpless set. Our plan was to assist them as much as possible, and when we get things into the proper train for sending them on, to get the assistance of the husband and wife who have no children, but are uncle and aunt to the woman with five, in taking with them one of the younger children, leaving fewer for the mother. Of the lads, or young men, there is also one who we thought capable of accompanying one of the older girls to one of whom he is paying attention, they told us. Would it not be the best way to get those in Norristown under your own care? It seems to me their being sent on could then be better arranged. This however is only a suggestion.

Hastily Yours,

G. A. LEWIS.

The above party of eleven is described in the account of Eusebius and Sarah P. Barnard.

SCHUYLKILL, 11th mo. 29th, 1855.

DEAR FRIEND, WILLIAM STILL:—Those boys will be along by the last Norristown train to-morrow evening. I think the train leaves Norristown at six o'clock, but of this inform thyself. The boys will be sent to a friend at Norristown, with instructions to assist them in getting seats in the last train that leaves Norristown to-morrow evening. They are two of the eleven who left some time since, and took with them some of their master's horses. I have told them to remain in the cars at Green St., until somebody meets them.

E. F. PENNYPACKER.

SCHUYLKILL, 11th Mo. 7th, 1857.

WILLIAM STILL, RESPECTED FRIEND:—There are three colored friends at my house now, who will reach the city by the Philadelphia and Reading train this evening. Please meet them.

Thine &c.,   E. F. PENNYPACKER.

We have within the past two months, passed forty-three through our hands, transported most of them to Norristown, in our own conveyance.   E. F. P.

WILMINGTON, 3d Mo. 23d, 1856.

DEAR FRIEND, WILLIAM STILL:—Since I wrote thee this morning informing thee of the safe arrival of the eight from Norfolk, Harry Craig has informed me that he has a man from Delaware that he proposes to take along, who arrived since noon. He will take the man, woman and two children from here with him, and the four men will get in at Marcus Hook. Thee may take Harry Craig by the hand as a brother, true to the cause; he is one of the most efficient aids on the Railroad, and worthy of full confidence. May they all be favored to get on safe. The woman and three children are no common stock. I assure thee finer specimens of human-ity are seldom met with. I hope herself and children may be enabled to find her husband who has been absent some years, and the rest of their days be happy together.

I am as ever, thy friend,

THOMAS GARRETT.

WILMINGTON, 10th Mo. 31st, 1857.

ESTEEMED FRIEND, WILLIAM STILL:—I write to inform thee that we have either seventeen or twenty-seven, I am not certain which, of that large gang of God's poor, and I hope they are safe. The man who has them in charge informed me there were twenty-seven safe, and one boy lost during the last night, about fourteen years of age, without shoes; we have felt some anxiety about him, for fear he may be taken up and betray the rest. I have since been informed there are but seventeen, so that at present I cannot tell which is correct. I have several looking out for the lad; they will be kept from Philadelphia for the present. My principal object in writing thee at this time is to inform thee of what one of our constables told me this morning; he told me that a colored man in Philadelphia, who professed to be a great friend of the colored people, was a traitor, that he had been written to by an abolitionist in Baltimore to keep a look out for those slaves that left Cambridge this night week; told him they would be likely to pass through Wilmington on Sixth-day or Seventh-day night, and the colored man in Philadelphia had written to the master of part of them telling him the above, and the master arrived here yesterday in consequence of the information, and told one of our constables the above. The man told the name of the Baltimore writer, which he had forgotten, but declined telling the name of the colored man in Philadelphia. I hope you will be able to find out who he is, and should I be able to learn the name of the Baltimore friend, I will put him on his guard respecting his Philadelphia correspondents.

As ever thy friend, and the friend of humanity, without regard to color or clime.

THOMAS GARRETT.

———

9th Mo. 26th, 1856.

RESPECTED FRIEND, WILLIAM STILL:—I send on to thy care this evening by railroad, five able-bodied men, on their way North ; receive them as the Good Samaritan of old, and oblige thy friend.

THOMAS GARRETT.

RESPECTED FRIEND, WILLIAM STILL :—I now have the pleasure of consigning to thy care four able-bodied, human beings, from North Carolina, and five from Virginia—one of which is a girl twelve or thirteen years of age—the rest all men. After thee has seen and conversed with them, thee can determine what is best to be done with them. I am assured they are such as can take care of themselves. Elijah F. Pennypacker some time since informed me he could find employment in his neighborhood for two or three good hands. I should think those from Carolina would be about as safe in that neighborhood as any place this side of Canada. Wishing our friends a safe trip, I remain thy sincere friend.

THOMAS GARRETT.

After conferring with Harry Craig, we have concluded to send five or six in the cars to-night, and the balance, if those go safe, to-morrow night, or in the steam boat, Second-day morning, directed to the anti-slavery office.

WILMINGTON, 5th Mo. 11th, 1856.

ESTEEMED FRIENDS, M'KIM AND STILL :—I propose sending to-morrow morning by the steam-boat, a woman and child whose husband, I think, went some nine months previous to New Bedford. She was furnished with a free passage by the same line her husband came in. She has been away from the person claiming to be her master some five months, we therefore think there cannot be much risk at present. Those four I wrote thee about, arrived safe up in the neighborhood of Longwood, and Harriet Tubman followed after in the stage yesterday. I shall expect five more from the same neighborhood next trip.

As ever your friend, THOMAS GARRETT.

WILMINGTON, 12th Mo. 1st, 1860.

RESPECTED FRIEND, WILLIAM STILL:—I write to
let thee know that Harriet Tubman is again in these
parts. She arrived last evening from one of the trips
of mercy to God's poor, bringing two men with her as
far as New Castle. I agreed to pay a man last evening
to pilot them on their way to Chester county. The wife
of one of the men, with two or three children, was left
some thirty miles below, and I gave Harriet ten dollars to
hire a man with carriage to take them to Chester county.
She said a man had offered for that sum, to bring
them on. I shall be very uneasy about them, until I
hear they are safe. There is now much more risk on
the road, till they arrive here, than there has been for
several months past, as we find that some poor worthless
wretches are constantly on the look out on two roads,
that they cannot well avoid, especially with carriage;
yet as it is Harriet, who seemed to have had a special
angel to guard her on her journey of mercy, I have
hope.

Thy friend,

THOMAS GARRETT.

N. B.—We hope all will be in Chester county, to-
morrow.

AMERICAN ANTI-SLAVERY SOCIETY.

FIRST CONVENTION OF THE AMERICAN ANTI-SLAVERY
SOCIETY, HELD IN PHILADELPHIA DECEMBER 4TH,
5TH AND 6TH, 1833.—ADOPTION OF CONSTITUTION
AND DECLARATION OF SENTIMENTS.

As the abolitionists, prior to the Rebellion, were vili-
fied, reviled and persecuted, their labors and purposes
misrepresented—sometimes through a want of proper
knowledge, and sometimes through malice—I have
deemed it advisable to insert in this work the *Constitu-*

tion of the American Anti-slavery Society, with the *Declaration of Sentiments* adopted by them as embracing the
principles and motives which actuated them in their
efforts in behalf of the slave.

Local anti-slavery societies had already been formed
in different parts of the Middle and New England
States, and Colonization Societies had been organized,
whose object was the gradual emancipation of slaves and
their colonization in Africa; but WILLIAM LLOYD
GARRISON, editor of *The Liberator*, felt that the time
had come for more united and vigorous action which
could best be set on foot by a call for a National Convention, having for its object *immediate emancipation
without expatriation*. His views met with approval, and
the convention was held in Philadelphia on the fourth,
fifth and sixth of December, 1833. As the time approached the fire of opposition and malice was kindled
through the columns of different newspapers. The
characters and purposes of the leading abolitionists were
grossly misrepresented, and the fury of the mob element
was ready to be aroused in that City of Brotherly Love,
whose commercial interest in the South leagued them in
feeling together.

On the day prior to the convention, several delegates
and others were on board the steamer from New York
to Philadelphia, coming to attend it, and some earnest
discussions were held by different parties respecting it.
One person, addressing himself to Samuel J. May, inquired, " What, sir, are the abolitionists going to do in
Philadelphia ? " Samuel replied that " they intended to
form a National Anti-slavery Society." This elicited
an outpouring of those common-place and oft-reiterated

Q*

objections that had grown familiar to the ear, when William Lloyd Garrison, who was sitting near by, took part in the conversatien, and expounded in a very lucid and admirable manner the doctrines and purposes of those who believed with him that the slaves—the blackest of them—were men, entitled as much as the whitest and most exalted men in the land to their liberty, to a residence here if they chose, and to acquire as much wisdom, as much property, and as high a position as they might.

After a long conversation which attracted as many as could get within hearing, the gentleman said, courteously: "I have been much interested, sir, in what you have said, and in the exceedingly frank and temperate manner in which you have treated the subject. If all abolitionists were like you there would be much less objection to your enterprise. But, sir, depend upon it, that hair-brained, reckless, violent fanatic, Garrison, will damage, if he does not shipwreck any cause." Samuel J. May, stepping forward, said: "Allow me, sir, to introduce to you Mr. Garrison, of whom you entertain so bad an opinion. The gentleman you have been talking with is he." The look of incredulous surprise when this announcement was made can easily be imagined.

When they arrived in the city in the evening, brick bats, rotten eggs, tar and feathers, etc., were being talked of. The mayor and police had notified the Philadelphia abolitionists that they could not protect them in the evening, and therefore their meetings must be held by daylight.

It was deemed advisable, as more likely to insure

peace, that their meetings be presided over by some
prominent citizen of Philadelphia. But none who were
spoken to would accept, and finally Rev. Beriah Green,
of New York, was chosen President.

After drafting and adopting a Constitution, it was
unanimously agreed that it was needful to give to the
country and to the world a fuller declaration of the
sentiments and purposes of the American Anti-slavery
Society than could be embodied in its Constitution, and
which should be to them in their efforts to secure liberty to the slave in this country, what the Declaration
of Independence was to our Revolutionary Fathers in
their efforts to "secure liberty to themselves and their
posterity." It was therefore resolved "that Messrs.
Atlee, Wright, Garrison, Joselyn, Thurston, Sterling,
Wm. Green, Jr., Whittier, Goodell and May, be a committee to draft a Declaration of Principles of the American Anti-slavery Society for publication, to which the
signatures of the members of this Convention shall be
affixed."

This committee, feeling that the work assigned them
ought to be most carefully and thoroughly done,
embodying as far as possible the best thoughts of the
whole Convention, invited about half of their members
to meet them at the office of their chairman, Dr. Edwin
P. Atlee. This was done, each one expressing the sentiment, or announcing the purpose, which he thought
ought to be given in the declaration. After a session
of more than two hours, in which great unanimity prevailed, a sub-committee of three was appointed to prepare a draft of the proposed declaration, consisting of
William L. Garrison, John G. Whittier and Samuel J.

May, and to report next morning at 9 o'clock to the whole committee. As Garrison was looked up to by them as their Coryphæus, they left the writing of the document with him, and retired to meet him at 8 o'clock in the morning. At ten that night he sat down to the work, and when the committee arrived at the appointed hour they found him with shutters closed and lamps still burning, just writing the last paragraph. The declaration was read before the Convention, and carefully considered in all its parts, and with very few changes adopted.

Samuel J. May, in speaking of the earnestness, solemnity and Christian character which marked the proceedings of that Convention throughout, said: "If there was ever a praying assembly I believe that was one."

Of the sixty-one members who signed that Declaration, but two are now living: John G. Whittier and Robert Purvis.

CONSTITUTION OF THE AMERICAN ANTI-SLAVERY SOCIETY.

WHEREAS, The Most High God "hath made of one blood all nations of men to dwell on the face of the earth," and hath commanded them to love their neighbors as themselves; and

WHEREAS, Our national existence is based upon this principle, as recognized in the Declaration of Independence, "that all men are created equal, and that they are endowed by their Creator with certain inalienable rights, among which are life, liberty and the pursuit of happiness; and

WHEREAS, After the lapse of sixty years, since the faith and honor of the American people were pledged to this avowal before Almighty God and the world, nearly one-sixth part of the Nation are held in bondage by their fellow-citizens ; and

WHEREAS, Slavery is contrary to the principles of natural justice of our American form of government and of the Christian religion, and is destructive of the prosperity of the country, while it is endangering the peace, union and liberties of the States ; and

WHEREAS, We believe it the duty and interest of the masters immediately to emancipate their slaves, and that no scheme of expatriation, either voluntary or by expulsion, can remove this great and increasing evil; and

WHEREAS, We believe that it is practicable, by appeals to the consciences, hearts and interests of the people, to awaken a public sentiment throughout the Nation that will be opposed to the continuance of slavery in any part of the republic, and by effecting the speedy abolition of slavery, prevent a general convulsion ; and

WHEREAS, We believe we owe it to the oppressed, to our fellow-citizens who hold slaves, to our whole country, to posterity, and to God, to do all that is lawfully in our power to bring about the extinction of slavery ; we do hereby agree, with a prayerful reliance on the Divine aid, to form ourselves into a society, to be governed by the following constitution:

ARTICLE I.—This society shall be called the AMERICAN ANTI-SLAVERY SOCIETY.

ARTICLE II.—The objects of this society are the entire abolition of slavery in the United States. While it admits that each State in which slavery exists has by the Constitution of the United States the exclusive right to legislate in regard to its abolition in said State, it shall aim to convince all our fellow-citizens, by arguments addressed to their understandings and consciences, that slave-holding is a henious crime in the sight of God, and that the duty, safety and best interests of all concerned, require its immediate abandonment, without expatriation. This society will also endeavor, in a constitutional way, to influence Congress to put an end to the domestic slave-trade, and to abolish slavery in all those portions of our common country which come under its control, especially in the District of Columbia, and likewise to prevent the extension of it to any State that may be hereafter admitted to the Union.

ARTICLE III.—This society shall aim to elevate the character and condition of the people of color by encouraging their intellectual, moral and religious improvement, and by removing public prejudice, that thus they may, according to their intellectual and moral worth, share an equality with the whites of civil and religious privileges, but this society will never in any way countenance the oppressed in vindicating their rights by resorting to physical force.

These three articles give the object of the society. The seven articles which follow relate to the duties of officers only, and are therefore omitted.

DECLARATION OF SENTIMENTS OF THE AMERICAN ANTI-SLAVERY SOCIETY.

More than fifty-seven years have elapsed since a band of patriots convened in this place to devise measures for the deliverence of this country from a foreign yoke. The corner-stone upon which they founded the TEMPLE OF FREEDOM was broadly this, "that all men are created equal, and they are endowed by their Creator with certain unalienable rights; that among these are life, LIBERTY, and the pursuit of happiness." At the sound of their trumpet call three millions of people rose up as from the sleep of death, and rushed to the strife of blood, deeming it more desirable to die instantly as freemen, than desirable to live one hour as slaves.

They were few in number—poor in resources; but the honest conviction that TRUTH, JUSTICE and RIGHT were on their side, made them invincible.

We have met together for the achievement of an enterprise, without which that of our fathers is incomplete; and which, from its magnitude, solemnity, and probable results upon the destiny of the world, as far as transcends theirs as moral truth does physical force.

In purity of motive, in earnestness of zeal, in decision of purpose, in intrepidity of action, in steadfastness of faith, in sincerity of spirit, we would not be inferior to them.

Their principles led them to wage war against their oppressors, and to spill human blood like water, in order to be free. *Ours* forbid the doing of evil that good may come, and lead us to reject, and to entreat the oppressed to reject the use of all carnal weapons for deliverance from bondage; relying solely upon those which are spiritual and mighty through God · to the pulling down of strongholds.

Their measures were spiritual resistance—the marshalling in arms—the hostile array—the mortal encounter. *Ours* shall be such only as the opposition of moral purity to moral corruption—the destruction of error by the potency of truth—the overthrow of prejudice by the power of love—and the abolition of slavery by the spirit of repentence.

Their grievences, great as they were, were trifling in comparison with the wrongs and sufferings of those for whom we plead. Our fathers were never slaves—never bought and sold like cattle—never shut out from the light of knowledge and religion—never subjected to the lash of brutal taskmasters.

But those for whose emancipation we are striving—constituting at the present time at least one-sixth part of our countrymen—are recognized by the law, and treated by their fellow-beings as marketable commodities, as goods and chattels, as brute beasts; are plundered daily of the fruits of their toil without redress—really enjoying no constitutional nor legal protection from licentious and murderous outrages upon their persons; are ruthlessly torn asunder; the tender babe from the arms of its frantic mother, the heart-broken wife from her weeping husband, at the caprice or pleasure of irresponsible tyrants. For the crime of having a dark complexion they suffer the pangs of hunger, the infliction of stripes and the ignominy of brutal servitude. They are kept in heathenish darkness by laws expressly enacted to make their instruction a criminal offense.

These are the prominent circumstances in the condition of more than two millions of our people, the proof of which may be found in thousands of indisputable facts, and in the laws of the slave-holding States.

Hence we maintain that in view of the civil and religious privileges of this Nation, the guilt of its oppression is unequalled by any other on the face of the earth; and therefore that it is bound to repent, to undo the heavy burdens, to break every yoke and to let the oppressed go free.

We further maintain that no man has a right to enslave or imbrute his brother; to hold or acknowledge him for one moment as a piece of merchandise, to keep back his hire by fraud, or to brutalize his mind by denying him the means of intellectual, social and moral improvement.

The right to enjoy liberty is inalienable; to invade it is to usurp the prerogative of Jehovah. Every man has a right to his own body; to the products of his own labor; to the protection of law, and to the common advantages of society. It is piracy to buy or steal a native African, and subject him to servitude. Surely the sin is as great to enslave an AMERICAN as an AFRICAN.

Therefore we believe and affirm, that there is no difference *in principle* between the African slave-trade and the American slavery.

That every American citizen who retains a human being in involuntary bondage as his property is, according to Scripture, (Ex. xxi. 16) a MAN STEALER.

That the slaves ought instantly to be set free, and brought under the protection of the law.

That if they lived from the time of Pharoah down to the present period, and had been entailed through successive generations, their right to be free could never have been alienated, but their claims would have constantly risen in solemnity.

That all those laws now in force, admitting the right of slavery, are, therefore, before God utterly null and void, being an audacious usurpation of the Divine prerogative; a daring infringement on the laws of nature, a base overthrow of the very foundations of the social compact, a complete extinction of all relations, endearments, and obligations of mankind, and a presumptuous transgression of all holy commandments; and, that, therefore they ought instantly to be abrogated.

We further believe and affirm—That all persons of color who possess the qualifications which are demanded of others, ought to be admitted forthwith to the enjoyment of the same privileges, and the exercise of the same prerogatives as others; and that the paths of preferment, of wealth and of intelligence should be opened as widely to them as to persons of a white complexion.

We maintain that no compensation should be given to the planters emancipating the slaves.

Because it would be a surrender of the great fundamental principle that man should not hold property in man;

Because SLAVERY IS A CRIME, AND THEREFORE IS NOT AN ARTICLE TO BE SOLD.

Because the holders of slaves are not the just proprietors of what they claim; freeing the slaves is not depriving them of property, but restoring it to its rightful owners; it is not wronging the master, but righting the slave—restoring him to himself.

Because immediate and general emancipation would only destroy nominal, not real property: it would not amputate a limb or break a bone of the slaves, but by infusing motives into their breasts, would make them doubly valuable to the masters as free laborers, and

Because, if compensation is to be given at all, it should be given to the outraged and guiltless slaves and not to those who have plundered and abused them.

We regard as delusive, cruel and dangerous any scheme of expatriation which pretends to aid, either directly or indirectly, in the emancipation of the slaves,

or to be a substitute for the immediate and total abolition of slavery.

We fully and unanimously recognize the sovereignty
of each State to legislate exclusively on the subject of
the slavery which is tolerated within its limits; we concede that congress, *under the present national compact*, has
no right to interfere with any of the slave States in relation to this momentous subject.

But we maintain that Congress has a right, and is
solemnly bound, to suppress the domestic slave trade
between the several States, and to abolish slavery in
those portions of our territory which the Constitution
has placed under its exclusive jurisdiction.

We also maintain that there are at the present time
the highest obligations resting upon the people of the
free States to remove slavery by moral and political
action as prescribed in the Constitution of the United
States.

They are now living under pledge of their tremen-
dous physical force, to fasten the galling fetters of
tyranny upon the limbs of millions in the Southern
States; they are liable to be called at any moment to
suppress a general insurrection of the slaves; they author-
ize the slave-owner to vote on three-fifths of his slaves as
property, and thus enable him to perpetuate his oppression; they support a standing army at the South for its
protection; and they seize the slave who has escaped
into their territories, and send him back to be tortured
by an enraged master, or a brutal driver. This relation
to slavery is criminal, and full of danger, and IT MUST
BE BROKEN UP.

These are our views and principles; these our designs
and measures. With entire confidence in the over-
ruling justice of God, we plant ourselves upon the Declaration of our Independence, and the truth of Divine
revelation as upon the Everlasting Rock.

We shall organize Anti-slavery Societies, if possible,
in every city, town and village in our land.

We shall send forth agents to lift up their voice of
remonstrance, of warning, of entreaty, of rebuke.

We shall circulate, unsparingly, and extensively, anti-slavery tracts and periodicals.

We shall enlist the pulpit and the press in the cause of the suffering and the dumb.

We shall aim at a purification of the churches from all participation in the guilt of slavery.

We shall encourage the labor of freemen rather than that of slaves, by giving a preference to their productions, and

We shall spare no exertions nor means to bring the whole nation to speedy repentence.

Our trust for victory is solely in God. *We* may be personally defeated, but our principles never. TRUTH, JUSTICE, REASON, HUMANITY, must and will gloriously triumph. Already a host is coming up to the help of the Lord against the mighty, and the prospect before us is full of encouragement.

Submitting this DECLARATION to the candid examination of the people of this country, and of the friends of liberty throughout the world, we hereby affix our signatures to it, pledging ourselves that under the guidance and by the help of Almighty God we will do all that in us lies, consistently with this Declaration of our principles, to overthrow the most execrable system of slavery that has ever been witnessed upon the earth—to deliver our land from its deadliest curse—to wipe out the foulest stain which rests upon our national escutcheon—and to secure to the colored population of the United States all the rights and privileges which belong to them as men and as Americans—come what may to our persons, our interests, or our reputation—whether we live to witness the triumph of LIBERTY, JUSTICE and HUMANITY, or perish untimely as martyrs in this great, benevolent and holy cause.

Done at Philadelphia, the sixth day of December, A. D. 1833.

[Signed.]

MAINE.

David Thurston,
Nathan Winslow,
Joseph Southwick,
James Frederick Otis,
Isaac Winslow.

NEW HAMPSHIRE.

David Campbell.

VERMONT.

Orson S. Murray.

MASSACHUSETTS.

Daniel S. Southmayd,
Effingham L. Capron,
Joshua Coffin,
Amos A. Phelps,
John G. Whittier,
Horace P. Wakefield,
James B. Barbadoes,
David T. Kimball, Jr.,
Daniel E. Jewett,
John R. Campbell,
Nathaniel Southard,
Arnold Buffum,
William L. Garrison.

RHODE ISLAND.

John Prentice,
George W. Benson,
Ray Potter.

CONNECTICUT.

Samuel J. May.
Alpheus Kingsley,
Edwin A. Stillman,
Simeon S. Jocelyn,
Robert B. Hall.

NEW YORK.

Beriah Greene, Jr.,
Lewis Tappan,
John Rankin,
William Greene, Jr.,
Abm. L. Cox,
William Goodell,
Elizur Wright, Jr..
Charles W. Denison,
John Frost.

NEW JERSEY.

Jonathan Parkhurst,
Chalkley Gillingham,
John McCullough,
James White.

PENNSYLVANIA.

Evan Lewis,
Edwin A. Atlee,
Robert Purvis,
Jas. McCrummill,
Thomas Shipley,
Bartholomew Fussell,
David Jones,
Enoch Mack,
James McKim,
Aaron Vickers,
James Loughhead,
Edwin P. Atlee,
Thomas Whitson,
John R. Sleeper,
John Sharp, Jr.,
James Mott.

OHIO.

John M. Sterling,
Milton Sutliff,
Levi Sutliff.

CLAUSE IN THE CONSTITUTION OF THE UNITED STATES.

FUGITIVE SLAVE LAW.

ARTICLE IV, SECTION 2.—No person held to service or labor in our State, under the laws thereof, escaping into another, shall, in consequence of any law or regulation therein, be discharged from such service or labor, but shall be delivered up on claim of the party to whom such service or labor may be due.

There was much wrangling over the adoption of this clause in the Constitution which its framers were devising for a Government whose professed purpose was to guarantee liberty and protection to its people. But the idea of extending the blessings of that liberty to the African race then held as slaves in this country, did not seem to enter the minds of some of those patriotic fathers. It will, however, be observed that the terms *slave* and *slavery* were carefully omitted, and the term *service or labor* used instead.

On the 18th of September, 1850, Congress passed the law known as the "Fugitive Slave Law of 1850."

It was pretty definitely understood by the friends of that bill in Congress, that if they passed it, Zachary Taylor, then President, would veto it. Before it was voted upon General Taylor died, and Millard Fillmore, who succeeded him, when the bill passed Congress, affixed his signature to it, and it became a law.

THE FUGITIVE SLAVE LAW.

THOSE PARTS WHICH RELATE TO THE CAPTURE AND RETURN OF SLAVES.

SECTION 3.—*And be it further enacted,* That the Circuit Courts of the United States, and the Superior Courts of each organized Territory of the United States, shall from time to time enlarge the number of Commissioners, with a view to afford reasonable facilities to reclaim fugitives from labor, and to the prompt discharge of the duties imposed by this act.

SECTION 4.—*And be it further enacted,* That the Commissioners above named shall have concurrent jurisdiction with the Judges of the Circuit and District Courts of the United States, in their respective circuits and districts within the several States, and the Judges of the Superior Courts of the Territories, severally and collectively, in term-time and vacation ; and shall grant certificates to such claimants, upon satisfactory proof being made, with authority to take and remove such fugitives from service or labor, under the restrictions herein contained, to the State or Territory from which such persons may have escaped or fled.

SECTION 5.—*And be it further enacted,* That it shall be the duty of all marshals and deputy marshals to obey and execute all warrants and preceps issued under the provisions of this act when to them directed ; and should any marshal or deputy marshal refuse to receive such warrant or other process when tendered, or to use all proper means diligently to execute the same, he shall on conviction thereof be fined in the sum of one thousand dollars to the use of such claimant, on the motion of such claimant, by the Circuit or District Court for the district of such marshal, and after arrest of such fugitives by such marshal, or his deputy, or whilst at any time in his custody under the provisions of this act should such fugitive escape, whether with or without the assent of such marshal or his deputy, such marshal shall be liable on his official bond to be prosecuted for the benefit of such claimant, for the full value of the service or labor of said fugitive in the State, Territory or District whence he escaped ; and the better to enable the said Commissioners, when thus appointed, to execute their duties faithfully and efficiently, in conformity with the requirements of the Constitution of the United States, and of this act, they are hereby authorized and empowered within their counties respectively, to appoint in writing under their hands, any one or more suitable persons, from time to time, to execute all such warrants and other process as may be issued by them in the lawful performance of their respective duties; with authority to such Commissioners or the persons to be appointed by them to execute process as aforesaid, to summon or call to their aid the bystanders or *posse comitatus* of the proper county, when necessary to insure a faithful observance of the clause of the Constitution referred to, in conformity with the provision of this act, and all good citizens are commanded to aid and assist in the prompt and efficient execution of this law, whenever their services may be required, as aforesaid for that purpose, and said warrants shall run and be executed by said officers anywhere in the State, within which they are issued.

SECTION 6.—*And be it further enacted*, That when a person held to service or labor in any State or Territory in the United States has heretofore or shall hereafter escape into any other State or Territory of the United States, the person or persons to whom such service or labor may be due, or his, her, or their agent or attorney, duly authorized, by power of attorney, in writing, acknowledged and certified under the seal of some legal officer or Court of the State or Territory in which the same may be executed, may pursue and reclaim such fugitive person, either by procuring a warrant from some one of the courts, Judges or Commissioners as aforesaid, of the proper circuit, district or county for the apprehension of such fugitive from service or labor, or by seizing and arresting such fugitive, where the same can be done without process, and by taking, or causing such persons to be taken, forthwith before such court, Judge or Commissioner, whose duty it shall be to hear and determine the case of such claimant in a summary manner, and upon satisfactory proof being made, by disposition or affidavit, in writing, to be certified to such court, Judge or Commissioner, or by other satisfactory testimony, duly taken and certified by some court, magistrate, justice of the peace, or other legal officer, authorized to administer an oath and take deposition under the laws of the State or Territory from which such person owing service or labor may have escaped, with a certificate of such magistracy or other authority, as aforesaid, with the seal of the proper court or officer thereto attached, which seal shall be sufficient to establish the competency of the proof, and with proof also by affidavit of the identity of the person whose service or labor is claimed to be due as aforesaid, that the person so arrested does in fact owe sevice or labor to the person or persons claiming him or her, in the State or Territory from which such fugitive may have escaped as aforesaid, and that said person escaped, to make out and deliver to such claimant, his or her agent or attorney, a certificate setting forth the substantial facts as to the service or labor due from such fugitive to the claimant, and of his or her escape from the State and Territory in which he or she was arrested, with authority to such claimant, or his or her agent or attorney, to use such reasonable force and restraint, as may be necessary, under the circumstances of the case, to take and remove such fugitive person back to the State or Territory whence he or she may have escaped as aforesaid. In no trial or hearing under this act shall the testimony of such alleged fugitive be admitted in evidence, and the certificates in this and the first section mentioned shall be conclusive of the right of the person or persons in whose favor granted, to remove such fugitive to the State or Territory from which he escaped, and shall prevent all molestation of such person or persons by any process issued by any court, judge, magistrate or other person whomsoever.

SECTION 7.—*And be it further enacted*, That any person who shall knowingly and willfully obstruct, hinder, or prevent such claimant, his agent or attorney, or any person or persons lawfully assisting him, her, or them, from arresting such a fugitive from service or labor, either with or without process, as aforesaid; or shall rescue, or attempt to rescue, such fugitive from service or labor, from the custody of such claimant, his or her agent or attorney, or other person or persons lawfully assisting as aforesaid, when so arrested, pursuant to the authority herein given and declared; or shall aid, abet, or assist such person so owing service or labor as aforesaid, directly or indirectly, to escape from such claimant, his agent or attorney, or other person or persons legally authorized as aforesaid; or shall harbor or conceal such fugitive, so as to prevent the discovery and arrest of such person, after notice or knowledge of the fact that such person was a fugitive from labor or service as aforesaid, shall for either of said offences, be subject to a fine not exceeding one thousand dollars, and imprisonment not exceeding six months, by indictment and conviction before the District Court of the United States for the district in which such offense may have been committed, or before the proper court of criminal jurisdiction, if committed within any one of the organized Territories of the United States; and shall moreover forfeit and pay, by way of civil damages to the party, injured by such illegal conduct, the sum of one thousand dollars for each fugitive so lost as aforesaid, to be recovered by action of debt, in any of the District or Territorial Courts as aforesaid, within whose jurisdiction the said offence may have been committed.

SECTION 8.—*And be it further enacted*, That the marshals, their deputies, and the clerks of the said District and Territorial Courts, shall be paid for their services the like fees as may be allowed to them for similar services in other cases; and where such services are rendered exclusively in the arrest, custody, and delivery of the fugitive to the claimant, his or her agent or attorney, or where such supposed fugitive may be discharged out of custody for the want of sufficient proof as aforesaid, then such fees are to be paid in the whole by such claimant, his agent or attorney, and in all cases where the proceedings are before a commissioner, he shall be

R

entitled to a fee of ten dollars in full for his services in
each case, upon the delivery of the said certificate to the
claimant, his or her agent or attorney; or a fee of five
dollars in cases where the proof shall not in the opinion
of such commissioner warrant such certificate and delivery, inclusive of all services incident to such arrest and
examination, to be paid, in either case, by the claimant,
his or her agent or attorney. The person or persons
authorized to execute the process to be issued by such
commissioners for the arrest and detention of fugitives
from service or labor as aforesaid, shall be entitled to a
fee of five dollars each for each person he or they may
arrest and take before any such commissioner as aforesaid, at the instance and request of such claimant, with
such other fees as may be deemed reasonable by such
commission for such other additional services as may be
necessarily performed by him or them; such as attending at the examination, keeping the fugitive in custody,
and providing him with food and lodging during his
detention, and until the final determination of such
commissioner; and in general for performing such other
duties as may be required by such claimant, his or her
attorney or agent, or commissioner in the premises, such
fees to be made up in conformity with the fees usually
charged by the officers of the courts of justice within the
proper district or county, as near as may be practicable,
and paid by such claimant, their agents or attorneys,
whether such fugitives from service or labor be ordered
to be delivered to such claimants by the final determination of such commissioners or not.

SECTION 9.—*And be it further enacted*, That upon
affidavit made by the claimant of such fugitive, his or
her agent or attorney, after such certificate has been
issued, that he has reason to apprehend that such fugitive will be rescued by force from his or their possession
before he can be taken beyond the limits of the State in
which the arrest is made, it shall be the duty of the
officer making the arrest to retain such fugitive in his
custody, and to remove him to the State whence he

fled, and there to deliver him to said claimant, his agent, or attorney. And to this end, the officer aforesaid is hereby authorized and required to employ so many persons as he may deem necessary to overcome such force, and to retain them in his service so long as circumstances may require. The said officer and his assistants, while so employed, to receive the same compensation, and to be allowed the same expenses as are now allowed by law for transportation of criminals, to be certified by the judge of the district within which the arrest is made, and paid out of the Treasury of the United States.

LINCOLN'S CAUTION AND CONSCIENTIOUSNESS.—LETTER TO HORACE GREELEY.—VISIT FROM DELEGATION OF MINISTERS.—PROCLAMATION OF EMANCIPATION.—EXTRACTS FROM MESSAGES IN REFERENCE TO IT.—AMENDMENTS ABOLISHING AND PROHIBITING SLAVERY.

During the early period of the war President Lincoln was severely and mercilessly criticised, not only by his political opponents, for the measures he had taken to crush the rebellion, but by his impetuous anti-slavery friends, who thought him too tardy in availing himself of an opportunity to declare freedom to the slave, which they claimed was then within his power, and which it was his duty to enforce.

Although the Southern States were in rebellion, and had seceded when he assumed the duties of President of the United States, he felt that he was conscientiously bound to preserve the union of States, if possible, by the best means he could employ, according to the Constitution, and in fulfillment of the following *oath of office*:

" I do solemnly swear (or affirm) that I will faithfully

execute the office of President of the United States, and will, to the best of my ability, preserve, protect and defend the Constitution of the United States."

He had neither time nor inclination to harrow up his mind by considering the many hostile letters and articles in newspapers, aimed like so many arrows at him and his policy, preferring to direct his attention to acquiring a full knowledge of the entire situation of the whole country, and in accordance with that knowledge to adapt the best means to the best ends.

Sitting upon the highest place in the National Government, he had a better opportunity of seeing and knowing the varied condition of affairs, and what movements to make, than many in lower positions who presumed to knew more.

> " His soul, whose vision, place nor power could dim
> Moved slow and reverently, that he might scan,
> And not mistake the part assigned to him
> In the Creator's plan."

He was always looking toward emancipation, and was ready to issue such a proclamation when he felt that it would be sustained by the army and by the States not then in rebellion. Hence he said : " *Agitate* the question. Get the people ready. AGITATE, AGITATE." But Horace Greeley, growing impatient, published a letter in the New York *Tribune*, directed to Lincoln, to which he made the following reply :

"EXECUTIVE MANSION,
WASHINGTON, Aug. 22, 1862. }

HON. HORACE GREELEY—*Dear Sir :* I have just read yours of the 19th addressed to myself through the *New York Tribune.* If there be in it any statements or assumptions of fact which I may know to be erroneous, I do not now and here controvert them. If there be in it any inferences which I may believe to be falsely drawn, I do not now and here argue against them. If there be perceptible in it an impatient and dictatorial tone, I waive it in deference to an old friend, whose heart I have always supposed to be right.

"As to the policy I 'seem to be pursuing,' as you say, I have not meant to leave any one in doubt.

" I would save the Union. I would save it the shortest way under the Constitution. The sooner the National authority can be restored, the nearer the Union will be 'the Union as it was.' If there be those who would not save the Union unless they could at the same time *save* Slavery, I do not agree with them. If there be those who would not save the Union unless they could at the same time *destroy* Slavery, I do not agree with them. My paramount object in this struggle *is* to save the Union, and is *not* to save or destroy Slavery. If I could save the Union without freeing *any* slave, I would do it, and if I could do it by freeing *all* the slaves I would do it, and if I could do it by freeing some and leaving others alone I would also do that. What I do about Slavery and the colored race, I do because I believe it helps to save the Union, and what I forbear, I forbear because I do *not* believe it would save the Union. I shall do *less* whenever I shall believe what I am doing hurts the cause, and I shall do *more* whenever I shall believe doing more will help the cause. I shall try to correct errors when shown to be errors, and I shall adopt new views so fast as they shall appear to be true views. I have here stated my purpose according to my view of *'official* duty,' and I intend no modification of my oft-expressed *personal* wish that all men, everywhere, could be free.

" Yours, A. LINCOLN."

When Horace Greeley published his letter he was ignorant of the fact that Lincoln had already matured a definite policy of emancipation, ready to be announced at a suitable moment.

R*

He was waited upon some time after that by a church delegation from Chicago, to urge upon him the necessity, and to impress upon him that it was his duty to issue a proclamation of emancipation. It was Lincoln's policy in all cases before taking an important and advanced step, to weigh the arguments on both sides, and the chances of failure or success, and to act accordingly. He therefore presented the adverse arguments and facts which had all along confronted him, especially in the army, and in the border States, and asked them to confute those arguments, and to show to him that the way was clear, that the obstacles he had shown to be in the way would no longer be a barrier, but that the mass of the people would support the proclamation. His object was to draw from them any new thought, or any fact he had not himself considered. But he discovered they had nothing new to give him, that they did not know all the opposition he had to contend with, that their chief line of argument was the oft-reiterated declaration that it was clearly his duty to abolish, by proclamation, the institution of slavery. He listened to their advice, but gave them no satisfaction as to what he would do, and they left him, saying there was no use in pleading further with him. One of them, however, returned immediately and said : " Mr. Lincoln, I cannot leave you yet; I have a message *direct from God to you, and that is that you set his people free.*"

"Well, now," said Lincoln, " if God intended that message to come ' direct to me,' why didn't he send it to me directly, instead of sending it away around by that terribly wicked city of Chicago ? " The minister turned and left, and thus ended the visit.

Little did they know that in his coat-pocket was then folded that important document which in a short time was to go out upon the wings of the American press, proclaiming freedom to four millions of slaves whose sweat had bedewed American soil.

On the twenty-second day of September, 1862, he issued that memorable PROCLAMATION, that " on the first day of January, in the year of our Lord one thousand eight hundred and sixty-three, all persons held as slaves within any State, or any designated part of a State, the people whereof shall then be in rebellion against the United States, SHALL BE THEN, THENCE-FORWARD, AND FOREVER FREE."

On the first of January, 1863, he issued the following Proclamation, which was to supplement that of September, 1862, and which crowned the Temple of American Liberty with the completeness of its architectural design:

WHEREAS, On the twenty-second day of September, in the year of our Lord, one thousand eight hundred and sixty-two, a proclamation was issued by the President of the United States containing, among other things, the following, to wit:

That on the first day of January, in the year of our Lord, one thousand eight hundred and sixty-three, all persons held as slaves within any State, or any designated part of a State, the people whereof shall then be in rebellion against the United States, shall be thenceforward and forever free, and the Executive Government of the United States, including the military and naval authority thereof, will recognize and maintain the freedom of such persons, or any of them, in any efforts they may make for their actual freedom.

That the Executive will on the first day of January aforesaid, by proclamation, designate the States and parts of States, if any, in which the people thereof respectively shall then be in rebellion against the United States, and the fact that any State, or the people thereof, shall on that day be in good faith represented in the Congress of the United States by members, chosen therefor at elections, wherein a majority of the qualified voters of such State shall have participated shall, in the absence of strong countervailing testimony, be deemed conclusive evidence that such State and the people thereof are not then in rebellion against the United States.

" Now, therefore, I Abraham Lincoln, President of the United States, by virtue of the power in me vested as Commander-in-Chief of the Army and Navy of the United States, in time of actual armed rebellion against the authority and Government of the United States, and as a fit and necessary war measure for repressing said rebellion, do, on this First day of January, in the year of our Lord one thousand eight hundred and sixty-three, and in accordance with my purpose so to do, publicly proclaimed for the full period of one hundred days from the day of the first above-mentioned order, designate as the States and parts of States, wherein the people thereof respectively are this day in rebellion against the United States, the following, to wit : Arkansas, Texas, Louisiana, except the parishes of St. Bernard, Plaquemines, Jefferson, St. John, St. Charles, St. James, Ascension, Assumption, Terre Bonne, Lafourche, St. Mary, St. Martin, and Orleans, including the city of New Orleans, Mississippi, Alabama, Florida, Georgia, South Carolina, North Carolina, and Virginia except the forty-eight counties designated as West Virginia, and also the counties of Berkely, Accomac, Northampton, Elizabeth City, York, Princess, Ann and Norfolk, including the cities of Norfolk and Portsmouth, and which excepted parts are, for the present, left precisely as if this proclamation were not issued.

"And by virtue of the power and for the purpose aforesaid, I do order and declare, that all persons held as slaves within said designated States and parts of

States, are and henceforward shall be free; and that
the Executive Government of the United States, in-
including the military and naval authorities thereof,
will recognize and maintain the freedom of said persons.

"And I hereby enjoin upon the people so declared to
be free, to abstain from all violence, unless in necessary
self-defense, and I recommend to them, that in all
cases, when allowed, they labor faithfully for reasonable wages.

"And I further declare and make known that such
persons of suitable condition will be received into
armed service of the United States, to garrison forts,
positions, stations, and other places, and to man vessels
of all sorts in said service.

"And upon this, sincerely believed to be an act of
justice, warranted by the Constitution upon military
necessity I invoke the considerate judgment of mankind
and the gracious favor of Almighty God."

At the close of the annual message to Congress,
December, 1864, Lincoln said:

" I repeat the declaration made a year ago, that while
I remain in my present position, I shall not attempt to
retract or modify the Emancipation Proclamation, nor
shall I return to slavery any person who is free by the
terms of that Proclamation or by any of the Acts of
Congress.

" If the people should, by whatever mode, or means,
make it an Executive duty to re-enslave such persons,
another, and not I, must be the instrument to perform it."

In his second Inaugural Address, speaking of the
North and the South, and the continuance of the war,
he said:

" Both read the same Bible, and pray to the same
God, and each invokes His aid against the other. It
may seem strange that any man should dare to ask a
just God's assistance in wringing his bread from the
sweat of other men's faces. But let us judge not that
we be not judged."

    *   *   *   *   *   *

" Fondly do we hope, fervently do we pray that this mighty scourge of war may speedily pass away. Yet if God wills that it continue until all the wealth piled by the bondsman's two hundred and fifty years of unrequited toil shall be sunk, and until every drop of blood drawn by the lash shall be paid by another drawn by the sword as was said three thousand years ago, so still it must be said that the judgments of the Lord are true and righteous altogether.

With malice towards none, with charity for all, with firmness in the right as God gives us to see the right, let us strive on to finish the work we are in, to bind up the nation's wounds, to care for him who shall have borne the battle, and for his widow and his orphans, to do all which may achieve and cherish a just and lasting peace among ourselves and with all nations."

AMENDMENTS TO THE CONSTITUTION, ABOLISHING AND PROHIBITING SLAVERY.

XIIITH AMENDMENT, PASSED 1865.

SECTION 1.—Neither slavery nor involuntary servitude, except as a punishment for crime, whereof the party shall have been duly convicted shall exist within the United States, or any place subject to their jurisdiction.

XIVTH AMENDMENT.

SECTION 1.—All persons born or naturalized in the United States, and subject to the jurisdiction thereof, are citizens of the United States, and of the State wherein they reside. No State shall make or enforce any law which shall abridge the privileges or immunities of citizens of the United States. Nor shall any State deprive any person of life, liberty or property without due process of law, nor deny to any person within its jurisdiction the equal protection of the laws.

XVTH AMENDMENT.

SECTION 1. The right of citizens of the Uniten States to vote shall not be denied or abridged by the United

States or by any State, on account of race, color, or previous condition of servitude.

These Amendments were ratified by the requisite number of States according to the requirements of the Constitution, and certified to as follows:

Secretary Seward certified to the ratification of the 13th Amendment on December 18th, 1865; and to that of the 14th Amendment, July 20th, 1868.

Secretary Fish certified to the ratification of the 15th Amendment March 30th, 1870. On the same day Gen. Grant sent a message to Congress, in which he said, " I consider the adoption of the 15th Amendment to the Constituton completes the greatest civil change, and constitutes the most important event that has occurred since the nation came into life."

The adoption of an Amendment dates from the certification of the Secretary of State.

"It is the Lord's doings and marvelous in our eyes."

THE END.

INDEX.

Aaron, Rev. Samuel_____30, 219.
Adams, John Quincy_____102.
Adamson, Charles_____198, 212.
Adamson, Mary C._____212.
Agnew, Allen_____32.
Agnew, Maria_____32.
Allen, Abram_____187.
Ames, Charles G._____145.
Ashmead, J. W._____130.

Badaracka, Dido_____353.
Baer, William_____70, 90, 98, 127.
Barber, Robert_____27, 47.
Barnard, Eusebius_____33, 131, 141, 282, 288, 297.
Barnard, Eusebius R._____282, 290, 293.
Barnard, Joseph_____288.
Barnard, Richard_____288.
Barnard, Richard M._____288.
Barnard, Sarah D._____33, 288.
Barnard, Sarah M._____33, 138, 141, 297.
Barnard, Sarah P._____289, 297.
Barnard, Simon_____33, 185, 253, 276, 282, 285, 301, 326, 342.
Barnard, William_____33, 253, 282, 289, 297, 301, 304.
Bayard, James A._____239.
Bell, Sally_____28.
Bell, Thomas S._____196, 334.
Benezet, Anthony_____143.
Bessick, Thomas_____47.
Birdsall, Sylvester_____268.
Blunson, Samuel_____27.
Bonsall, Abraham_____90, 99, 100, 245.
Bonsall, Thomas_____30, 57, 73, 78, 90, 100, 101, 102, 103, 105, 138, 193.
Bodey, Jacob_____224.
Bond, Samuel_____233.
Boston, Abraham_____56.
Boude, Gen. Thomas_____27, 28.
Bradburn, George_____187.
Brinton, Caleb_____95, 132.
Brinton, Joseph_____33.
Brinton, Joshua_____80, 89, 132.

8

Brinton, Samuel_____99.
Brooks, Isaac_____29.
Brosius, Mahlon_____810.
Brosius, William_____312.
Brown, David Paul_____359, 360.
Brown, Ellwood_____77.
Brown, John_____167.
Brown, John (colored)_____323, 337.
Burleigh, Charles C.____64, 176, 205, 235, 260, 264, 278, 282, 283, 287, 340.
Burleigh, Cyrus_____287.
Burleigh, Gertrude K._____191, 204.
Burleigh, William_____287.
Burrowes, Dr. Francis S._____61.
Burvis, Samuel D._____355.
Bushong, Henry_____71, 73, 74, 75, 233.
Bushong, Jacob_____67, 71, 72, 75, 104.
Bushong, John_____75.

Cain, Dr. Augustus W._____33, 99, 126.
Cain, John_____99.
Carter, Henry_____77.
Carter, Jacob_____136.
Carter, Joseph_____136.
Carter, Richard_____136.
Chamberlain, Marsh_____90, 98.
Cland, Pusey_____273.
Clark, John_____99.
Clark, James Freeman_____279.
Clendenon, Joshua_____341.
Coates, Deborah S._____87.
Coates, Edwin H._____98, 355.
Coates, Emmeline_____86.
Coates, Elizabeth_____348.
Coates, Levi_____32.
Coates, Lindley___30, 57, 64, 67, 75, 78, 80, 84, 87, 89, 90, 94, 96, 99, 101, 102, 103, 113, 128, 132, 135, 186, 138, 164, 193, 227, 231.
Coates, Moses_____212.
Coates, Sarah W._____212.
Coates, Simmons_____86.
Cochran, ———._____28.
Collyer, Robert_____235, 279.
Commegys, Andrew_____326.
Compton, Wilson_____51.
Cooper, Truman_____83.
Corson, Lawrence E._____224.
Corson, Dr. William_____30, 219, 223.
Cox, Hannah P._____33, 260, 273, 275, 278.
Cox, John_____33, 260, 273, 278, 301, 302.

Cox, J. William_____276, 302.
Cummichael, James_____161.
Curtis, George William_____188.
Cuyler, Theodore_____124.
Dannaker, James T._____344, 346, 347, 349, 351, 352, 353.
Darlington, Chandler_____33, 263, 279, 301, 308.
Darlington, Hannah M._____ __ _____301, 308.
Dawsey, James._____81.
Dayton, William L._____45, 60.
Dorsey, Araminta._____ ___ _____328.
Dorsey, Basil._____356.
Dorsey, Charles._____356.
Dorsey, John._____328.
Dorsey, Thomas_____356.
Dorsey, William._____356.
Douglass, Frederick_____181, 187, 188, 287.
Dugdale, Joseph A._____256.

Earle, Mary_____61.
Earle, Thomas_____61, 89, 235, 345.
Eshleman, Dr. J. K._____30, 33, 59, 63, 66, 138, 290, 295, 301, 304.
Evans, Nathan_____33, 135, 136, 286, 301, 304, 338, 340, 342, 346.
Everett, Hamilton_____36.
Everhart, Hon. William_____268.

Ferree, Diller._____128.
Fisher, Joel._____39, 45.
Flint, Isaac S._____31.
Franklin, Benjamin_____52, 143.
Freeman, Benjamin_____333, 337, 338.
Fremont, John C._____45, 60
Fulton, James, Jr._____30, 33, 77, 80, 131, 134, 135, 138, 248, 310, 341.
Fulton, Joseph_____85, 90, 91, 93, 126, 132.
Furniss, Oliver_____31, 227, 232.
Fussell, Bartholomew._____169, 260, 261.
Fussell, Dr. Bartholomew__32, 169, 170, 182, 187, 201, 252, 260, 261, 289, 297.
    301, 302, 326, 342.
Fussell, Dr. Edwin_____30, 33, 168, 175, 182, 186, 187, 188, 189, 268.
Fussell, Emma J._____188, 190.
Fussell Joshua L._____269, 272.
Fussell, Lydia Morris_____260, 263, 267, 269.
Fussell, Dr. Morris._____269.
Fussell, Rebecca Bond._____269.
Fussell, Rebecca Lewis_____171, 186, 187, 188.
Fussell, Solomon._____173.
Fussell, William_____30, 33, 175.

Garfield, James A._____145.
Garrett, Davis, Jr._____341, 342.

Garrett, Sarah_____237.
Garrett, Thomas__31, 164, 227, 237, 239, 243, 244, 249, 250, 251, 266, 270, 289,
    291, 297, 301, 302, 308, 326, 329, 330, 332, 355.
Garrigues, Benjamin_____326.
Garrison, William Lloyd_____68, 88, 131, 167, 205, 235, 278, 287, 354.
Gause, Jonathan_____59.
Gay, Sidney Howard_____167.
Gibbons, Daniel__29, 30, 37, 38, 46, 53, 55, 56, 59, 64, 69, 72, 74, 77, 85, 90, 96,
    100, 102, 103, 105, 135, 138, 164, 187, 192, 216, 235, 288.
Gibbons, Hannah W_____37, 53, 55, 59.
Gibbons, James_____53.
Gibbons, Dr. Joseph_____58, 59, 60, 61, 62, 73, 136.
Gibbons, Phebe E_____59, 61.
Gibbs, Richard_____140.
Giddings, Joshua R_____287.
Gilbert, Amos_____102.
Gilbert, Joshua_____71.
Goodell, William A_____131.
Goodrich, William C_____45.
Gorsuch, Dickerson_____107, 119, 205.
Gorsuch, Edward_____108, 115, 116, 117, 119, 123, 129, 216.
Grew, Mary_____279.
Griffith, Jarvis_____305.
Griffith, William_____306.
Groff, John A_____192, 193.

Haines, Joseph_____30, 138, 217, 218.
Hall, William_____158.
Hambleton, Charles_____32, 312.
Hambleton, Eli_____32, 82, 102, 312.
Hambleton, Thomas_____32, 102, 134, 312.
Hanway, Castner_____107, 118, 124, 128, 129, 217, 322.
Harris, George_____272.
Harris, Henry_____95.
Hardy Elizabeth_____188.
Hardy, Neal_____188.
Harris, Isaac_____196.
Harris, Rachel_____191, 195, 201, 328.
Harvey, Dr. Elwood_____182, 268.
Hawley, Joseph_____302.
Hayes, Esther_____33, 301, 304.
Hayes, Jacob_____304.
Hayes, Mordecai_____33, 85, 138, 301, 304, 342.
Haynes, Jacob_____164.
Henson, Josiah_____32.
Hewes, Rebecca C_____267.
Hibbard, William, Jr_____342.
Hickman, Dr. Joseph_____340.

Hood, Caleb C. _____30, 80, 81, 82.
Hood, John _____83.
Hood, Joseph _____80.
Hood, Thomas _____83.
Hoopes, Joshua _____59.
Hopkins, Henry C. _____126.
Hopkins, Thomas _____98.
Hopper, Isaac T. _____143, 150, 159, 279, 287.
Howard, William _____81, 82.
Hunn, Ezekiel _____326.
Hunn, John _____238, 244.
Hutchinson, James _____198.

Ingram, Dr. Thomas _____196.
Irwin, Samuel _____319.

Jackson, Alice _____321.
Jackson, Isaac _____314.
Jackson, Israel _____316.
Jackson, John _____250, 253, 326.
Jackson, Thomas _____74.
Jackson, William _____34, 223, 326.
Jamison, Samuel _____223.
Janney, Richard _____164.
Jeffries, Hannah _____201.
Johnson, Abraham _____77, 115, 248, 251.
Johnson, Benjamin _____93.
Johnson, Moses _____74, 75.
Johnson, Susan P. _____90, 106.
Johnson, Hon. Reverdy _____348, 350.
Johnson, William H. _____200, 223, 326, 328, 358.
Jones, "Ben," _____151.
Jones, Benjamin _____68, 85.
Jones, John _____47.
Jones, "Tom," _____152, 153.
Jourdon, Cato _____46.

Kelley, Abby _____254, 279.
Kent, Benjamin _____34, 301, 309.
Kent, Daniel K. _____310.
Kent, Edwin _____310.
Kent, Elizabeth _____312.
Kent, Hannah S. _____34, 301, 309.
Kent, Henry _____311.
Kidd, John _____75.
Kimber, Abigail _____191, 202.
Kimber, Emmor _____30, 33, 85, 97, 191, 194, 196, 202, 315, 326, 333.
Kimber, Susanna _____204.
Kirk, Isaac _____100.

s*

Kirk, Jacob---236.
Kirk, William---71.
Kline, Henry H--116.

Lamborn, Jacob---249, 254.
Landrum, Abner---143, 151.
Lee, Henry---341.
Lemoyne, Dr. F. J---45, 60.
Lewis, Dr--39.
Lewis, Elijah--118, 124, 129, 217.
Lewis, Elizabeth R--33, 171, 179.
Lewis, Enoch--301, 312.
Lewis, Esther---30, 32, 33, 169, 170, 171, 172, 173, 177, 184, 186, 191, 304, 334.
Lewis, Evan---317.
Lewis, Graceanna--------33, 138, 171, 174, 180, 192, 201, 202, 253, 292, 326.
Lewis, Isaac---178.
Lewis, James----------------------------340, 342, 344, 346, 347, 350, 351.
Lewis, John, Jr-----------------------------------168, 169, 170, 171, 186.
Lewis, Hon. Joseph J-----------------------------------168, 169, 314, 321.
Lewis, Mariann---33, 170.
Lewis, Samuel--223.
Lewis, Thomas---206, 217.
Lewis, William---224.
Lincoln, Abraham--63, 244, 382.
Lindley, Jacob-------------------------------------100, 227, 245, 246, 326.
Livermore, Mary A--256.
Logan, James---256.
Loney, Robert---49, 51, 77.
Long, Charles--81.
Long, John--126.
Lowell, James Russell-----------------------------------254, 279, 287.
Lundy, Benjamin---90, 299, 354.

Maris, Norris--30, 33, 174, 191, 193.
Marsh, Gravner-------30, 32, 101, 131, 137, 138, 140, 141, 142, 164, 301, 304.
Marsh, Hannah--131, 137, 138, 142.
Marshall, Lewis--302.
Martin, Elizabeth R--51.
May, Samuel J---279.
Mendenhall, Aaron--256, 257.
Mendenhall, Benjamin---256.
Mendenhall, Dinah H------------------32, 223, 249, 252, 259, 289, 297, 326.
Mendenhall, Isaac-32, 223, 248, 249, 250, 251, 253, 255, 256, 259, 289, 297, 326.
Mendenhall, Joseph---256.
Mendenhall, Rachel---237.
Meredith, Isaac--------------------------------------33, 266, 297, 301, 302.
Meredith, Thamazine P--33, 301.
McGill, Jonathan--223.

Mifflin, John _____48.
Mifflin, Jonathan _____48.
Mifflin, Samuel W _____36, 45, 48, 50, 51, 52.
Mifflin, Susan _____48.
Mickle, Samuel _____75.
Miller, David _____73.
Miller, Robert _____133.
Mitchener, Dr. Ezra _____268.
McKim, J. Miller _____143, 158, 159, 167, 189, 218, 235, 268, 332.
McKim, Lucy _____167.
McKinley, John _____155.
Moore, Charles, _____33, 34, 143, 163.
Moore, Gainer _____75.
Moore, Hamilton _____71.
Moore, James _____30.
Moore, Jeremiah _____33, 67, 77, 78, 84.
Moore, Joseph _____33, 132.
Morrison, John _____231.
Mott, James _____158, 159.
Mott, Lucretia _____235, 279, 287.
Munroe, James _____187.
Myers, Michael _____131, 132, 134.

Neall, Daniel _____355.

Owen, Griffith _____258.

Painter, Cyrus _____200.
Painter, James _____330.
Painter, Joseph _____342.
Painter, Samuel M. _____200, 201, 328, 332, 334, 336, 337.
Parker, Theodore _____279, 287.
Parker, William _____92, 97, 107, 108, 129, 248, 251.
Patterson, Dr. A. P. _____120.
Paxson, Abigail _____143.
Paxson, Dr. Jacob L. _____30, 198, 206, 222, 224, 225, 226, 326.
Peart, Lewis. _____174, 191, 192, 196.
Peart, Thomas _____30, 73.
Pearson, Sarah _____249, 254.
Peirce, Joseph _____76.
Penn, John _____59.
Penn, Richard _____59.
Penn, William _____258.
Pennell, Robert _____258.
Pennock, Moses _____301.
Pennock, Samuel _____178, 301.
Pennypacker, Elijah F. _30, 32, 33, 174, 192, 206, 208, 209, 210, 214, 326, 340.
Pennypacker, Hannah _____212.
Phillips, Wendell _____167, 287.

Pierce, Gideon_____30, 33, 131, 134, 310.
Pierce, Eli D._____326.
Pierce, Jacob_____156.
Pierce, Lukens._____135, 341.
Pilsbury, Parker._____225.
Pinkney, Alexander_____92, 115, 248, 251.
Pownall, E. B._____121.
Pownall, Levi._____107, 115, 120, 121, 125.
Pownall, Levi, Jr._____120.
Pownall, Sarah._____115, 121, 123.
Pownall, Thomas._____124.
Preston, Amos._____34, 248, 301, 305, 326.
Preston, Ann._____248, 268.
Preston, Isaac._____133.
Preston, Mahlon._____34, 301, 305.
Price, Benjamin_____33, 199, 301, 323, 328, 329, 331.
Price, Eli K._____168.
Price, Isaiah._____201, 323, 328.
Price, Dr. Jacob._____331.
Price, Jane._____323, 331.
Price. John._____175.
Price, Philip._____100, 323, 331.
Pugh, James_____253.
Pugh, Sarah._____279.
Purvis, Robert._____344, 353.
Purvis, William._____354.

Quiggs, Hannah._____83.
Quincy, Edmund._____287.

Rakestraw, William._____75, 247.
Read, Thomas._____206, 218, 219, 221.
Reckless, Hester._____346.
Remond, Charles Lennox._____187.
Richards, Henry._____193.
Richardson, Abel._____173.
Ridgway, John._____151.
Roberts, Anthony E._____128.
Roberts, Isaac._____30, 219.
Roberts, John._____30, 219.
Roberts, Mary R._____219, 221.
Robinson, Joshua._____157.
Ross, Daniel._____30, 206, 219.
Russell, John N._____77, 227, 233.
Russell, Slater B._____234.

Scarlett, Elizabeth._____215, 216.
Scarlett, Joseph P._____119, 128, 129, 206, 215, 216.
Schofield, Benjamin._____164.

Sellers, John--326
Sellers, S.--345.
Shadd, Abraham D.--33, 323, 337.
Sharpless, Joshua--335.
Sharpless, Mary--237.
Sharpless, Philip P.--199
Shippen, Edward--256.
Shoemaker, Tacy--232.
Slack, Isaac---86.
Smith, Allen---74, 83.
Smith, Gerrit---131.
Smith, Joseph-----------------------------------31, 80, 227, 228, 231, 232, 312.
Smith, P. Frazer--333.
Smith, Rachel---231.
Smith, Stephen---26, 46, 50.
Spackman, Thomas--141.
Speakman, Micajah-----------------------------30, 33, 94, 134, 138, 143, 164.
Speakman, Sarah A (McKim)--143, 167.
Speakman, William A----------------------------------30, 89, 134, 143, 164.
Stevens, Thaddeus--36, 38, 46, 89.
Still, William--176, 178, 218, 253.
Stowe, Harriet Beecher--32.
Stone, Lucy---235, 279.
Sugar, John---326.
Sugar, William--289.

Tappan, Arthur--69.
Taylor, Bayard--168, 279.
Taylor, Charles---29.
Taylor, Franklin---268.
Taylor, Joseph C.---76, 285.
Taylor, James N.--227, 247, 248, 251.
Thomas, Richard---152.
Thomas, Zebulon.-----------------------------------30, 33, 282, 291, 299.
Thorne, J. Williams--33, 131.
Todd, Francis.--354.
Torrey, Charles T---52, 80, 233.
Townsend, Mary---181.
Trimble, William---34, 150.
Truth, Sojourner.---256.
Tubman, Harriet---249, 250.
Tyson, Elisha.---------------------------------------90, 100, 245, 262, 264.

Urick, John---72.

Vickers, Aaron---154.
Vickers, Abby.---158.
Vickers, John--30, 32, 33, 64, 73, 101, 105, 138, 139, 143, 146, 148, 151, 152, 153,
    154, 156, 157, 158, 160, 161, 162, 191, 201, 206, 252, 253, 286, 291, 301, 304,
    310, 326, 333, 334, 335, 338.

Vickers, Mary_____153,
Vickers, Paxson_____143, 162.
Vickers, Sarah_____150, 151.
Vickers, Thomas_____90, 143, 148, 150.
Wallace ———_____46.
Wallace, William_____71, 72.
Walker, Enoch_____100.
Walker, Joseph G_____243.
Walton, Asa_____102.
Ward, Levi B_____227, 247.
Washington, James_____171.
Waters, Henry_____195.
Waters, Isaac_____229.
Webb, Benjamin_____31.
Webb, Thomas_____31.
Webb, William_____31.
Webster, George_____74, 75.
Webster, George Jr,_____75.
Webster, Jesse_____73.
West, J. Pierce_____253.
Whipper, Benjamin_____97.
Whipper, William_____46.
White, Jacob C_____335.
White, William A_____187.
Whitehead, William_____340.
Whitson, Micah_____77.
Whitson, Moses_____83, 90, 94, 95, 96, 97, 99. 102.
Whitson, Samuel_____99.
Whitson, Thomas_36, 63, 64, 66, 67, 69, 70, 85, 90, 101, 102, 131, 132, 164, 193.
    227, 235, 312.
Whittier, John G._____131, 258, 278, 279, 280, 287.
Wierman, Joel_____40, 43, 44.
Williams, James_____33, 85, 132, 215.
Williams, William_____128.
Wilkinson, Perry_____50.
Williamson, James_____132.
Williamson, Seymour C_____83, 131, 134.
Willis, Samuel_____48.
Wills, Allen_____138.
Wilson, Josiah_____250.
Wilson, Mary_____250.
Wood, Day_____247.
Wood, James_____198.
Woodrow, James_____76.
Woodward, Maris_____301, 341.
Worthington, John T_____197, 198, 200.
Wright, John_____27, 31.

Phebe_____37, 40, 41, 42, 43, 52, 170.

Samuel_____27.

William (of Columbia)_____25, 28, 31, 46, 48, 78.

William (of Adams county)_____36, 37, 89, 41, 42, 43, 45, 52.

, William_____45.

THE JOURNAL.

A Paper Devoted to the Interests of the Society of Friends.

"FRIENDS, MIND THE LIGHT."—GEORGE FOX.

PUBLISHED AT

PHILADELPHIA AND LANCASTER.

The Journal is now nearing the middle of its eleventh volume. Its conductors consider this a fitting time and opportunity at which to urge its claims to recognition and support upon Friends. They feel at liberty so to do because they have, to the best of their ability, made it a paper worthy of such recognition and support; such a paper, in fact, as should be in every Friend's family. The report of Philadelphia Yearly Meeting of 1883 is one of the best reports of a Woman's Meeting that has ever appeared in any paper. Numerous other interesting and valuable reports of meetings appear in its columns from time to time, making it just such a vehicle of news, of a religious character, as Friends need. A number of Friends contribute to its columns articles upon vital and important subjects bearing upon our principles and testimonies. In addition to these contributions, the editors have obtained the consent of Graceanna Lewis, of Philadelphia, the distinguished naturalist, to write occasionally for its columns. The first of her contributions, an interesting account, in three parts, of the beaver, is now in process of publication. Such are a few of the features that render The Journal a paper that every Friend should read and support. Its conductors trust that Friends will do everything in their power to assist in extending its circulation and influence.

The terms are, as they have long been, Ten Copies for $20, one year; 1 copy free to the getter up of the club. Five Copies for $11.25, one year; 1 copy free for six months to the getter up of the club.

JOSEPH GIBBONS,

Editor and Proprietor,

Bird-in-Hand, Lancaster county, Pa.

Business Letters to be addressed to

125 North Ninth St., Philadelphia, Pa.

9 781375 491105